Samurai in the Land of the Gaucho

Samurai in the Land of the Gaucho

Transpacific Modernity and Nikkei Literature in Argentina

KOICHI HAGIMOTO

VANDERBILT UNIVERSITY PRESS
Nashville, Tennessee

Copyright 2023 Vanderbilt University Press
All rights reserved
First printing 2023

Library of Congress Cataloging-in-Publication Data
Names: Hagimoto, Koichi, 1983– author.
Title: Samurai in the land of the Gaucho : transpacific modernity and
  Nikkei literature in Argentina / Koichi Hagimoto.
Description: Nashville : Vanderbilt University Press, 2023. | Includes
  bibliographical references and index.
Identifiers: LCCN 2023001764 (print) | LCCN 2023001765 (ebook) | ISBN
  9780826505699 (paperback) | ISBN 9780826505705 (hardcover) | ISBN
  9780826505712 (epub) | ISBN 9780826505729 (pdf)
Subjects: LCSH: Argentina—Relations—Japan. | Japan—Relations—Argentina.
  | Japanese literature—Argentina—History and criticism. | Spanish
  literature—Argentina—History and criticism. | Comparative
  literature—Spanish and Japanese. | Comparative literature—Japanese and
  Spanish. | Japanese—Argentina—Intellectual life. |
  Japanese—Argentina—History.
Classification: LCC F2833.5.J3 H34 2023 (print) | LCC F2833.5.J3 (ebook)
  | DDC 982/.004956—dc23/eng/20230221
LC record available at https://lccn.loc.gov/2023001764
LC ebook record available at https://lccn.loc.gov/2023001765

To Daisaku Ikeda

In memory of David William Foster
and Elena Gascón-Vera

Contents

Acknowledgments ix
Foreword by Ignacio López-Calvo xiii

Introduction 1

PART I: TRANSPACIFIC MODERNITY: AN ASIA–LATIN AMERICA PERSPECTIVE

Chapter 1. Argentine Chronicles on Japan: Hygiene, Aesthetics, and Spirituality in Eduardo Wilde and Jorge Max Rohde 23

Chapter 2. Empire across the Sea: Narratives of Japanese Imperialism in the Writings of Manuel Domecq García and Yoshio Shinya 44

PART II: NIKKEI LITERATURE AS COUNTERNARRATIVE

Chapter 3. Hybrid Nikkei Identity: Héctor Dai Sugimura's *Buscadores en mis últimas vidas* and Maximiliano Matayoshi's *Gaijin* 67

Chapter 4. Gendering Orientalism and Female Agency: Anna Kazumi Stahl's *Flores de un solo día* and Alejandra Kamiya's *Los árboles caídos también son el bosque* 84

Chapter 5. Visual Representations of Japan in Contemporary Argentine Cinema 101

Conclusion 121

Notes 125
Bibliography 153
Index 165

Acknowledgments

This book would not have been possible without the extraordinary support and guidance of many people. While it is impossible to thank everyone individually, I would like to mention some of them here. First, I want to thank Ignacio López-Calvo for writing a generous foreword for this book. His vast scholarship on transpacific studies has inspired me on many occasions, and I am grateful for his continuous mentorship and friendship. I also want to thank Gene Bell-Villada who meticulously read the manuscript and provided valuable feedback.

In the last seven years I have been fortunate to be invited to discuss my project at various universities. My gratitude goes to the following colleagues and their institutions: Rosario Hubert (Trinity College), Houchang Chehabi (Boston University), Aníbal González-Pérez (Yale University), Shigeko Mato (Waseda University), and Araceli Tinajero (CUNY Graduate Center). The fruitful dialogues that emerged from these talks allowed me to improve the quality of this book. In addition, I received indispensable feedback at a number of academic conferences, such as the "Japanese Diaspora to the Americas" at Yale University in 2019. I want to thank Seth Jacobowitz, the organizer of the Yale conference, as well as other participants, including Jeffrey Lesser, Eiichiro Azuma, Louise Young, Andre Haag, Nayoung Aimee Kwon, Sidney Xu Lu, Ana Paulina Lee, Zelideth Rivas, and Facundo Garasino. It was an honor to present my work on Argentina's Nikkei history and literature alongside such distinguished scholars of Japanese diaspora studies. In 2019 I gave a keynote address about Japan through the eyes of Eduardo Wilde and Jorge Luis Borges at the Romanistentag conference in Kassel, Germany. I offer my thanks to Ineke Phaf-Rheinberger, Alexandra Ortiz Wallner, and Hanna Nohe for the kind invitation and for the stimulating dialogues that led to the publication of *Geografías caleidoscópicas: América Latina y sus imaginarios intercontinentales* (2022).

The Asia and the Americas section of the Latin American Studies Association gave birth to many of the conversations that shaped my thinking about this project. In particular, I want to express my gratitude to Evelyn Hu-DeHart, Debbie Lee-DiStefano, Axel Gasquet, Kathleen López, Monica DeHart, Martín Camps, Juan E. de Castro, Gorica Majstorovic, Melissa Fitch, Laura Torres-Rodríguez, Junyoung Verónica Kim, Chisu Teresa Ko, Kim Beauchesne, Svetlana Tyutina, Aarti Smith Madan, and Paula Park. Most recently, I attended the virtual LASA/ASIA 2022, the first LASA Continental Congress. I am grateful for the exchanges I had with Youngkyun Choi, Jungwon Park, Héctor Hernán Díaz Guevara, Miguel Angel Urrego Ardila, Sarah Soanirina Ohmer, and Minni Sawhney.

In Argentina, many thanks go to the staff at *La Plata Hochi*, Centro Okinawense, Federación de Asociaciones Nikkei en la Argentina, Jardín Japonés, and Biblioteca del Congreso. I had an opportunity to meet with the crew of *Samurai*, including the director Gaspar Scheuer and the actor Jorge Takashima. I feel lucky to have worked with Anna Kazumi Stahl who invited me to give a talk at NYU-Buenos Aires and who showed me a genuine sense of comradeship from the first time we met. When I think of Buenos Aires, the memories of the late David William Foster invariably come to my mind. He was an extraordinary mentor and friend who taught me, among other things, the richness of Argentine culture and history. In Japan, my research benefited not only from the resources at JICA and the Instituto Cervantes Tokio, but also from my conversation with Alberto Matsumoto, who specializes in the history of Japanese immigration in Latin America. I am also thankful for the time I spent at Waseda University and for the dialogues I had with Roxana Shintani, Patricia Takayama, Pedro Erber, Chie Ishida, and Matías Ariel Chiappe Ippolito.

Wellesley College has always provided me with necessary support during the completion of this book. Conference travel funds, faculty research awards, and the sabbatical program gave me crucial writing time and research support. The publication of this book is made possible thanks to the Huntington Fund. I express my gratitude to Eve Zimmerman for inviting me to participate in the Newhouse Center where I had the opportunity to share my research with a diverse group of colleagues from across campus. I feel fortunate to work with amazing colleagues and friends in the Spanish and Portuguese Department: Carlos Ramos, Carlos Alberto Vega, Marjorie Agosín, Joy Renjilian-Burgy, Evelina Gužauskytė, Inela Selimović, Nancy Abraham Hall, Antonio J. Arraiza Rivera, António Igrejas, Maria del Mar Bassa Vanrell, Jael Matos, and the late Elena Gascón-Vera. I thank my seminar students for giving me challenging questions about Asian Latin American identity. I am grateful to my talented assistant, Regina Gallardo, who helped me with translations and copyediting.

I am indebted to Zachary S. Gresham at Vanderbilt University Press for believing in this project. His enthusiastic support has been truly inspiring since the beginning of our relationship. I am grateful to other staff in the editorial team, including Joell Smith-Borne, Jenna Phillips, and Patrick Samuel. Special thanks go to Gianna Mosser for her superb copyediting. I also want to express my gratitude to the anonymous readers for their careful reading of the manuscript and their valuable feedback. Needless to say, I take full responsibility for all mistakes and shortcomings.

My deepest appreciation goes to my friends and family for their constant support, love, and encouragement. I feel fortunate to be surrounded by an incredible group of friends who have supported me along the way: Junot Díaz, Marjorie Liu, Elena Creef, Thomas Hodge, Robert Goree, Kyung Park, Amitesh Kumar, Kie Shimizu, and Tom Fast. My wife, Alaina Farabaugh, has not only shown tremendous patience during the long duration of this book, but also read parts of the manuscript and offered crucial insights. Our children, Taishi and Mina Hagimoto, never fail to give us joy and laughter with their ever-growing creativity. I want to express my sincere gratitude to the rest of my family in Tokyo, Okayama, Monroe, San Francisco, Pittsburgh, and Detroit. They have been an integral part of this project in ways they never imagined. Lastly, as with my first book, this book is dedicated to my mentor Daisaku Ikeda who has always encouraged me to have faith in myself and in others.

A shorter version of Chapter 1 was published as "Contrapuntos estéticos e higiénicos: Japón y China en las crónicas de viaje de Eduardo Wilde" in *Revista de Crítica Literaria Latinoamericana* (87 [2018]: 161–78). Excerpts from Chapters 3 and 4 appeared as "Beyond the Hyphen: Representation of Multicultural Japanese Identity in Maximiliano Matayoshi's *Gaijin* and Anna Kazumi Stahl's *Flores de un solo día*" in *Transmodernity: Journal of Peripheral Cultural Production of the Luso-Hispanic World* (3, 2 [Spring 2014]: 83–108). I thank both editors, José Antonio Mazzotti and Ignacio López-Calvo, for their permission to include them in this book.

Foreword

Ignacio López-Calvo
UNIVERSITY OF CALIFORNIA, MERCED

When one thinks about Nikkei communities in Latin America, the first countries that come to mind are usually Brazil with its 1.9 million Japanese descendants and Peru with 100,000 Nikkeijin. Yet studies like Koichi Hagimoto's remind us that there are other Nikkei communities in Latin America, such as those in Argentina and Mexico, which, despite being much smaller, have also left an indelible mark on their respective host countries. In *Samurai in the Land of the Gaucho: Transpacific Modernity and Nikkei Literature in Argentina*, we learn how, in contrast to Edward Said's notion of Orientalism in the Levant, the Argentine intelligentsia's utopian (mis)conceptions of Japanese culture and ethics helped mold what they saw as an alternative modernity to that offered by the West—this is the "transpacific modernity" referenced in the title of Hagimoto's insightful study.

Laura Torres-Rodríguez, in her 2019 book *Orientaciones transpacíficas: La modernidad mexicana y el espectro de Asia*, explored how Mexican intellectuals such as José Juan Tablada, José Vasconcelos and, more recently, Roger Bartra, decided at one point to exchange their transatlantic, occidentalist gaze to find, instead, a transpacific, orientalist inspiration in the modernization and far-away cultures of India, China, and Japan. Similarly, in the first half of his book, Hagimoto demonstrates how early-twentieth-century Argentine thinkers such as Eduardo Wilde and Manuel Domecq García found an alternative path for their country's progress in the Japanese model of modernization following the Meiji Restoration. In this sense, while concentrating on immigration narratives and Japan, *Samurai in the Land of the Gaucho* complements three previous studies about Argentine travelers' literary Orientalism: Martín Bergel's *El Oriente desplazado* (2015), Axel Gasquet's *Oriente al Sur: El orientalismo literario argentino de Esteban Echeverría a Roberto Arlt* (2007), and *El llamado de Oriente. Historia cultural del orientalismo argentino, 1900–1950* (2015). As Gasquet explains in the cultural history compiled in this last book, after World War I Argentines began to question the alleged universality of European values, looking instead at the cultures, philosophies, and mysticism of "the Orient." This peripheral, ideological Orientalism ended up being key in the discursive articulation of the Argentine national imaginary of a modern state.

Perhaps one of the most interesting and original contributions of Hagimoto's study resides in its disclosure of the very different immigrant experience that the Japanese had in Argentina, in contrast with other countries like Brazil, Peru, or Mexico, where Nikkeijin had to endure deportation (Peru), state-sponsored persecution (Peru and Brazil), and relocation (Peru, Brazil, and Mexico). According to Hagimoto, the cultural integration of the Japanese in Argentina was much less challenging than that of other Nikkei communities in Latin America, albeit not entirely free from racism and discrimination. He suggests several reasons for this difference, including their smaller size, even though it is still the third largest Nikkei community in Latin America; Argentina's neutrality during World War II; and the fact that the Japanese immigrant society in Argentina was less endogamic and segregated than those in Brazil or Peru. Intermarriage and conversion to Catholicism were more common in part because many settled in Buenos Aires instead of isolated rural areas. More importantly, according to Hagimoto, beginning in the late nineteenth century, the Argentine elite conceived of Japan as a civilizational model, thus regarding Japanese immigrants as "modern" and "desirable."

Indeed, in Brazil, during the Estado Novo regime led by President Getúlio Vargas, a "Brazilianization" campaign targeted Axis Powers nationals, who began to be seen as "enemy aliens." Particularly after Brazil declared war on Japan in 1942, this resulted in the relocation of Nikkeijin living in Santos and other coastal areas, as well as in an attempted epistemicide: the Brazilian government tried to impose Western worldviews, Brazilian culture, and Portuguese language by eliminating Japanese culture and language. It forbade the teaching of Japanese language in schools, possession of Japanese-language publications, and even speaking the language in public. Anti-Japanese hysteria was more pronounced in Peru, in part because this country has a Pacific coast that could be used as a hostile landing for the Imperial Japanese Navy, as the US World War II anti-Japanese propaganda warned. After an incident in a Japanese barber shop in which a Peruvian woman was accidentally killed in May 1940, a rioting mob looted many Japanese homes and businesses. Even worse was the kidnapping and deportation, without any legal procedure, of 1,771 Peruvian Nikkeijin to internment camps in New Mexico and Texas during World War II, where they remained interned for more than two years. Pressured by Washington, the Peruvian government led by President Manuel Carlos Prado y Ugarteche not only willingly allowed these deportations, but also confiscated Japanese-Peruvian property. In the end, only seventy-nine of the deported Japanese nationals and residents were allowed to return to Peru. By contrast, Nipponophobia was not as glaring in Mexico as it was in Peru and Brazil. Unlike Peru and several other Latin American countries, Mexico refused to send its Japanese residents to internment camps in the United States. However, it did relocate them, particularly those residing by the Pacific Coast and the US border, to Mexico City and Guadalajara.

Fortunately, as Hagimoto makes clear, fewer traumatic episodes and less epistemic violence of this kind took place in Argentina; instead, he claims, there is a history of "positive prejudice" toward Japanese immigrants. This study thus contributes to dispelling reductionist historical accounts about the uniformity in diasporic experience of the Japanese and their descendants in the Americas. Hagimoto also argues that their integration was much easier than those of the Chinese and Koreans, who have been traditionally less accepted and even considered a threat to Argentine national culture. Similarly, the Japanese community in Mexico endured much less discrimination and persecution than their Chinese counterparts, who suffered several massacres and were also deported from the states of Sonora and Sinaloa in the early 1930s.

In what is, in my view, this study's most important contribution to the understanding of the reception of Japanese modernization in Latin America, Hagimoto demonstrates that Argentine intellectuals' surprising interest in Japan actually responded to a desire to claim their country's Western identity: because of Japan's perceived desirable traits, Japanese immigrants were reconceptualized as symbols of an alternative whiteness that could be transposed to Argentine people. It is, then, because of this "honorary whiteness" that Japanese immigrants were more welcome than their mainland Asian counterparts. Hagimoto, therefore, finds common ideological denominators in Argentina's discourse of whiteness and Japan's desire for Westernization since the Meiji Restoration. Just as Japan claimed its exceptionalism (a sense of superiority with respect to the surrounding nations, especially Korea and China), so did Argentina in Latin America, albeit without an overt aspiration to global domination. As is well known, this claim to exceptionalism was supposed to teleologically justify the so-called Greater East Asia Co-Prosperity Sphere, that is, the Empire of Japan's right to lead Asia's decolonization from Western powers, with the ensuing colonial subjugation of the Asian continent to Tokyo.[1] This South-South exploration of the Argentine racial imaginary based on a cultural history of the country's conceptualization of far-away Japan is then contextualized with the current, hegemonic discourse of whiteness in the country.

Within the analysis of the idealization of Japan among Argentines of European ancestry in the first half of the book, Hagimoto examines how Argentine travelers unproblematically praised Japanese idiosyncrasies, including its hygiene culture, aesthetic and spiritual tradition, and imperial trajectory. The *modernista* Eduardo Wilde, for example, found in Japanese hygiene culture—both in terms of physical/public and spiritual/private cleanliness—a model of civilization that he contrasted with the perceived barbarism and dirtiness of China. For his part, another *modernista*, Jorge Max Rohde, romanticized the artistic, religious, and spiritual traditions of "old Japan." Both *modernistas* eroticized East Asian women in their Orientalist writings, at times comparing the beauty of Japanese and Chinese women, while also accepting a hierarchical relationship between a glorified Japan and a criticized China, which implicitly justified the former's imperial expansionism. Hagimoto interprets the disparagement of China as "a reflection of an undesirable and primitive Argentina" in their writings (31); that is, in the civilization-barbarism dichotomy that anchored numerous cultural debates at the time in Argentina, Japan represented civilization while China was the barbarous country.

In turn, both Argentine Admiral Manuel Domecq García, who was invited by the Japanese government to observe the Russo-Japanese War, and Yoshio Shinya, the first officially registered Japanese immigrant in Argentina, praised the Japanese Empire's military conquests, imperial expansion, collective patriotism, and Western characteristics (read: its purported whiteness) as a potential model of transpacific modernity for Argentines. As a secondary effect, Shinya's discourse in favor of Japanese immigration contributed to the myth of the "model minority" in Argentina.

Interestingly, Hagimoto reveals that, whereas Japanese imperialism was perceived as a threat by several Latin American governments—Nikkei communities throughout the region were often seen as a fifth column that could potentially spy for the Empire of Japan or provide logistic and military support for Japan's invasion—that was not the case in Argentina. Instead, Hagimoto finds a shared outlook on expansionism during the 1870s as reflected in the similar ways in which both Japanese and Argentine governments portrayed the invasion of Taiwan and the so-called Conquest of the Desert respectively as civilizing missions. Along these lines, Hagimoto finds echoes of Shinya's propagandistic discourse supporting Japan's expansion in China and Korea in Argentine politicians' arguments for the discrimination against people of African and indigenous ancestry as a path to modernization. In both cases, the pursuit of a unified national identity, cultural superiority, and territorial expansion went hand in hand.

Incidentally, these Western idealizations of a harmonious Japanese culture would later give way to the theory of *Nihonjinron* in Japan. Disseminated by Inazō Nitobe's *Bushido: The Soul of Japan* (1899) and similar contemporary books about Japan, this philosophy, in a strategic essentialist move, willingly adopted outsiders' celebratory romanticization of the purported uniqueness of the Japanese character, particularly in contrast with Western cultures. All these Western, nineteenth-century, positive stereotypes and fantasies about the Japanese national psychology (group-oriented mentality, unbreakable stoicism and self-restrain, cultural and linguistic exceptionalism, a special relationship with nature, racial homogeneity, the resiliency of the *ganbare* spirit) contributed to the rebuilding of a Japanese national identity and pride that had been recently shattered by the outcome of World War II.

Moving on to the early twenty-first century, Hagimoto shows in the second half of his study how diasporic Nikkei authors such as Héctor Dai Sugimura and Maximiliano Matayoshi, are offering more realistic counternarratives by problematizing these earlier thinkers' uncritical simplifications of Japanese modernity, ethics, and culture, understood as monolithic. They propose, instead, more nuanced and sophisticated literary representations of Japan. In their works, Hagimoto explores the pioneering literary imagery of a transnational, hybrid, and hyphenated Japanese Argentine subjectivity. Far from the vision of Japaneseness as an alternative type of whiteness presented a century earlier by Euro-Argentine intellectuals, Sugimura and Matayoshi respond with a more reflective literary representation of Japanese culture. Likewise, the fluid immigrant and diasporic identities of their characters helped disrupt the grand narrative of modernity. By writing about Argentine Nikkeijin, their experience with racism and xenophobia, and their struggles to integrate into mainstream society, Hagimoto concludes, Sugimura and Matayoshi challenge the hegemonic, Eurocentric idea of what it means to be an Argentine in contemporary times.

For their part, narratives of gendered Orientalism by Nikkei women authors Anna Kazumi Stahl and Alejandra Kamiya offset, according to Hagimoto, the androcentric gaze that characterized the writing of their male counterparts, which stereotypically defined female characters' identities through their romantic relationship to male characters. This essentialized literary portrayal of Japanese and Nikkei women is now replaced by a feminine gaze, together with examples of anti-patriarchal resistance and female solidarity that concomitantly challenge the hegemonic rhetoric of racial homogeneity summoned by the ideology of whiteness in Argentina. Their female characters are independent and resilient, and the denunciation of domestic psychological abuse at the hands of patriarchal husbands moves the texts far from the idealizations of Japanese culture that Hagimoto analyzes in the first half of the book. In his view, Stahl and Kamiya have created a discourse of counter-modernity against both the ideology of white supremacy and patriarchy.

The closing chapter of *Samurai in the Land of the Gaucho* complements these literary representations of modernity, nation-building, and immigrant identity by analyzing visual renderings of these same topics in three contemporary feature and documentary films dealing with the Nikkei experience by the non-Nikkei Argentines Clara Zappettini, Gaspar Scheuer, and Pablo Moyano. Besides addressing issues such as identitarian uncertainties, intergenerational conflicts, and the tragedy of Nikkei families who lost relatives during Argentina's 1970s military dictatorship, Hagimoto claims that these films, like Nikkei literature, open the national imaginary to the realities of racial diversity and the need for social inclusivity. He also examines the representation of the Japanese protagonist in Gaspar Scheuer's 2010 film *Samurai* as a contemporary symbol of what he previously termed "transpacific modernity," in contrast with the simplified, negative, and dehumanized image of Chineseness in Sebastián Borensztein's 2011 feature film *Un cuento chino*.

As he does in his analysis of Nikkei literature, in the discussion of the films Hagimoto concentrates on the power and multiple meanings of silence, interpreting it within the framework of Japanese culture: "Unlike the West, Japan has long embraced and even institutionalized silence as an essential mode of communication. At the same time, silence is also regarded as a moral principle based on the Confucian ethics of obedience, hierarchy, and honor" (115). In the 2015 documentary *Silencio roto: 16 Nikkeis*, for example, Nikkei families seem to be reluctant to openly denounce the disappearance of their relatives at the hands of the military junta in part because, in their view, Nikkei participation in subversive activities was shameful and dishonorable—in the parents' view, Nikkeijin were supposed to be grateful to a government that had hosted them in its country. Incidentally, Jeffrey Lesser describes this same type of generational gap in his 2007 study on Japanese Brazilians, *A Discontented Diaspora: Japanese Brazilians and the Meanings of Ethnic Militancy, 1960–1980*. Moreover, in contrast with Argentine thinkers' glorification of all things Japanese, this documentary denounces the Japanese government's refusal to help these families by arguing that the disappeared Nikkeijin were "foreigners" and, therefore, the embassy could not interfere in domestic political issues. The embassy thus silenced its citizens.

Altogether, this eye-opening book covers a wealth of materials, including travel writing, newspapers, military reports, essays, novels, short stories, and film. It explores, first, a range of aesthetic idealizations and then, more realistic representations of Japan by both Nikkei and non-Nikkei Argentines. Beginning at the end of the nineteenth century, Argentine intellectuals of European ancestry, through what Hagimoto calls "the discourse of transpacific modernity," idealized Japan in uncritical, romanticized descriptions of its culture and society, which contributed to the creation of the model minority myth in Argentina. However, a new generation of twenty-first-century Nikkei authors are de-Orientalizing this idealized image of Japan by unveiling, in sophisticated literary representations, a more realistic society with numerous problems, including patriarchal attitudes, intergenerational conflicts, and a government that neglected to defend its citizens from persecution at the hands of a foreign state.

With this impressive study, Hagimoto makes an important contribution to Transpacific Studies from a Latin Americanist perspective, using an Asia–Latin America heuristic approach that reveals the particularities of this hybrid cultural production.

Introduction

On September 11, 1954, *La Plata Hochi*, the local newspaper for the Japanese community in Buenos Aires, published a poem by Ángel Sirimarco, a local Argentine gaucho. It depicts Argentina as a country of freedom and equality for all immigrants, with a particular emphasis on those coming from Japan:

> It is nice to see and admire
> communities from foreign countries
> who enjoy themselves and are happy
> as in their homeland.
> In this land they are content
> without ignoring their beloved homeland
> that gave them hope and life
> upon looking at the light of the world:
> they only remember mothers and relatives
> whom they left behind in the land of the Rising Sun.[1]

These words were meant to celebrate the diversity in a country where people from across the world "enjoy themselves and are happy." It is well-known that beginning in the late nineteenth century Argentina presented itself as a *crisol de razas* (melting pot) through a massive scale of immigration, mostly from Europe. As a result, different national and ethnic groups came into contact and created a multicultural society. Although the Japanese represented a very small fraction of this diverse population, Sirimarco regarded the people from the Far East as important constituents of modern Argentina. Like him, other Argentines have come to ascribe positive characteristics to "the land of the Rising Sun" in their vision of nation-building since the beginning of the twentieth century.

In this book, I explore how different literary and cultural approaches to Japan have shaped the concept of modernity in Argentina. The purpose of my project is twofold. On the one hand, I study how the historical imaginings of Japan enabled some Argentines to envision the narrative of what I call "transpacific modernity" in the early twentieth century. As I show in Part I, intellectuals such as Eduardo Wilde (1844–1913) and Manuel Domecq García (1859–1951) celebrated Japanese ethos as important values that could be integrated into Argentine society. On the other hand, my study also examines the way in which a new generation of Nikkei or Japanese Argentines is rewriting this traditional narrative in the twenty-first century.[2] Part II then is devoted to how Nikkei writers are challenging the earlier, uncritical view of Japan based on their literary recreation of immigrant and diasporic experiences. Through an analysis of diverse genres (travel writing, newspapers, military reports, essays, novels, short stories, and films), my discussion yields a multi-layered study in order to underline the particular role that Japan has played, and continues to play, in both defining and defying the notion of Argentine modernity.

An important piece of this project is the largely unknown history of Japanese immigration in Argentina. In recent years, scholars have engaged with the conversation about Nikkei literary and cultural production in several Latin American countries.[3] In Argentina, however, the contribution of Japanese or any other Asian immigrants has received scant attention to date.[4] To fill this lacuna, my book presents the first systematic study on the representation of Japan created by Argentines of European descent as well as by Nikkei Argentines.[5] At the same time, my discussion seeks to highlight the history of the Japanese diaspora in Argentina in contrast with Brazil and Peru, as I will explain further. By comparing Argentina to its neighboring countries, my study averts the temptation to homogenize the Japanese diasporic experience in the continent or to simplify their experience through historical reductionism.

With its focus on the Nikkei experience in Argentina, the present study makes a key contribution not only to Transpacific Studies, but also to what Jeffrey Lesser and Raanan Rein have called the New Ethnic Studies in Latin America.[6] In this sense, my project proposes an alternative to the conventional understanding of the area studies model, especially as it relates to

Asian American Studies in US academia. The field of Asian American Studies was created after decades of student activism, and it is primarily concerned with the question of ethnic representation within the United States. Rather than US-centered Asian American Studies, my book suggests the notion of "Asian Latin American Studies," with which I follow some recent studies on the Asian diaspora in Latin America, particularly what Chisu Teresa Ko calls "Asian Argentine Studies."[7] In her essay titled "Asia-Latin America as Method: The Global South Project and the Dislocation of the West," Junyoung Verónica Kim also argues that "Asia-Latin America entails a negotiation between the epistemological frameworks of area studies and ethnic studies."[8] Along these lines, the transnational and interdisciplinary approach that I employ in this book suggests a new kind of framework that is not limited to Asian Americans in the US, but includes Asians in the Americas in the hemispheric sense. Hence, what I propose is not only the redefinition of "Asian American Studies" as a field, but also the expansion of "American Studies" in general. As Vicente Rafael and Mary Louise Pratt have recently noted, "American studies, we believe, stands to benefit greatly from incorporating language, linguistic difference, translation, and multilingualism as basic parameters of analysis across its interdisciplinary terrain."[9] I am aware that by attempting to mediate between two academic fields, Asian American Studies and Latin American Studies, my study risks dissatisfying both sides that I seek to dialogue with. However, my hope is to contribute to the growing scholarship that finds points of convergence, divergence, and contradictions between Asia and Latin America. Therefore, among the purposes of this book is to raise awareness about the history of the global Asian diaspora and their relationship to the multilingual, (trans) national politics of immigration in the Americas.

Historical Background

A brief history outlining the differences between the Japanese immigrant experience in Argentina compared with that in Brazil and Peru illustrates multiple layers of historical narrative in the region. Besides the sheer size of immigration (Brazil became the behemoth of Japanese immigration in the 1920s), one of the most notable distinctions is the degree of state-sponsored persecutions. In Brazil, the anti-Japanese movement known as "Campanha Anti-Nipônica" (Anti-Japanese Campaign) was notoriously influential in the 1920s. Miguel Couto, the most vocal proponent of this movement, believed that immigration from Japan was a devious plot to overtake the Brazilian nation.[10] Under the regime of Getúlio Vargas, there was a state-wide discrimination against people of Japanese descent through the politics of "Estado Novo" (New State). Of particular importance was the 1939 program to encourage "Brasilidade" (Brazilianization), which represented "the state-driven homogenization program sought to protect Brazilian identity from the encroachment of ethnicity by eliminating distinctive elements of immigrant culture."[11] When Brazil declared war on Japan in 1942, Vargas's anti-Japanese propaganda intensified further, turning the Japanese (as well as Italians and the German) into "enemy aliens" who became the targets of systematic oppression.[12]

In the same vein, the Japanese in Peru also endured the trauma of anti-Japanese racism and political persecution by the state. Two specific events are worth mentioning. First is the major riot that took place in May 1940 in which protestors looted more than 600 Japanese businesses and homes in downtown Lima. As Ayumi Takenaka points out, this incident was the worst rioting in the history of independent Peru and became "a symbol of racial hatred" in the country.[13] Another episode of anti-Japanese hysteria was the history of more than 1,700 Japanese nationals and Peruvian citizens of Japanese ancestry who were kidnapped and sent to US internment camps during World War II. As a close ally of the United States, the Peruvian government arrested Nikkei Peruvians and deported them to American soil without any legal procedure. When the war ended, only 79 individuals were permitted to return to Peru. President Manual Carlos Prado y Ugarteche's apparent refusal to accept the re-entry of the majority of these internees shows that he saw this moment as an opportunity to remove the Japanese presence from the country.[14]

It is true that different immigrant histories exist between Brazil and Peru (for example, unlike Peru, Japanese immigrants could only enter Brazil in family units, not as individuals). Nonetheless, what the two countries share are the episodes of systematic political persecution against people of Japanese descent. On the other hand, the Japanese in Argentina generally lived under a more agreeable sociopolitical climate, although this does not mean that they were completely spared from racism or discrimination. What I mean is that they did not experience the kind of epistemic violence and erasure from the national consciousness that occurred in Brazil and Peru. Instead, to use the anthropologist Marcelo Higa's words, the Japanese in Argentina were treated with "positive prejudice" (prejuicio positivo) in their history of immigration.[15] As Higa puts it, "they [Argentines] created an image that associated the Japanese with characteristics of positive connotations (silence, respect, hygiene, honesty, work and self-sacrifice, etc.), a semantic universe not exempt from discriminatory connotations but that immigrants appropriated and knew how to take advantage of years later."[16]

It must be emphasized that in Argentina the scale of the Japanese community was much smaller than in Brazil and Peru: according to the Association of Nikkei and Japanese Abroad and the Ministry of Foreign Affairs of Japan, there are currently 65,000 people of Japanese descent in Argentina, which represents the third largest Nikkei community in Latin America, after Brazil (1.9 million) and Peru (100,000).[17] The small number of Nikkei Argentines can be explained in several ways. To begin with, their initial process of immigration was based not on a government-subsidized contract (*keiyaku imin*), but on their own spontaneous decisions and free will (*jiyu imin*). Upon arrival, most Japanese had neither the information about rural conditions, nor a large sum of capital investment to start a business.[18] Despite these obstacles, they found employment in transportation, hotels, and restaurants.[19] Some wealthy residents of Buenos Aires hired Japanese immigrants as domestic servants, especially as chauffeurs and gardeners.[20] As these immigrants moved toward self-employment in the early twentieth century, *tintorería*, or dry cleaner, became a thriving business. First established in 1921, this industry attracted many Japanese people because, unlike agriculture, it required minimum funds and experience to set up a store.[21] Because of the efficient service at *tintorería*, the Japanese gradually gained respect and trust in society, establishing upper-working class families. It is worth mentioning that Argentina maintained stronger commercial ties to Japan than other Latin American nations before World War II, and the country had one of the largest Japanese communities in the region after the war.

Their successful assimilation can also be attributed to at least three social factors. First, the Japanese were generally open to the local community, admitting native Argentines to their recreational events (e.g., sports activities) and hiring local residents in their businesses. This openness is in sharp contrast to the inward-looking nature of the Japanese communities in Brazil and Peru, where the industrial and commercial districts were strictly segregated.[22] For instance, whereas local Peruvians showed suspicion toward the exclusive character of the Japanese community, Japanese immigrants were often welcomed in Argentine society. It is also true that Argentina's rapid industrialization in the early twentieth century allowed Japanese immigrants, many of whom settled in Buenos Aires, to directly interact with urban residents rather than living in isolated rural areas.²³ Importantly, interracial marriage with Europeans was not uncommon for these early settlers, even for Issei or first-generation immigrants. For instance, Kinzo Makino, the first Japanese individual to arrive in Argentina, married a European woman, Amalia Rodriguez, and together they had four children with European names: Armando, Roger, Pedro, and José.²⁴ It goes without saying this kind of mixed marriage was also seen as an instrument for social mobility. The contrast with Brazil and Peru is evident in this regard as well: unlike in Argentina, most of the Japanese men who first migrated to Peru tended to avoid intermarriage by bringing "picture brides" from their homeland.²⁵ Another crucial element was the willingness to accept the Catholic faith, especially among Nisei (the second-generation) Japanese.²⁶ In the 1940s there was a campaign led by the Argentine government and Father Virgilio Filippo to convert Nikkei Argentines to Catholicism in order to facilitate their social integration.²⁷ During the postwar era the majority of Nikkei Argentines received higher education and became Catholic. These converts made annual pilgrimages to the sanctuary of the Virgin of Luján located in the province of Buenos Aires.²⁸ Although some people may not have remained active members of the Catholic Church, it is possible to assume that the general adoption of the country's religion played a significant role in their successful integration into the new society.

The positive reception of Japanese immigrants also reflects how Argentina's political and intellectual circles consistently showed interest in creating a close relationship with Japan. In the 1920s, President Marcelo T. de Alvear implemented a policy that encouraged Japanese immigration as a way to advance agriculture and the fishing industries.²⁹ His administration also sent emergency funds to Japan in support of the damages caused by the great Tokyo earthquake of 1923. During World War II, Argentina kept a neutral stance and only declared war at the last minute on March 27, 1945, when pressured by the United States. As Gary Y Okihiro explains, "World War II had little effect on the Japanese in Argentina, mainly because of the pro-Axis sympathies of the government."³⁰ As a result, while some restrictions were applied (e.g., a ban on meetings), it is understood that most Japanese residents did not suffer serious damages. For instance, Japanese-language newspapers were not censored until the last months of the war, and there was no evidence of the destruction of their property.³¹ While Japanese Brazilians were systematically labeled as "enemy aliens," Japanese Argentines were merely regarded as "foreigners under vigilance."

Based on these historical accounts, I ask, why were the perceptions of

Japan and Japanese immigrants so positive in Argentina? What were the factors that contributed to their "easier" process of integration and assimilation in comparison to their countrymen and women in Brazil and Peru? What made them more "acceptable" than other Asians, such as Koreans or Chinese?[32] I argue that the answer to these questions lies in varying degrees of modernity in Argentina, as perceived by local Argentines as well as early Japanese immigrants. There is no doubt that the Japanese were successfully integrated into Argentine society through diligence, perseverance, and hard work. Their small number certainly helped avoid unnecessary conflicts both within themselves and against the locals. According to Marcelo Higa, "these circumstances speak to the peaceful insertion of the Japanese into Argentinian society, without the traumatic experience they suffered in other regions like Hawai'i, the west coast of the United States, Peru or even Brazil."[33] Similarly, Isabel Laumonier explains the "low profile" of Nikkei Argentines as the following: "Japanese immigrants had deliberately kept a low profile. Quietly settled in the community, they were recognized for their honorableness and dedication to their work. Their social lives unfolded mainly within their own circles, and for the most part they did not participate in national politics."[34] Built upon the unique history of Japanese immigrants in Argentina, the first part of this book looks at how Argentine writers and intellectuals envisioned the integration of these newcomers through their own national imaginary. Specifically, I am interested in examining the political interests of Argentina's elite class that sought to portray Japan as an alternative model of civilization as early as the late nineteenth century. Unlike some other non-European immigrant groups, Japanese were perceived as a "civilized," "modern," and therefore "desirable" people. To put differently, their socioeconomic status was in some way comparable to the reality of being "white" in Argentina.

Discourse of Whiteness in Argentina

One of my central arguments in this book is that Argentina's century-old interest in Japan represents a disguised way to (re)claim its Western identity. In order to understand the positive perception of Japan and Japanese immigrants in Argentine history, I turn to the current debate on race in Argentina, particularly as it relates to the discourse of whiteness.[35] If we look at the history of Argentine nationalism, it is easy to find moments that indicate a penchant for becoming a white, European nation. An obvious example is the country's inclination toward the reception of European immigrants, mostly from Italy and Spain, beginning in the nineteenth century. The Argentine Constitution of 1853 explicitly referred to the government's preference for European immigration, even though equal rights were given to all inhabitants.[36] Between 1880 and 1916, approximately 2.9 million immigrants settled permanently in Argentina, making nearly one-third of the country's population foreign-born by the end of this period.[37] The national project to sponsor European immigration in an effort to whiten the population was advocated by such political figures as Juan Bautista Alberdi (1810–84), Domingo F. Sarmiento (1811–88), and José Ingenieros (1877–1925).[38] As George Reid Andrews argued in his groundbreaking work on Afro-Argentines, these intellectuals formulated their worldview based on European racial theories while ignoring the social reality that surrounded them.[39]

Another notable manifestation of Argentina's discourse of whiteness is the military campaign in the 1870s, known as the Conquest of the Desert. This project of territorial expansion was carried out based on the belief that indigenous people were not only "savages" but also destined to become extinct in a country that projected itself through a European lens. In fact, as Ignacio Aguiló discusses in his book *The Darkening Nation: Race, Neoliberalism and Crisis in Argentina* (2018), whiteness has always been a symbol of the hegemonic ideal in Argentine society.[40] According to him, the discourse of whiteness has historically forced people of color into the homogenous vision of a colorless nation. Consequently, "[w]hiteness became common sense and taken for granted: Argentina was hailed as a 'race-less' country while, in everyday reality, the inequalities that race produced contributed to the longevity of social hierarchies."[41]

Already in 1895, the official census declared that the Indigenous, African, and Asian races were practically non-existent in Argentina.[42] This national obsession with whiteness meant that the category of race almost entirely disappeared from public discussion, even though racial ideas continued to operate as the official modality to reinforce differences in one's skin color. In this way, whiteness was linked to the idea of racial homogeneity, which in turn became the model of progress and civilization. On the surface, Argentina portrayed itself as a *crisol de razas*, but in reality, this was an illusory representation of the mixture of different racial groups, mostly European, who were protected as the dominant class.

The narrative of whiteness went through a critical evolution during Juan Domingo Perón's presidency in the 1940s. His political movement marked a transformation from a mainly agricultural society to an industrial one.⁴³ In particular, Perón's regime successfully integrated the working-class population into national affairs. His politics, known as "justicialismo," was designed to reject both American capitalism and Eastern European communism in order to advance his nationalist agenda. It was a classic example of populist nationalism in Latin America: one that allowed the working class to participate in politics alongside the alliance between a military leadership and the entrepreneurial middle-class.

Importantly, the so-called Peronism revealed racial anxiety among many middle-class Argentines. During this period, *porteños* (residents of Buenos Aires) enjoyed new social status, high standards of living, better education, as well as economic prosperity. In terms of racial identification, they defined themselves as "white" as opposed to the dark-skin, lower-class masses from the underdeveloped provinces, who were associated with the racist term *cabecita negra* (black head).⁴⁴ The way middle-class Argentines embraced a white identity ensured the continuity of the discourse of whiteness through the second half of the century. Historians have long argued that Perón's main concern was the articulation of "the people" as a unified political subject and that racial or ethnic conflicts were of minor importance to his agenda. However, recent scholarship has reevaluated the role of racial politics in Peronist and anti-Peronist representations within the larger framework of the history of race and nation in Argentina.⁴⁵ As I will discuss in Chapter 3, Perón maintained a close relationship with the Japanese community in Buenos Aires, which illustrates how Peronism gave certain privileges and political entitlement to this racial minority in the mid-twentieth century.

What is striking about Argentina's historical narrative of whiteness is how the maintenance of the hegemonic ideal depends on the fluid nature of whiteness itself.⁴⁶ In many instances, racial homogeneity was achieved alongside a nebulous idea of what it meant to be "white" in Argentina. Within this scheme, some non-white people could symbolically belong to the national community, while continuing to manifest racial differences in reality. According to Aguiló,

> Imaginaries of racial homogeneity and the ambiguity of racialized subjectivities in Argentina meant that non-white groups could use them to distance themselves, at least momentarily, from stigmatized identities.... In this sense, Argentina's vague ideas about whiteness also had an inclusive component.⁴⁷

His discussion of the flexible nature of whiteness is suggestive because it underlines how non-white people can negotiate with the characteristics associated with whiteness in Argentina. For example, Aguiló studies Bolivian immigrants in contemporary Argentina as signifiers of non-whiteness that can be politically appropriated to celebrate racial diversity under the name of neoliberal multiculturalism.[48]

While Aguiló's study focuses on immigrants from other Latin American countries (Bolivia, Paraguay, Peru, and the Dominican Republic), my project examines Japanese immigrants as symbols of alternative whiteness. I argue that some Argentine intellectuals perceived Japanese immigrants as closer to their association of whiteness than other ethnic minorities because of the desirable characteristics they recognized in Japan.[49] This does not mean, of course, that these Asian immigrants were treated as equal to their European counterparts (e.g., the pejorative term *ponja* that was used to refer to the people of Japanese descent).[50] Nor am I suggesting that Japanese immigrants themselves acted as if they were "white" in relation to other minority groups. By the same token, it would be wrong to blindly ascribe "whiteness" to Nikkeijin living abroad, considering the history of racism and discrimination they suffered in other parts of the world (e.g., the internment of Japanese Americans during World War II). Instead, what I propose is that in the specific case of Argentina the discourse of whiteness can serve as a useful tool to understand positive perceptions of Japan and its people. It can shed new light on the way in which the experience of Nikkei Argentines differed from that of Nikkei Brazilians or Nikkei Peruvians in terms of the lack of state-wide discrimination.[51] At the same time, their presumed "whiteness" can also be compared to the "non-white" characteristics of other Asian groups, such as Chinese and Koreans. From this perspective, my study offers a critique of Argentina's racial imaginary, which is manifested in their (mis)conceptualization of Japan. In other words, Asians are presumably nonexistent in the country, except when they exhibit certain aspects of whiteness.

History of Westernization in Modern Japan

Similar to how the discourse of whiteness has operated as the hegemonic ideal in Argentina, Japan in the prewar period often looked to the West as a political and ideological model. While the historical context of this book primarily focuses on Argentina, the following overview is meant as a guide for readers who are unfamiliar with the history of modern Japan. Although the full scale of westernization in modern Japan is difficult to assess, it is safe to say that the Meiji period (1868–1912) was a radically transformative moment in Japanese history because of the overflow of Western influence.[52] The 1868 Meiji Restoration was decisive in terms of how a country opened itself to Western civilization after 214 years of isolation, following a foreign policy known as *sakoku*, meaning "locked country," from 1603 to 1868, during the Tokugawa shogunate.[53] Under the slogan *fukoku kyōhei* (Enrich the Country, Strengthen the Military), the early Meiji era can be defined by the process of rapid modernization as well as a revolutionary transformation of political, economic, social, and cultural institutions.[54] The leaders from this period, including Ōkubo Toshimichi, Kido Takayoshi, and Itō Hirobumi, passionately studied Western countries in order to adopt new methods and technologies that would help industrialize the country (e.g., creation of a new constitution, establishment of a parliamentary government, and introduction of compulsory public education).[55] In 1885, the Japanese newspaper *Jiji Shimpō* published an editorial called *Datsu-A-Ron* (Escape Asia) authored by Fukuzawa Yukichi (1835–1901), one of the leading intellectuals of the Meiji period.[56] This influential essay argued that Japan should distance itself from other Asian countries in order to grow closer to the Western world. In particular, Fukuzawa proposed replacing the civilizational model of classical, Confucian China with new models of Western technology, education, and nation-state.

Meanwhile, in 1889 the Meiji government promulgated Japan's first modern constitution, making a reference to the Great Empire of Japan, and the expansionist view of the Empire would clearly manifest itself during the Sino-Japanese War of 1894–95. Hence Japan's early process of modernization/Westernization went hand in hand with its imperial trajectory in East Asia. In some ways the country sought to imitate the West (and protect itself against the West) by reproducing its own system of control and oppression. For example, Japan's expansionism was seen in the occupation of Hokkaido (1869) and the Ryukyu Kingdom (1879), the colonization of Taiwan (1895), the annexation of Korea (1910), and the invasion of Manchuria (1931). As a result, the first half of the twentieth century is primarily understood as the history of imperial Japan. With the emperor serving as the absolute symbol of Japan's nationalism and imperialism, the country did not hesitate to show its hunger for international status and global power. In his study of the transnational history of Japanese immigrant settler colonialism, Eiichiro Azuma underlines "the exchanges of migrant bodies, expansionist ideas, colonial expertise, and capital in the Asia-Pacific basin before World War II."[57] As Azuma explains, Japan's modern history was closely linked with imperial aspirations:

> After the restoration of imperial rule (known as the Meiji Restoration) in 1868, the new nation-state self-consciously sought to build a modern monarchy patterned after western models, especially Prussia and Britain. From the outset, not only were Japan's new leaders concerned with establishing the structures and policies that would signal to the West that Japan was not a candidate for colonization, but they also actively set out to engage in imperialistic practices. In this sense, to be a modern nation-state was to be a modern empire.[58]

Takeuchi Yoshimi (1910–77), an eminent Sinologist and one of the most famous Japanese intellectuals of the twentieth century, believed that Japan's imperialist policies in Asia derived from the colonial interests of the West. For Takeuchi, Japan was willing to accept and appropriate the Western logic in order to occupy the position of regional superiority through violence.[59] One of Takeuchi's points of reference is the political debate known as *Seikanron* (Advocacy to invade Korea) (1873), which was a failed plan to invade Korea in 1873. Takechi saw this as an early example of Japan's interest in employing violence as a means to expand its territorial influence and to create a modern nation-state.[60] As I explain in Chapter 2, the Russo-Japanese War of 1904–1905 clearly demonstrated Japan's eagerness to be recognized as a global power with equal expansionist rights to the Anglo-Saxons.

Transpacific Modernity: An Asia-Latin America Perspective

My study follows this modern history of Japan, especially as it relates to the complex process of Westernization at the turn of the century. By juxtaposing Argentina's discourse of whiteness and Japan's history of Westernization, we begin to see how the two countries share the same aspiration to belong to the West in their respective ways. At the heart of this resemblance is the notion of exceptionalism. The general idea of exceptionalism constitutes an integral part of national imagination based on a sense of superiority over other people, countries, or any other institutions. As far as Argentina is concerned, as we have seen, the narrative of exceptionalism is often translated into the discourse of whiteness. Such an "exceptional" characteristic has been used as a point of reference when describing Argentina's "superior" position in comparison to other Latin American nations. Meanwhile, Japan's own version of exceptionalism has historically been defined in relation to its neighbors, especially China and Korea. To use Naoki Sakai's word, Japanese people can be characterized as "whites of Asia."[61] As described earlier, the radical shift toward Westernization in the late nineteenth century played a role in imagining Japan's "exceptional" characteristic. Similarly, another element of Japanese exceptionalism can be attributed to the country's economic success in the postwar era. Based on this comparison, we can argue that both Argentina and Japan see themselves as "exceptional" countries that are willing to claim their status as part of the West, even though their historical position has been peripheral in relation to Europe. One of the goals of my project is to investigate this particular South-South relationship in order to examine how a South American country came to identify with an East Asian country through their shared ambition for Westernization.

Related to exceptionalism, I argue that it is the concept of modernity that drew Argentina closer to Japan. According to the conventional Eurocentric understanding of modernity, the beginning of modern society can be traced back to the large scale of social and ideological transformation in Western Europe during the seventeenth and eighteenth centuries.[62] This process was defined by several major factors, such as the end of feudalism, industrialization, growth of the middle-class population, secularization, expansion of political participation, and the formation of "the people" as the subject of the nation-state. Most important, these features of modern society are attributed to an imagined symbol of cartography called "the West."

In the nineteenth century, this Western-style modernity became a model for the elites across the world, including the newly independent Latin American nations. In Argentina, Domingo Faustino Sarmiento's *Facundo* (1845) offered a famous paradigm of "civilization and barbarism," which played a fundamental role in defining the politics of modernity in Argentina during the nineteenth century and beyond. As Patrick Dove points out, "one of the central concerns of *Facundo* is to deliver a perspective, or more specifically a form of self-reflexivity, that would in turn engender or establish the bearings for Argentine modernity."[63] For Sarmiento, "civilization" was associated with the ideals of the European Enlightenment that were practiced in the metropolitan city of Buenos Aires. On the contrary, his notion of "barbarism" symbolized the backwardness of the native tribes, particularly gauchos, that were found in the countryside. This dialectic between civilization and barbarism became a prominent theme in the literature and culture of Argentina as well as those of Latin America. Most notably, it is the proposed contention itself that corresponds to the essence of a modern nation-state in Argentina. According to Dove, "As a thesis on Argentine modernity, *Facundo* posits a difference (the 'civilized' versus the 'barbaric') that derives its determinant force and its inscription of value not from eternal truths but from the *structure of opposition* itself."[64]

The experience of mass immigration from 1880 to 1930 also contributed to building a modern state based on the narrative of whiteness I discussed earlier. The anthropologist Arnd Schneider defines Argentine modernity through the nation's selective immigration process. He explains how "the whole experience of migration itself was a metaphor for modernity as it seemed to embody the promises of progress and upward mobility in a dislocated time (the *future*) and space (*America*, or in this case, Argentina)."[65] Used as a metaphor for progress, immigration served as a key instrumental for nation building with close ties to the notion of prosperity.[66] Moreover, as Julia Albarracín's recent study makes it clear, there is always a range of economic, cultural, and international factors that influence state decision-making processes in the establishment of Argentina's immigration policies.[67]

At the same time, immigration also gave birth to new cultural institutions that were crucial to the development of Argentine modernity during the first decades of the twentieth century. In her landmark book *Una modernidad periférica: Buenos Aires 1920–1930* (A peripheral modernity: Buenos Aires 1920–1930) (1988), Beatriz Sarlo offers an insightful study of the process of urbanization during the 1920s and the 1930s. Through an interdisciplinary approach, her book examines how Argentine intellectuals grappled with the urban transformation of Buenos Aires, which was manifested in feminist discourse, the aesthetics of avant-garde literature, and various forms of political discussion. One of her central arguments is that the cultural scene of the early-twentieth-century Buenos Aires was a "culture of mixture" (cultura de mezcla) in which "defensive and residual elements coexist with renovating programs."[68] According to Sarlo, Argentine modernity can be characterized as "peripheral" because it represented "a scene of loss but also of restorative fantasies."[69]

In order to highlight a different component of what Sarlo calls a "culture of mixture" in Argentina, my study refers to the term *transpacific modernity*, which, unlike earlier narratives of modernity, emphasizes a shift toward the Pacific.⁷⁰ I use the term to describe how Argentina's intellectuals looked toward Japan in search of an alternative, non-European model of civilization at the beginning of the twentieth century. Like Argentina, Japan constituted the locus of the periphery from the Western perspective. As such, transpacific modernity offers a different kind of "peripheral modernity" than Sarlo's original thesis. In the first part of this book, I discuss how Argentine writers and travelers sought to conceptualize a utopian vision of the "Japanese model" through their travel literature.⁷¹ The aforementioned paradigm of "civilization and barbarism" remains relevant to my discussion since the Argentine intelligentsia sought to characterize "civilized" Japan in opposition to its "barbaric" neighbors, whether it is China or Russia. In Chapter 1, I study the writings of the physician and politician Eduardo Wilde (1844–1913), who observed Japan's hygiene culture during his visit in 1897. By emphasizing the physical cleanliness as well as the spiritual integrity of Japanese people, Wilde's *Por mares y por tierras* (By seas and by land) (1899) explores a wide range of sociocultural issues, only to suggest that Japan can offer an example of modernization for Argentina. In addition, Chapter 1 analyzes *Viaje al Japón* (Journey to Japan) (1932) by another Argentine writer who traveled to Japan, Jorge Max Rohde (1892–1979). In his text, Rohde glorifies Japan's religious and spiritual traditions, following in the steps of the Greek-Irish American writer Lafcadio Hearn (1850–1904). As shown in this chapter, a comparative analysis of travel writings by Wilde and Rohde reveals the ways in which Argentina's elite class came to idealize the Asian nation, without necessarily losing their desire for Westernization.

Meanwhile, another manifestation of transpacific modernity is the high regard of Japanese militarism within Argentine society. As Keiko Imai explains, Argentina celebrated Japan's 1905 victory against the Russian Empire in major newspapers such as *La Nación*, *La Prensa* and *El País*.⁷² In Chapter 2, I examine how the rising Japanese empire was viewed as an example of civilization that could be translated into an Argentine context. My study focuses on Manuel Domecq García (1859–1951), an Argentine admiral who witnessed the Russo-Japanese War in person, and Yoshio Shinya (1884–1954) who was Domecq García's associate and the first documented Japanese immigrant in Argentina. Specifically, I analyze Domecq García's military reports in *Guerra Ruso-Japonesa 1904–1905: Estudio sobre la preparación y eficiencia de la Marina Japonesa* (1917; Russo-Japanese war 1904–1905: A study of the readiness and efficiency of the Japanese navy) alongside Shinya's book *Imperio del sol naciente: Su maravillosa evolución moderna* (1934; Empire of the rising sun: Its marvelous modern evolution). When read together, these texts illustrate how the two authors sought to promote positive images of Japan in Argentina by referring to the presumed "whiteness" of Imperial Japan. I contend that Japan's military success made its brand of territorial expansion a plausible model of transpacific modernity in Argentina's elite society. In their writings, Domecq García and Shinya ardently suggested that Argentina should learn from Japan in terms of its military forces, collective patriotism, expansionist agenda, and "Western" characteristics.

Nikkei Literature as Counternarrative

The concept of transpacific modernity is significant insofar as it reflects the celebration of Japan and its people in the early twentieth century. From this perspective, it comes as no surprise that other Argentine writers such as Leopoldo Lugones (1874–1938) and Jorge Luis Borges (1899–1986) also used their literary work to praise different aspects of Japanese culture, such as haiku and samurai.[73] However, the image of Japan portrayed in the narrative of transpacific modernity is often essentialized and homogenous, much like the discourse of whiteness in Argentina. Only in the twenty-first century has the literary representation of Japan in Argentina become more nuanced and complicated thanks to the contributions by Nikkeijin. While Part I of this book mostly deals with the perceptions of Japan among Argentines of European descent (except for Shinya), Part II grapples with how a new generation of Nikkei writers is challenging this earlier discourse of modernity. Unlike Brazil or Peru, where there is a long history of Nikkei literary and cultural production, Argentina has not seen a widespread creation of Nikkei literature. It is partly due to the national emphasis on multiculturalism in the last two decades that significant literary works by minority groups have been published in Argentina. As I show in Part II, a small group of Nikkei writers has begun to tell their own stories of immigration and present counternarratives to the traditional imagery of Japan that was created almost a century ago.

For my discussion of Nikkei literature in Argentina, I establish a dialogue with Ignacio López-Calvo, who characterizes Asian-Latin American literature as an alternative form of *Weltliteratur*. According to López-Calvo, "Asian-Latin American literature, as a paramount non-Eurocentric body of work, can extend links and bridges to soften, beyond withered orientalist approaches, this purported rivalry between the Asian and Euro-American world-systems vying for literary hegemony in the twenty-first century."[74] I would argue that an emphasis on Nikkei literature in Argentina has the potential to complicate the country's hegemonic discourse of whiteness. Because of the non-Eurocentric aspect of the transnational literature involving Japan and Argentina, this kind of cultural product puts into question the framework of racial homogeneity invoked by whiteness. The discussion of Japanese Argentine characteristics can challenge the nation's historical identity as a homogenizing and unifying force of culture. To borrow Walter Mignolo's word, I am interested in exploring the possibility of "pluriversal" subjectivity as opposed to the white, Eurocentric, and monocultural universality.[75] By analyzing contemporary Nikkei literary texts, my study seeks to highlight a non-Western, post-national form of citizenship and identity formation.[76]

In Chapter 3, I study the representation of a transnational, hybrid identity in two of the pioneering works of Nikkei literature in Argentina, namely Héctor Dai Sugimura's *Buscadores en mis últimas vidas* [Seekers in My Last Lives] (1995) and Maximiliano Matayoshi's *Gaijin* [Foreigner] (2003). These novels are among the first literary works that address the formation of what can be considered Japanese Argentine subjectivity. By focusing on the paradigm of hyphenated hybridity in their novels, Sugimura and Matayoshi articulate a different concept of "Japaneseness" than the one proposed by the Argentine writers I study in the previous chapters. At the same time, the analysis of the fluid nature of immigrant identity in both novels indicates a critical approach to Argentina's historical narrative. Rather than adhering to the idealized vision of Japan viewed through the lens of whiteness, the two Nikkei authors in this chapter present a more nuanced and reflective perspective on the country of their ancestors.

Chapter 4 turns to Nikkei female writers, Anna Kazumi Stahl and Alejandra Kamiya.[77] While Sugimura and Matayoshi paved the way for a new kind of Japanese immigrant literature in Argentina, Stahl and Kamiya take it a step further because their writings purposefully create space to rethink Nikkei cultural identities beyond the male-centered point of view. By analyzing Stahl's novel *Flores de un solo día* (2002; Flowers in a single day) and Kamiya's short stories in *Los árboles caídos también son el bosque* (2016; Fallen trees are the forest, too), I examine how these writers embody resistance to the essentialist depictions of women. The protagonists in their works demonstrate instances of female solidarity as well as critiques of patriarchal values through the notion of what I call "gendering Orientalism." Despite their diverse personal and sociohistorical circumstances, these characters equally defy the conventional understanding of what it means to be Japanese or Nikkei daughters, mothers, wives, and grandmothers. I argue that the counternarratives offered by Stahl and Kamiya can be understood in two ways: their literature symbolizes resistance against the ideology of whiteness, on the one hand, and against the system of patriarchy, on the other.

Finally, Chapter 5 investigates the representation of Japanese immigrants and their descendants in three contemporary Argentine films, which I compare with another film about the experience of Chinese immigrants. Clara Zappettini's documentary *La otra tierra: japoneses en Argentina* (1986; The other land: The Japanese in Argentina) provides one of the earliest visual manifestations of the Nikkei experience in Argentina. Some of the themes I discuss in Chapters 3 and 4 recur in this film, including the conflict between Japanese and Argentine identities, as well as generational differences within the Nikkei community. This chapter will also compare two feature films from the 2010s: Gaspar Scheuer's *Samurai* (2013) and Sebastián Borensztein's *Un cuento chino* (2011; Chinese take-away). While these movies similarly present Asian immigrants as constituents of Argentina's multicultural society, they also show how the Japanese are portrayed in a more positive light than their Chinese counterparts. In my view, the Japanese protagonist in *Samurai* represents the contemporary symbol of transpacific modernity, while the Chinese immigrant character in *Un cuento chino* is reduced to an object of dehumanization. Lastly, in order to understand the lasting legacy of the Nikkei community in Argentina, I examine the documentary, *Silencio roto: 16 Nikkeis* (2015; Broken silence: 16 Nikkeis), directed by Pablo Moyano. This film narrates, for the first time, the story of Nikkei Argentines who lost family members during Argentina's military dictatorship in the late 1970s. As shown in this chapter, the study of visual representations can complement the earlier analysis of literary work because they each seek to redefine the traditional narratives of modernity, nation-building, and immigrant identity.

As I have noted, there have been different representations of Japan in Argentine literature and culture. In the past, the images of Japan were often constructed by writers of European descent, and these images sought to promote a monolithic and homogenous view of the Asian nation. As the writers I study in Part I envision an alternative model of modernity based on such a celebratory view, the Argentine government also portrayed Japanese immigrants as a privileged "model minority" in order to paint the portrait of a diverse multiracial nation. It is only through the emergence of literary production from the Nikkei community itself that the representation of their homeland becomes more nuanced. Collectively, these Nikkei projects in Argentina serve as a counterpoint to the essentialized notion of Japan that claims historical teleology in parallel with the discourse of whiteness. In other words, the decolonization of knowledge allows the people of Japanese descent to disavow the grand narrative of modernity. The purpose of this book is not to set forth a comprehensive historical recollection of Japanese immigration in Argentina. Rather, my goal is to provide a critical tool through which to problematize the traditional paradigms of race, ethnicity, and nationality, while proposing a new understanding of transnational Nikkei subjectivity in Latin America.

PART I

TRANSPACIFIC MODERNITY

An Asia–Latin America Perspective

CHAPTER 1

Argentine Chronicles on Japan

Hygiene, Aesthetics, and Spirituality in Eduardo Wilde and Jorge Max Rohde

This chapter examines the chronicles by two Argentine intellectuals who offered some of the earliest accounts of Japan and its cultural traditions at the turn of the twentieth century. Eduardo Wilde and Jorge Max Rohde traveled to Japan and wrote about their experience in *Por mares y por tierras* (1899) and *Viaje al Japón* (1932), respectively. While both are crucial texts for understanding how uncritical views on Japan were constructed and shared with the Argentine audience as early as 1899, they made appeals based on differing aspects of Japanese society. Wilde focuses on Japan's aesthetic values by emphasizing the hygiene culture in both private and public spaces. His interest in the "cleanliness" of Japan is also contrasted with the "dirtiness" he perceives in China. For Rohde, Japan's most desirable attributes can be found in the spiritual tradition of what he calls the "old Japan." By praising Japanese history through romantic glorification, Rhode saw himself as a natural successor to the Greek Irish-American writer Lafcadio Hearn (1850–1904), creating a European gaze that exoticized the Oriental other.[1] As I show in this chapter, a comparative analysis of travel writings by Wilde and Rohde reveals how Argentina's intellectual class came to idealize Japanese society as an alternative model of modernity.

It was Eduardo Wilde—a physician, politician, and writer—who spearheaded the long journey from Argentina to the other side of the globe at the end of the nineteenth century. During his visit in 1897, he observed the transformation of a traditional, long-isolated country into a modern society with pervasive Western influence. One of the aspects that caught his attention was the importance of hygiene. In his travel narratives published in *Por mares y por tierras*, Wilde affirms that the Japanese "practice *the hygiene of the soul* by maintaining tranquility in their spirit, just as they maintain the cleanliness of their bodies."[2] By highlighting personal hygiene as well as moral integrity, the Argentine traveler seeks to explore various aspects of Japanese society based on his scientific perspective.

Wilde's admiration for such practice of "the hygiene of the soul" contrasts with his perception of China, the country he visited prior to Japan. According to Wilde, despite the geographical proximity, the two countries represent opposite realities and values. His notes about Chinese society are mostly negative reflections, especially with regard to their hygiene culture. For example, he writes that "the hygienic conditions in China—public and private—are deplorable; the poverty, the misery, the abominable food quality, the dirtiness, the humidity as well as the exhausting work and lack of clothing, must be the causes of the notable annual decrease in population."[3] From social problems to moral issues, the Argentine author employs an exaggerated language to depict China as an antithesis to its neighboring country.[4]

Like Wilde, Jorge Max Rohde was a prolific writer who held a deep passion for travel. Between 1926 and 1931, he made four trips to Asia and authored books of chronicles, including *La senda del palmero* (1928), *Viaje al Japón* (1932), and *Oriente* (1933). Whereas Wilde was attracted to the modern technology and the social institutions of the island nation, Rohde was more interested in Japan's artistic and religious aspects. In particular, as I show in the second half of this chapter, his *Viaje al Japón* is filled with celebrations of the country's traditional virtues that have been lost in the Western world. For Rohde, the beauty of Japan and its people can be appreciated through the parameters offered by Lafcadio Hearn, whom he considered a "master." Reflecting on his Eurocentric view, I will also argue that his emphasis on the Japanese tradition is tied to his implicit acknowledgment of Japan's imperial agenda.

In comparison to the famous writers of Latin American *modernismo* such as Rubén Darío and José Martí, Wilde and Rohde are still relatively unknown figures in Latin American literary traditions. One of the goals of this chapter is to place the two Argentine writers within the pantheon of *modernistas* who turned to the Far East in search of new inspiration. As I show, both Wilde and Rohde share numerous characteristics with other *modernistas*, including their romanticized view of Asia and their sexualization of Asian women. Moreover, Wilde's chronicles not only deal with the cultural connections between Asia and Latin America, but also suggest a hierarchical relationship between Japan and China. In other words, his critique of Chinese society can be read as a strategic way to emphasize, in turn, the splendor of the Japanese nation. To use the famous dichotomy proposed by Sarmiento, it is possible to say that Wilde's China represents "barbarism," while his Japan symbolizes "civilization." For his part, Rohde at first does not directly suggest Japan's superiority over its neighboring country. His writings on Japan are mostly meant to celebrate its cultural history of spirituality. However, underneath his reflections is a tacit acceptance of Japanese expansionism, which also indicates his belief in the existence of hierarchy within the region. Read together, their chronicles demonstrate different ways in which Wilde and Rohde underscore their views on Japan in order to suggest the notion of transpacific modernity: an alternative model of civilization for the future of Argentina.

Latin American Travel Narrative on Asia

Before entering into a discussion of Wilde and Rohde, it is useful to situate their travel writings within the larger conceptual framework. *Writing Culture: The Poetics and Politics of Ethnography* (1986), edited by James Clifford and George Marcus, is without a doubt a fundamental text about the concept of "culture" that has influenced numerous fields, including history, anthropology, cultural studies, and postmodern theory. The argument about "the poetics and the politics of the ethnography," as suggested by the title, concerns how and with what purpose one can analyze the history of the foreign or exotic Other, questioning the authority of the Western worldview.[5] Like the project of New Historicism in the 1990s, one of the permanent legacies of *Writing Culture* is its contribution to the contemporary debate on the politics of representation, in particular the ability to speak about the culture of the marginalized subject.

Likewise, in *Imperial Eyes: Travel Writing and Transculturation* (1992), Mary Louise Pratt introduces the concept of "contact zone" to refer to the space of imperial encounters that allows previously separated subjects—whether by geography or history—to interact with each other.[6] The contact established in this space exposes relationships held in asymmetric situations of power between the colonizer and the colonized, between the traveler and the native, and between the center and the periphery. In contrast to the narrative of conquest and colonization created by an imperial project, her discussion focuses on the interactive dimension of the transoceanic encounter between Europe and the Americas, not in terms of their separation but "in terms of co-presence, interaction, interlocking understandings and practices, often within radically asymmetrical relations of power."[7] One of the central arguments of Pratt's study lays in the decentralization of the "planetary consciousness" of the West, leading to the restructuring of the hegemonic ideal.[8]

Latin American travel writings on Asia, including those of Wilde and Rohde, present a different dimension to Pratt's theory, which does not address any Asian countries in depth. *Imperial Eyes* defines some of the most critical concepts in terms of the power dynamics between the colonial subject and the subaltern Other. However, the bipolarity between Europe and the rest of the world may not be the most adequate tool to explore the relationship between Latin America and Asia, since both regions share similar histories of colonialism despite their geographic differences. In other words, the understanding of the historical and cultural ties between Latin America and Asia demands a different kind of theoretical approach that goes beyond the hegemonic intersection between the old and the new worlds.

In the last two decades, a new group of literary critics have developed a theoretical framework regarding the representation of Asia in Latin American travel narrative. In *Orientalismo en el modernismo hispanoamericano* (2003), Araceli Tinajero argues that Latin American *modernistas* who traveled to Asian countries toward the end of the nineteenth century played a key role in the cultural reconstruction of the transpacific network. By analyzing some of the most representative *modernista* chronicles, Tinajero's study revolves around the impossibility of understanding the Asian-Latin American relationship from a Western point of view. Tinajero proposes some provocative questions for postcolonial readers:

> What are the forms of representation that emerge from a discourse created from a "margin" of Western modernity to another "margin"? . . . What is the dynamic that emerges from this approach, from an "exotic subject" to another "exotic" subject; and through the *modernista* perspective what and who is exotic?[9]

Her study is in dialogue with Edward Said's classic text *Orientalism* (1994), which explains the power structure of the colonial discourse that seeks to both (re)produce and maintain Western hegemony. For Tinajero, *modernista* travelers are interested in creating a "productive conversation" with Asia through their symmetric and eclectic literature. Instead of imagining themselves through the lens of inequality, she argues, Latin Americans tried to find commonalities between their native countries and the Asian land they came to admire.

In the case of Argentina, my study owes an important debt to Axel Gasquet's *Oriente al Sur: El orientalismo literario argentino de Esteban Echeverría a Roberto Arlt* (2007), which is the first book to explore the representation of the Orient in Argentine literary texts. Gasquet studies many Argentine writers who traveled to the Middle East and East Asia, such as Domingo Faustino Sarmiento, Lucio Mansilla, Pastor Obligado, Leopoldo Lugones, Wilde, and Rohde.[10] Similar to Tinajero, Gasquet affirms that Argentine Orientalism differs from Said's theory because of its "reflective" and "introspective" nature.[11] He also argues that one of the differences between European orientalism and the Argentine version resides in how Argentina did not project economic or political interests in their approach to the Oriental world.[12] Instead, Gasquet proposes a cultural dialogue between the two regions without a European lens. As he puts it, in Argentina there was an authentic desire to know about foreign people and their cultures, outside the conventional binary of Europe versus Latin America.[13]

In the following pages, my analysis of Wilde's and Rohde's chronicles seeks to establish a conversation with the aforementioned studies, without ignoring their importance. It is true that both Argentine authors try to imagine a new cultural link between Asia and Latin America, the two regions that have shared the same peripheral history based on Hegel's view of the world.[14] However, a closer look into the comparative study of Wilde and Rohde allows us to go beyond the essentialist idea of what "Asia" symbolizes. I argue that though Wilde's and Rohde's writings seem to part from the Western perspective in terms of the Hegelian structure of hegemony, their texts manifest a different kind of hierarchy within Asia. In contrast to the other *modernista* writers, Wilde presents a scientific perspective to envision a political view through which to imagine Argentina's future by juxtaposing Japan's civilization and China's anti-civilization. In Wilde's mind, the power relationship exists in the "contact zone" not between Latin America and Asia but between Japan and China. Rohde, on the other hand, follows the step of his "master" Lafcadio Hearn as he glorifies Japanese traditions from a Eurocentric perspective, recreating the Orientalist vision of the exotic Other. In both cases, the notion of a symmetric cultural dialogue between Asia and Latin America based on respect and equality seems to reveal a problematic paradigm to analyze the works of Wilde and Rohde. I suggest it is necessary to question the singular perspective that tends to illustrate a homogenous Asia. At the same time, it is also important to discuss the multifaceted—and at times contradictory—nature of the Argentine perspective on the Far East.

Wilde on Japan and China: Civilization and Barbarism

Wilde belonged to the so-called "Generation of '80" whose main proposal lay in the consolidation of a liberal oligarchic regime in Argentina through positivist ideology and a European model of progress. Between 1880 and 1890, Wilde played an important role in national politics. In 1882 he was named Minister of Justice and Education under the presidency of Julio A. Roca, and with this position, he helped promote secular education as well as civil marriage in the nation. In addition, he also had a successful career as a physician, hygienist, professor, and writer.[15] As we will see, his concern with public health is a central theme in his chronicles on Japan, which makes him different from other *modernistas* from the period.

Following his political career, Wilde spent some time traveling around the world, beginning in Europe, across Africa, and arriving all the way to Asia. His letters appeared in *La Prensa*, one of the most popular newspapers in Buenos Aires at that time. Later, some of his diaries and notes were published in *Por mares y por tierras* (1899) and *Viajes y observaciones* (1939). During his travel through Europe, Wilde affirmed that European countries had lost their charm and that there was no innovative culture in the Old World. For example, when he visited Paris in 1890, he described the French city, which Walter Benjamin called "the capital of the nineteenth century," as a forgotten spectacle from the past. In one of his notes titled "Entre París y Bruselas" (Between Paris and Brussels) written in 1939, the Argentine author's pessimism is palpable. He expresses his deprecation by confessing that "the sediment of my short stay is a sensation of sadness" and that "Paris has appeared to me as a city in a daze, unaware of what is happening in the world."[16] With inspiration from the philosophy of positivism, Wilde saw himself as a modern man who despised the reminiscence of the past. For him, Europe was an ancient place that nostalgically lived in history and classic books, totally isolated from the rest of the world and the new development of modernity. As Lila Bujaldón de Esteves observes, this critique of the European model separates Wilde from other Argentine intellectuals of his generation.[17]

In sharp contrast, his 1897 visit to Japan was full of astonishment and excitement, which he did not hesitate to express in *Por mares y por tierras*. It seems as if the Asian country offered him a cultural archetype of civilization that he could not find in Europe. Upon his arrival to the Japanese capital, he declared that "all I see is real and positive, proper and genuine from this delicious place of the globe that I so wanted to visit."[18] It is important to note that since Wilde's trip took place decades after the Meiji Restoration of 1868, there were fundamental transformations in the nation in regard to its sociopolitical structure and cultural norms. The Japanese army defeated the Chinese Qing dynasty in 1895 after a bloody war, leading to the expansion of the Japanese Empire in East Asia. As I explain more in Chapter 2, another decisive moment took place when Japan managed to obtain an unexpected and striking victory in the war against Russia in 1905, making the country the only Asian nation to have defeated a Western power in modern times and thus shifting the regional geopolitics in a significant way.

China, on the other hand, was going through a period of crisis and confusion at the end of the nineteenth century. The defeat in the war of 1895 was a sign of major humiliation for the Qing dynasty, which had to pay significant reparations to the Japanese Empire. Even before the war, the country was suffering from systematic corruption in the government, partly due to the extensive use of opium and the existence of internal conflicts in the country. In contrast to Japan, China ended up losing its geopolitical power in the region, which is evident in Japan's annexation of the Liadong peninsula, the island of Taiwan, and the Manchuria region.

As I show in the following pages, Wilde can be studied alongside other *modernistas* from nineteenth-century Latin America. His observations about Japan concern not only political issues but also aesthetic and cultural themes. For him, Japan incarnates a society that has modernized itself successfully without shedding its traditional values. He describes the country's modern transformation in the following way:

> I attend the act of transformation of people and arrive at the supreme moment in which two civilizations touch each other, to say goodbye; the ancient one immersing itself in the memories of the past, opening way to the modern one with the approval by the children of the land who, if

they had no other virtue than to adapt to such radical changes, that alone would be enough to raise them before the eyes of all humanity and signal them as examples.[19]

In his view, Japan was able to celebrate the intersection between the past and the future, unlike European countries that were incapable of embracing modernity and tradition. Here Wilde uses a rhetorical tool to highlight Japan's historical significance based on his elite Latin American perspective.

Furthermore, the Argentine author compares Japanese and European art: "In Europe they may produce millions of analogous pieces, but almost in all of them we see commercial *pattern* but not divine *art*. A cane head in the old Western world is a vulgar object; in Japan it is a living being that speaks if it represents a human head, and trills if it imitates a bird."[20] It must be noted that this preference for Japanese art over European (especially French) art was not new to Latin American intellectuals of the time. In this sense, Wilde aligns himself with other *modernistas* who also traveled to Japan at the beginning of the twentieth century. For instance, when the Guatemalan Enrique Gómez Carrillo (1873–1927) arrived to Tokyo in 1905, he compared Japanese and Western cultures in *El Japón heroico y galante* (The heroic and gallant Japan): "And inside the tiny train, the smallest one, lighter than the trolley in Madrid, the peculiar movement of each arrival is announced, but not like in Europe, not with feverish impatience and childish curiosities, not with noise or joy but deeply and slowly."[21] For Gómez Carrillo, the Japanese train invokes such values as tranquility and delicacy, while he associates the European train with impatience and immaturity. In his *En el país del sol* (In the country of the sun), the Mexican writer José Juan Tablada (1871–1945) describes his experience in Japan in the same way: "the Russian artist and I exchanged our European garments for the national kimono, which is superior in *comfort* and elegance."[22] Tablada emphasizes the modernity achieved by the Japanese in their culture, focusing on the better quality of Japanese fashions and literally replacing his Western clothing for the kimono. Inspired by Japanese modernity as opposed to the European paradigm, many *modernistas* use their chronicles to reflect on the reality of their own countries in Latin America.[23]

What makes Wilde different from his contemporary *modernistas* is his scientific perspective as a physician and a hygienist. In order to fully understand Wilde's travel narrative on Asia, we need to examine his role as a leading public hygienist in Argentina between the 1880s and the turn of the century. Most important, his view on hygiene is related to the social circumstances of late-nineteenth-century Latin America, where such topics as "health," "cleanliness," and "hygiene," connected to "sexual morality," were becoming a constant obsession.[24] The massive publication of magazines and public announcements promoting physical energy and hygiene habits created a widespread concern for the maintenance of good health in both public and private discourses. It was not uncommon for popular magazines to publish warnings about unhygienic behaviors, such as kissing statues at religious institutions or using the telephone in public.[25] Indeed, the concept of "filthiness," in both moral and social sense, was one of the most representative metaphors of "barbarism" in the continental imaginary of the time. Beatriz González-Stephan explains how Latin America's modernity was intrinsically associated with the politics of cleansing, which produced the culture of surveillance and coercion through the imposition of pure and non-contaminated categories.[26] In Argentina, the concept of a "hygiene utopia" (utopía del higienismo) began to appear in the 1870s, when the country suffered from serious problems caused by pollution and decomposition.[27] Together with Wilde, other hygienists from this period, including Guillermo Rawson and Pedro Mallo, established a new epidemiological paradigm focusing on public education, social institutions, housing, and nutrition, among other issues.[28] As Kristin Ruggiero points out, one of Wilde's most important arguments was that while it was essential for public institutions to try to control disease and pollution, it was also crucial for people to change their habits, including how to properly dispose of their own waste, like cadavers, feces, and urine.[29] In Wilde's words, public health requires both institutional support and individual morality: "Instruction, morality, good nutrition, good air, sanitary precautions, public assistance, public benefits, work, and even free entertainments; in the end, attention to all that could constitute an obligation from each individual and all the inhabitants of a county or city."[30] Viewed from this perspective, Wilde's different perceptions on Asia can be understood in relation to his profound concerns for Argentine reality. As Clifford and Marcus remind us, the poetics and the politics of ethnography make one's account of the "other" also a construction of him/herself.[31] In metaphorical terms, then, it can be said that Wilde's China is a reflection of an undesirable and primitive Argentina. He sustains that "the Chinese are alien to all the elements of civilization on the management of their cities" and that "Chinese cities are a labyrinth of tortuous, dirty, and narrow streets."[32] He further writes that there are no hygienic arrangements in such places because the creation of public space is not based on scientific knowledge but rather on superstitions and supernatural beliefs.[33] Epidemics like cholera, smallpox, typhus, and the bubonic plague can enter and exit the country at any given time due to its overwhelming population and the penetrating dirtiness in the streets.[34] Later on, he asks, why is it that there are not so many deaths caused by diseases as expected? The only rational explanation, the author believes, is that "the microbes of the habitual negligence are stronger that those of epidemics."[35] For Wilde, China represents an abominable space where poverty and misery are the inevitable consequences of the absence of social consciousness in regard to hygiene practices.

While the Asian barbarism represented by China signals a dangerous image for the future of a country, Japan seems to offer him an oasis of hygiene and order. If, as Ruggiero argues, one of the central aspects of Argentine modernity was "a raised consciousness of the public good and a commitment to science as the warranty of progress," then Wilde discovered in Japan a potential solution to the problem of public hygiene.[36] During his stay, he describes everything in terms of beauty in the streets, schools, and hospitals. For example, he visits a local home in Kamakura and is impressed by its cleanliness: "Leaving Daibutsu we entered a small Japanese wooden house; it is like a toy, I said, by its distribution and cleanliness."[37] Apart from the building's sanitation, the Argentine traveler also refers to the "pure" nature of the Japanese people, which he calls "the hygiene of their altruism" (la higiene de su altruismo).[38] For him, the importance of hygiene is both pragmatic and metaphorical because his concerns include not only physical cleanliness but also moral integrity. Wilde visits various Japanese schools and universities in order to learn the ways in which "the hygiene of the soul" is taught and practiced.[39] Whereas in China he observes the world of superstitious beliefs, in Japan he perceives a scientific education that is meant to create a "refined" people: "With elements of education transmitted from ancestors to descendants and fostered from the cradle to the grave, there is nothing strange about how an affable, courteous, tolerant, sentimental, and artistic people with refined tastes have been formed; lovers of the beautiful and the good, genuinely honest and estimable from every point of view."[40] Wilde suggests that the ideal, universal form of human progress can be achieved through such culture of cleanliness and honesty. His reference to Japan's "affable, courteous, tolerant, sentimental, and artistic people with refined tastes" indicates a desire to see their example as a way to create a new sense of morality in Argentina. With its scientific education, his perception of modern Japan is the incarnation of a desirable model for his country's progress.

It comes as no surprise, then, that he wishes to promote Japanese immigration in Argentina. Referring to a meeting with Viscount Enomoto Takeaki (1836–1908), Wilde writes, "The viscount is currently in charge of sending immigrants to Brazil and Mexico. I urge him to also send them to the Argentine Republic and I offer to send him the laws and decrees relating to immigration."[41] While Fidélis Reis, an advocate of the anti-Japanese movement in Brazil, once described the Japanese as "the yellow cyst" that is unassimilable by blood, language, or religion, Wilde suggests that the hygienic culture of Japanese people will bring positive influence to his country. Curiously, the diplomatic relationship between Japan and Argentina was established in 1898—a year after Wilde's visit—with the Treaty of Friendship, Commerce and Navigation. Although it is difficult to calculate the exact influence of Wilde at the beginning of this bilateral relationship, it is safe to say that he was one of the first Argentine intellectuals to advocate for the potential impact of Japanese immigrants in the country. Significantly, it is clear that the positive image of the Japanese was created earlier than the start of the official immigration. In other words, these immigrants came to symbolize a "model minority" even *before* they had set foot in Argentina.

When it comes to China, Wilde's chronicles never mention the necessity to bring Chinese immigrants to Argentina. It seems evident that he would not support such a project, believing as he did in the "barbaric" characteristic of Chinese people who practice what he calls "the primitive cult of nature."[42] Considering this undeserved criticism, it is ironic that the Chinese community represents the majority of the Asian population in today's Argentina, far more than the Japanese or the Koreans.[43] Even though Chinese immigration was quite limited at the beginning of the twentieth century, the last wave of Chinese (and Taiwanese) immigrants starting in the 1990s has surpassed those of other Asian immigrants. However, a massive integration of the Chinese into Argentine society does not imply that they were free from racist and xenophobic experiences, as I will show in Chapter 5. Wilde's critical perspective on China during the nineteenth century revealed some of the negative stereotypes that Chinese immigrants would later endure in the twenty-first century.

Furthermore, Wilde's contrasting views regarding Japan (civilization) versus China (barbarism) also become apparent in his depictions of women. For him, the physical beauty of Japanese women is indisputable: "almost all young Japanese girls are pretty, funny, happy and affectionate; their most notable physical attraction is their neck, followed by their hands and feet."⁴⁴ This characterization is also manifested in José Juan Tablada's essay "La mujer japonesa" (The Japanese woman), where he writes, "in all parts, the *musumé* [young woman] is enchanting, flower of the outdoors and of palatial refinement, vibrant cicada or golden pheasant."⁴⁵ In their imaginations, both Wilde and Tablada exoticize Japanese women as objects from a male point of view. However, unlike his Mexican contemporary, Wilde offers a more scientific view based on his medical background and pays close attention to the female body. He details, for example, the size of the women's hands, the posture of their arm, or the specific form of their feet. What is noteworthy is his obsession with Japanese women's necks, which he describes as an "insurmountable aesthetic form" (insuperable forma estética).⁴⁶ It almost seems as if Wilde's scientific and masculine gaze sought to perform an imaginary anatomy in the female body when he writes, "[i]t is true that maybe I would find such qualities in a neck separated from its corresponding head and chest."⁴⁷

In contrast to Japanese women, Wilde portrays Chinese women in extremely negative terms. First, he poses a comparison between Chinese and European females, insisting that "many Chinese women behave with their husbands like European and American women," suggesting that China remains as "backward" as Europe.⁴⁸ Later he mentions, without evidence, that the Chinese women mistreat their husbands because "they cheat on them, ridicule and spoil them, and force them to work their entire lives; they demand everything from them and they pay their sacrifices with ingratitude, disloyalty, and disregard."⁴⁹ Although Wilde is aware that many women find themselves in a position of servitude with their husbands or fathers, he never seems to shy away from discussing the "disloyal" and "ungrateful" characteristics of Chinese women. As a result, he concludes that Chinese women do not represent an ideal model of femininity inasmuch as they lack any sentiment or feeling. Unlike the delicate and sensitive women of Japan, he sees how "because of her position and the lack of form through which to develop herself, the [Chinese] woman cannot have affectionate feelings, not for her parents, her siblings, or men she does not know."⁵⁰ Furthermore, Wilde's medical attention to the female body characterizes what he calls "the repellent monstrosity" (la repelente monstruosidad) of the deformed feet of Chinese women.⁵¹ It becomes evident that his depiction of the "monstrous" Chinese women is in direct opposition to the "insurmountable" beauty of Japanese women described earlier. In this way, Wilde seems to create a hierarchy of aesthetics in which Chinese "monstrosity" serves as a point of contrast to Japanese "beauty." At the same time, Wilde claims that the Chinese woman's "ugliness" is also reflected in the very culture of the country. He refers to the absence of creativity and innovation based on the false assumption that the imaginative capacity is nonexistent in China.[52] When it comes to Chinese sculpture, for example, he characterizes it as "grotesque, eccentric, monstrous, and unpleasant" (grotesco, estrafalario, monstruoso, desagradable).[53] By emphasizing the notion of "monstrosity" or barbarism in China, Wilde maintains that China and Japan represent cultural and aesthetic counterpoints within the Oriental space.

Nevertheless, it must be recognized that his writings about both countries share the same exoticized fetishization of Asian femininity, which is the problem of what Ann Cheng calls "ornamentalism."[54] In Japan, Wilde visits a famous house of prostitution in Yoshiwara, Tokyo, ensuring to the reader, in a form of public confession, that his visit was "for information only."[55] His notes describe the enclosed condition of the Japanese women in Yoshiwara: "There are the houses of courtesans with their cage-like display of monstrosity, where instead of birds there are young women, the prettiest ones, all well-dressed, honest in appearance, kindly smiling, and without doing anything improper."[56] After illustrating the interior of the house and the women he met—named "Hamawogi" and "Wakataque"—Wilde examines the reason why he believes these women are involved in prostitution.[57] According to him, "the girls who prostitute themselves at home do not think they are doing anything wrong; they do it with the consent of their parents."[58] However, the real history tells us that many of the Yoshiwara women were victims of forced labor. The majority of courtesans were sold by their parents to enter prostitution when poverty did not leave them any other options. As Hiromi Stone points out, the girls were usually between ten and fifteen years old when they were sold like commercial products, but some of them were barely seven or eight years old.[59] The living condition of these young women and girls was dreadful: they suffered from chronic malnutrition and lack of sleep, which explains why many of them ended up dying before they reached twenty. In addition to poverty, they also suffered from sexually transmitted diseases. According to the official registry at the Jokanji temple, the site where the corpses of many prostitutes were left in abandonment, syphilis and other related diseases were the most common causes of their deaths.[60] Taking into consideration these extremely severe circumstances in which the Yoshiwara courtesans lived, one can only conclude that Wilde's account stands far from the historical reality of the country.[61]

Wilde discusses prostitution in China from another point of view. His writings show that "the common houses of prostitution, at least the genuinely Chinese ones, are miserable."[62] He sees many "ugly" women and some "almost pretty."[63] He refers to how Chinese prostitution has "the stamp of poverty, necessity, habit, abandonment and indolence, little respect, I will say, for one's own body."[64] As Gasquet notes, Wilde finds in Chinese prostitution an institution that lacks voluptuousness, almost deprived of sexual symbols.[65] Such a negative characterization is considerably different from Wilde's earlier observation of Japanese prostitution. For him, the innate beauty of Japanese women is not stained even in the house of prostitution, although his visit seems contradictory to his belief in hygiene habits. The only way to reconcile these two opposing sides—the practice of promiscuity and the faith in cleanliness—is through his emphasis on the cleanliness of the place. In Wilde's mind, the "miserable" and "dirty" condition of the Chinese prostitution once again serves as a counterpoint to the "clean" and "healthy" space of Japanese prostitution: "In my reports I must say that in the great Yoshiwara of Tokyo and its simile of Yokohama, the rooms are large and clean, the food of the prostitutes healthy and abundant, and the dresses, to their satisfaction."[66] Regardless of the accuracy of his observation, the difference in perspectives is notable. In Japan, Wilde offers a favorable evaluation of the still vicious practice of prostitution and even shows sympathy for the "unhappy" women living in the institution. On the other hand, the conditions of Chinese prostitution are so dirty and deplorable that the author offers no sign of empathy or understanding. From his aesthetic-scientific point of view, the same practice of prostitution produces radically different perceptions as well as contradictory values he perceives within Asia.

Rohde's Perspective on Japanese Aesthetics and Spirituality

The way Wilde celebrated Japanese culture and society left an important mark for the next generation of Argentine writers, including Jorge Max Rohde. Rohde's trip to Japan took place thirty years after Wilde's, but some of the observations he set forth in *Viaje al Japón* are similar to Wilde's view.[67] Prior to Japan, Rohde traveled in the US for two months, visiting such cities as New Orleans, Houston, and Los Angeles. Interestingly, he offers negative accounts of American society, which would be contrasted with his positive impressions of Japan. As mentioned earlier, Japan witnessed a large-scale increase of modernization and industrialization with the 1868 Meiji Restoration. The country's transition into an industrial economy was largely completed by the early twentieth century. Hence, when Rohde arrived in Japan in 1931, the country had already received much Western influence in politics, education, architecture, and art. Upon his arrival to Yokohama, he expresses a certain discomfort in the way in which the West presents itself constantly in the country. As he depicts the Japanese port city, "the invalid city stands in a manly way to don a full suit in the American style."[68] His criticism of American influence also extends to the architecture he witnesses in Tokyo. Bewildered by the lack of "authentic" Japanese culture, he wonders, "Where is the Japanese soul?"[69] As it turns out, what he calls the "native spirit" (espíritu indígena) can be found in the "old Japan" untouched by the Western world. In his words, "the old Japan, with its beliefs and social differences, flows under the European mask and is offered to the naïve tourist."[70]

Whereas Wilde focuses on the modern aspect of Japan especially through hygiene culture, Rohde turns his attention to the country's past for inspiration. For instance, his interest in traditional Japanese arts is juxtaposed with his distaste for European art. During his visit to the Museum of Modern Art in Tokyo, he laments, "What a stupid fruit produced by the Western influence on this floor!"[71] Rohde believes that the "native spirit" of Japan still exists and can be manifested in a new form despite its foreign-looking surface:

> May the current era conclude with the renaissance and, therefore, the aesthetic predominance of the native spirit, already booming in the Nara period, which spans from 645 to 780, in those amazing paintings and sculptures that it embraces, especially, the Horyu-ji sanctuary, around the time when Europe becomes shadows in the cemetery where Latin civilization lies![72]

Here the idea of "renaissance" invokes a nostalgia for Japan's older society, particularly the Nara period, which, contrary to his claim, began in 710 and continued until 784. Also known as Heijo-kyo, this was an era in which art and culture flourished under the protection of a government that officially supported Buddhism. Many Buddhist temples were constructed during this period, including Todai-ji, Kofuku-ji, and Gango-ji. In the quoted passage, Rohde characterizes European civilization through the images of death/cemetery and shadow, while defining Japanese civilization through the notion of rebirth. It is through this emphasis on aesthetics that we can understand Rohde as an individual deeply interested in universal beauty and spirituality. Gasquet calls him a man of "renaissance humanism," highlighting that his vision represents a return to the aesthetic values of modern humanism in the late nineteenth century.[73]

Rohde admires the persistence of religious and artistic practices, described as a profound sense of spirituality in Japanese culture. At the same time, he also reminds the reader that Japanese aesthetics is a synthesis of diverse, foreign traditions:

> Let us remember that foreign influence entered this soil in the middle of the sixth century. Let us remember that some Korean priests bring the good news of truth, in other words, of beauty, undoubtedly moved by a transcendental design ... A journey, the final one, of aesthetic drama is fulfilled: India instills its consciousness, its lucid consciousness in the dormant China on the back of the mythical dragon.[74]

In this view, the essence of Japanese culture stems from the history of amalgamation involving different Asian elements, such as those introduced by Koreans, Indians, and Chinese.[75] Unlike Wilde, who clearly differentiates Japan from China based on his conceptualization of sociocultural hierarchy, Rohde does not seem to suggest that Japan is superior to China. Instead, he willingly accepts and celebrates the integration of Chinese influence into Japanese spirituality. His emphasis on cultural synthesis indicates that Japan's uniqueness lies precisely in its ability to borrow from other nations to reinvent itself. Perhaps it would not be an exaggeration to say that Rohde saw more heterogeneity in Japanese culture than Wilde did. Moreover, the idea of synthesis manifests itself in more abstract terms, as in the unification of the universal and the particular: "In the admiration that we leave in the astonishing sanctuary there remains the concept: the universal and the particular happily baptize the birth of Japanese art."[76] With a mixture of exultation and glorification that characterizes the general tone of the book, Rohde underlines the ostensible synthesis between the whole and the part in Japanese culture, a topic that would later be addressed by Octavio Paz in his reflections on India.[77]

Despite his exuberant idealization of Japanese culture and spirituality, a close analysis reveals how his representation is decidedly partial, because he recreates certain stereotypes of the country. In his travel narrative, Rohde follows the example proposed by Lafcadio Hearn, who is considered one of the most prolific writers about pre-modern Japan and is often portrayed as a purveyor of the Asian country for Western audiences. It is well-known that Hearn was a longtime admirer of Japan (he lived there for the last fourteen years of his life during which he married a Japanese woman, Koizumi Setsuko, and assumed Japanese nationality with the name Koizumi Yakumo).[78] Hearn was a definite role model for Rohde, as evidenced by the essay the latter dedicated to the former in *Humanidad y humanidades* (1969; Humanity and humanities). However, as Lila Bujaldón de Esteves observes, Rohde's admiration of Hearn began in his earlier text called *Casas ilustres* (Illustrious houses) published in 1930.[79] According to Bujaldón de Esteves, Rohde was impressed with Hearn's ability to immerse himself in Japanese culture, unifying the Asian values with the new demands of modern Europe.[80]

In *Viaje al Japón*, we see Hearn's life and work highlighted with an almost melodramatic tone, sometimes in comparison to other European writers and artists.[81] For Rohde, Hearn's Japan is a quintessential example of civilization because it represents the spiritual manifestation of the Asian country in the most idealistic sense. Rohde elucidates how Hearn discovers "the land of the spirit" in Japan. Most important, Rohde calls him a "master" who lived "the existence of the spirit in aesthetic and imperial annals."[82] What inspired Rohde was the way in which Hearn combined Oriental and Occidental elements through his depiction of Japan. During a visit to Hearn's house in Tokyo, Rohde shares a deep reflection on Buddhism, especially on the notion of reincarnation, which also influenced Hearn's notion of Japanese spirituality:

> Here we are in the garden of Lafcadio Hearn. Here we are in the garden of the liturgical rocks of the lamps that consecrate the race, the race itself— in a special sense—in the numerous existences with which the spirit that penetrates our flesh liked to incarnate itself through immeasurable time; of trees and flowers, whose nuances and perfumes make up the difficult poem clearly read by some predestined monks; of the threads of water that reflect the perpetual evolution of the cosmos, the eternal change of life.[83]

The Argentine traveler interprets Japanese nature through the eyes of his Greek Irish-American mentor in such a way that the two men's voices become almost indistinguishable. As a self-proclaimed disciple, Rohde feels that his mission is to continue the legacy of his master by promoting the positive images of Japan and its religious heritage. To use Hephzibah Roskelly's phrase, Rohde follows in Hearn's footsteps by serving as a "cultural translator" for Western and Latin American audiences.[84] His close association with Hearn indicates that, even though Rohde seems critical of Western influence in Japanese society, his view remains deeply ingrained in Eurocentric views.

Like Hearn, Rohde's perspective is that of an Orientalist who exoticizes the Oriental Other. His writings are much less factual renditions of Japan than imaginative glorifications of the remote country. This exoticization is most apparent in his observations of Japanese women, which are comparable to Wilde's masculine perspective I discussed earlier. For Rohde, Japan is a "paragon of culture," which is reflected in the beauty of its women:

> The Japanese woman is the paragon of culture; she is the harmonious triumph of civilization; she deifies human subject with the mystery—the ineffable mystery—of grace. Through her, especially through her, Japan is a refuge—the last remaining refuge of the universe—for the nostalgic traveler.[85]

The masculine gaze that turns to Japanese women in search of "ineffable mystery" can only be described as a fetishized desire to dominate the exotic Other. The Japanese spirituality he celebrated before is exemplified in the figure of these women, and it is in them where he discovers "the last refuge" from the rest of the world. However, it becomes clear that his treatment of women only exposes his inseparable ties to the Western point of view. To use Anne Cheng's word, Rohde as well as Wilde transform the Japanese woman into a "body ornament" and place her in the category of "perihumanity" in which "she represents feminine values but is often considered not a woman at all."[86]

Hence it should not be surprising that Rohde shows an obsession with the beauty of Japanese geishas. During a geisha performance in Kyoto, he expresses his fascination with how "[o]ur *geishas* gather in their physiognomies the softness dispersed by the world."[87] Struck by their grace, the Argentine traveler fantasizes himself as a "hero" of their dreams: "Let us thank them for the grace of farce: through them [their dreams] mercenary love is purified in the love of art; through them *we become heroes of the dream on a spring night.*"[88] In his view, women are assigned different roles in Japanese society. While mothers maintain the religious tradition of the "old Japan," young girls adhere to the culture of submission devoted to men. For their part, geishas serve to preserve, in his words, "the cult of art in the religion of beauty."[89]

The pervasive influence of his masculine gaze suggests that he celebrates the aesthetics of Japanese women only insofar as they are unmarked by European influence:

Will Western influence even reach Japanese women? Will they endure, like fairy-tale heroines, on the porcelain, the fan, and the folding screen? Will they pass on to the next generation the message of beauty that they received intact from the older generation raised in feudal courts? We think nostalgically about the future; we think that the feminine grace that the world still possesses can be obscured with the shadow of a world that was buried, a long time ago, in the daily struggle of life, in the sexual equality of rights and obligations, by the romantic secret of grace.[90]

Rather than advocating for gender equality, this self-declared "hero" argues that the Western value of individualism would destroy Japan's "feminine grace" when women claim their own rights or "sexual equality." From this perspective, it can be argued that his earlier criticism of Western modernity is actually a veiled attempt at preventing women from achieving equality and freedom.[91] A similar view is presented when Rohde visits a women's school in Tokyo. In a building he describes as "a pavilion of American style," he tells the reader that female students are receiving not the study of Japanese traditions, but Western-style instructions in sewing, literature, art, and music. Disappointed by the lack of "authenticity," he claims that "the formal education—especially the European one—that young women receive strikes us as wrong, as on the other hand they are obligated to accept the familiar prejudices of the old country."[92] By refusing to accept foreign influences, Rohde's position denies women's access to education. In fact, he argues that if a Japanese woman studied accounting, she would not be the ideal incarnation of femininity because she would cease to be "the flower that seduces us" (la flor que nos seduce).[93] It is clear that for the Argentine writer, the Japanese women are no more than sexual objects whose sole purpose is to seduce men, both local and foreign. In this sense, his call for the preservation of Japan's old values must be examined in a new light. His ostensive celebration of Japanese tradition is itself a calculated strategy to insert his Western, masculine subjectivity into the Oriental, feminine Other.

Moreover, Rohde's reflection on the significance of established customs reveals another aspect of society as he defines Japanese culture in terms of the history of imperialism. According to him, "[i]t is likely that tradition—a tremendous force in imperial society—will collide with daily life."[94] Celebrating the long tradition of the country is directly linked to embracing the imperial trajectory. Since Rohde aims to contribute to the celebration of Japan like Hearn, it is understandable that he never discusses other elements, avoiding the country's nation-building strategy that was vital to colonial expansion in Asia in the late nineteenth century. Rohde purposefully refuses to see a relationship between traditional Japanese culture and the growing militarism of the empire. As mentioned earlier, Japan began its imperial expansion in 1879 with the annexation of Hokkaido and the Ryukyu Islands (today's Okinawa), followed by the control of Taiwan, Manchuria, and Korea. While Hearn overtly approved of Japan's victories against China and Russia, Rohde does not offer explicit endorsement of Japan's imperial vision. However, his travel narrative never rejects Japanese militarism as a regional force, which again is closely related to Rohde's overall interest in the old tradition. He frequently refers to the natural beauty of Japan as a symbol of the empire. In Nikko, for example, he writes that "the empire that raised beauty in this place is powerful."[95] In Tokyo, he is impressed by the trophies earned during the wars against China and Russia, claiming that Japan is yearning for more victories in the region and that its territorial expansion has a vital meaning in history. When it comes to the potential power of the empire, Rohde even contradicts his earlier critique of Western influence: "I hope Japan only benefits from the West the arts of technology, science, and industry, which today flourish with extraordinary vigor in the glorious empire."[96] Although he does not entirely accept the Western presence in Japan, he seems to suggest that the "glorious empire" might actually benefit from Western "technology, science and industry." His proposal is noteworthy not only because it contradicts his earlier criticism about Western influence but also because the Japanese military already proved themselves as experts in Western-style weaponry during the Russo-Japanese War.[97]

As I have demonstrated in this chapter, Wilde and Rohde showed their admiration for different aspects of Japan through their travel writings, thus contributing to the narrative of transpacific modernity in Argentina. Like the discourse of whiteness itself, this blind admiration for Japan is male-centered as well as Western-oriented. For Wilde, the hygiene practices and the morality of the Japanese people are defined in opposition to what he perceives as the filth and the indecency of the Chinese. Of particular importance is how Japan and China constitute a sociopolitical paradigm of his national imaginary via the dichotomy between civilization and barbarism.

We can perceive a certain political agenda in Wilde's chronicles: to educate the Argentine reader for the improvement of their moral and social behaviors based on a new Asian model. With his ornate and descriptive language, Rohde also introduces the Argentine readership to various cultural practices and rituals of Japan. I concur with Gasquet in arguing that Rohde's view of Japan mirrors his vision of Argentina at the time, according to which he defended the aristocratic ideologies of the Generation of '80 and went against the progressive social agendas implemented by Hipólito Yrigoyen.[98] A close analysis of his chronicles reveals that, like Hearn, Rohde looks toward Japan based on a Eurocentric perspective that reproduces the Orientalist images of the Other. At the same time, his implicit approval of Japanese imperialism is indicative of how his interest in the "old Japan" parallels his indifference toward the geopolitical conflict in the region. In truth, the impact of Japan's emergence as a new superpower could be felt everywhere, even on the opposite end of the world. As I discuss in the next chapter, Japanese imperialism was embraced by both the Argentine admiral Manuel Domecq García, who witnessed the Russo-Japanese War, and his protégée, Yoshio Shinya, the first official Japanese immigrant in Argentina.

CHAPTER 2

Empire across the Sea

Narratives of Japanese Imperialism in the Writings of Manuel Domecq García and Yoshio Shinya

In the late nineteenth century, the elite classes in both Argentina and Japan were deeply invested in finding ways to bring progress and industrialization to their respective countries. In Argentina, decades of internal conflicts after independence were finally coming to an end when nationalist sentiment was consolidated during the war against Paraguay (1864–70). In addition, there was an attempt to eliminate the nation's indigenous people through the military campaign against Indian resistance on the frontier, known as the Conquest of the Desert (1879). In the name of modernization, "uncivilized" people of indigenous heritage were considered "savages" who were slated for extinction. Following this history of violence, Buenos Aires officially became the nation's capital in 1880, and the new president Julio A. Roca initiated a political transition into the new age of liberalism.

If we look at the other side of the globe, Japan was almost simultaneously undergoing the process of political and social transformation. The feudal military government of the Tokugawa shogunate was overthrown by supporters of the Meiji Restoration in 1868, ending two centuries of isolationist policy. As Japan opened itself to the outside world, the educated class tried to absorb as much Western influence as possible, not only by advocating individual rights and democracy, but also by emulating Western fashion and diet.[1] In her preface to the 1900 edition of *Unbeaten Tracks in Japan*, Isabella Bird, a British writer and explorer, mentioned the arrival of a "brilliant and successful Empire," that took its place "on equal terms in the family of civilized nations, the only Oriental power to which this intimate relationship has been conceded by the European and American Governments."[2]

In considering the similar process of modernization that took place concurrently in Argentina and Japan, this chapter studies the impact of the Russo-Japanese War (1904–05) as well as the representation of Japanese imperial power in early-twentieth-century Argentina. While Japanese imperialism would later be viewed as a domestic threat in other parts of Latin America (e.g., the terrorist group known as "Shindō Renmei" in Brazil during the 1940s), it did not produce such hostile reactions in Argentina.[3] After discussing some key historical moments that revealed the influence of Japan's rising power in Argentina and beyond, I will examine the military report by Manuel Domecq García, who observed the Russo-Japanese War in person. I will then turn my attention to Domecq García's close associate, Yoshio Shinya, who was the first documented Japanese immigrant in Argentina. Specifically, my comparative analysis focuses on Domecq García's *Guerra Ruso-Japonesa 1904–1905: Estudio sobre la preparación y eficiencia de la Marina Japonesa* (1917) and Shinya's *Imperio del sol naciente: Su maravillosa evolución moderna* (1934). Read together, these texts illustrate how the two authors similarly sought to promote positive images of Japan in Argentina in the first decades of the twentieth century. As I explain in this chapter, Japan's military success was seen as part of the narrative of transpacific modernity within Argentina's society. If rebellious Amerindians were relegated to the past in Argentina's national imaginary, civilized Japanese emerged as a new symbol of power for the nation. I argue that Domecq García and Shinya offered different perspectives on what Argentina could learn from Japan, including topics related to militarism, nationalism, and expansionism.

The Russo-Japanese War and the "Whiteness" of Japan

The Russo-Japanese War was a historical event on a global scale. Besides being the first international conflict of the twentieth century, it was the first time that wireless communications were deployed in a war. It was also the first war in which fleets of steel battleships faced each other on the high seas, as well as the first battle that included a long period of trench warfare.[4] Most important, it was the first time, in modern history, that an Asian country was able to overcome a Western power, which transformed the racial perceptions of Asians around the world. As Naoko Shimazu explains, the war inspired "the imagination of international contemporaries, representing many iconic clashes: West versus East, Europe versus Asia, Christian versus 'heathens,' tradition versus modern, and white race versus yellow race."[5] It is also worth noting that Japan's "surprising" victory influenced other non-European leaders, including the Indian Prime Minister Jawaharlal Nehru and the African American activist Mary Church Terrell. Pankaj Mishra suggests that the final battle of Tsushima had moral and psychological implications for many years in countries like Turkey (Ottoman Empire), Vietnam, India, and China.[6] In Western eyes, however, there were mixed reactions to this global event: while Japan was seen as a new threat to the geopolitical configuration of Asia, it was soon to be regarded as a nation of "honorary whites" in the network of colonial powers.[7]

Some historical context is necessary in order to understand the enormous significance of this world event. It is well-known that the 1890s witnessed the emergence of the so-called "Yellow Peril" in the Western world.[8] Although the categorization of Asian yellowness had already been invented by the German physician and anatomist Johann Friedrich Blumenbach in 1795, it was not until the late nineteenth century that modern science turned the notion into a widespread phenomenon. Large-scale, East Asian immigration to the West played a role in provoking pervasive fear of social degradation and potential military intervention. By the 1890s, many Western nations had willingly embraced the call to defend themselves against what they regarded as the invasion by the "Yellow race."[9]

In China, the notion of yellowness was traditionally accepted as an important historical and cultural signifier, which was evident in the naming of such symbols as the Yellow River or the mythical Yellow Empire, the presumed ancestor of the Han people.[10] In contrast, many Japanese resented the association with the yellow race and preferred to be associated with the European white race, especially at the conclusion of the Sino-Japanese War. The historian and economist Taguchi Ukichi noted in 1904 that "we can reject the ill repute that the Japanese are yellow" and that "those who maintain superiority and excellence in Japanese society are by no means of the yellow race."[11] His remark came shortly after Japan established an official alliance with the Great Britain in 1902, which signaled the country's insistence on securing global status on a par with the most powerful nation in the world. According to Taguchi's narrative, the "yellowness" of the Chinese must be distinguished from the "whiteness" of the Japanese, whom he compares to the Persians, the Greeks, and the Romans.[12] He proposes that Japanese men and women should wear hats to "whiten" their faces and to "ennoble their status."[13] Unlike other Japanese nationalists who sought to define their identity in opposition to the West, Taguchi and his colleagues claimed Japan's unique culture and its newly acquired military power through an equal relationship with the Western society. As a result, they willingly chose to distance themselves from their "yellow" neighbors from China and Korea.[14] In this sense, Wilde's assessment of Japan's "civilization" and China's "barbarism," which we examined in Chapter 1, was also adapted by Japanese intellectuals themselves in terms of their own colonialist discourse.

It is important to underline that Japan's presumed "whiteness" was already evident during the invasion of Taiwan in 1874, the so-called "Taiwan Expedition." The historian Robert Eskildsen elucidates how this national project revealed the Japanese government's attempt to appropriate principles of Western imperialism/civilization in order to advance their regional expansion. In his words, "the idea of exporting the Western civilizing impulse to the indigenous population of Taiwan helped justify, naturalize, and explain the concurrent effort to modernize Japan."[15] Western notions about power, control and hierarchy were widespread in Japanese society during the 1870s.[16] Interestingly, the way in which Japanese authorities saw this expedition as an effort to bring "civilization" to Taiwan is similar to how Argentina fought against the "uncivilized" natives during the Conquest of the Desert, which also took place in the 1870s.

Moreover, the self-definition of Japan as a nation comparable to a white Western country became a focal point of national debate when their imperial aspirations grew more apparent during the conflict against the Russian Empire. Subodhana Wijeyeratne appropriately characterizes the Russo-Japanese War as a "race war."[17] As he illustrates, some important Japanese thinkers from the early twentieth century—including the aforementioned Taguchi Ukichi, Katō Hiroyuki, Asakawa Kan'ichi, and Oka Asajirō—celebrated how Japan's victory shattered the conventional narrative of racial hierarchy that was created by Europeans and supported by Social Darwinism. According to these intellectuals, it was the Japanese race, not Russians, that was destined to become prosperous and civilized. For example, Asakawa Kan'ichi characterized Japan's potential as equal to that of other

Western countries. In his 1904 text about the ongoing Russo-Japanese War, he declared that his country was "the champion in the East of the rising civilization," which had joined the circle of the industrialized Western world in the aftermath of the conflict.[18] He further argued that Japan's history proved that the country had successfully become closer to other Anglo-Saxon nations.[19] Also in 1904, the newspaper *Yorozu chōhō* published an article that went so far as to mention Japan as a presumed savior of Western civilization:

> Russia is the shame of Europe, we need to defeat this nation in the name of civilization, in the name of peace, and in the name of humanity. Europe should be pleased that there is a new nation in the Far East which will bear the torch of their civilization and is suppressing the troublemaker, Russia.[20]

Desperate to grapple with the prevalent notion of the Yellow Peril, these Japanese intellectuals in the early twentieth century looked for ways through which to define their global power vis-à-vis Western notions of civilization and whiteness.[21] As Naoko Shimazu suggests, "the Japanese somehow became 'white' and adopted stereotypical Western attitudes toward Orientals, with the accompanying sense of racial and cultural superiority."[22]

Depictions of Japan's Imperial Power in Argentine Newspapers

After examining the early history of Japanese imperialism, we ask ourselves: what is the relevance of the Russo-Japanese War to Argentina? At first glance the remote conflict in East Asia seems to have no implications for Latin America. However, I believe that the Argentine public was paying close attention to this global event for at least two reasons. On a symbolic level, as I discussed earlier, Argentina had a history of national obsession with the discourse of whiteness, which can be applied to the "whites" of Asia. In a more practical sense, the country looked toward the rising power in the Far East because of its own interest in developing stronger military forces. Since the mid-nineteenth century, Argentina had been expanding its army through the process of nation building. The War of the Triple Alliance against Paraguay enabled the government to consolidate political control over the interior of the country. After participating in the war, the army general Julio A. Roca emerged as one of the leading figures in the political scene and served as president from 1880 to 1886 and from 1898 to 1904. Roca believed that the new Argentine army needed to play an important role in the process of national unification. Most important, the army provided the decisive means to resolve the "Indian problem" during the Conquest of the Desert. The success of this military campaign, which ultimately exterminated much of the indigenous population in the nation, was partly due to the introduction of new technologies, such as imported repeating rifles and telegraph lines that were used for rapid and efficient communication.[23] At the same time, the reinforcement of military forces was also Roca's strategic move toward defending the country from its neighbor, Chile. Convinced that a strong army was essential for a strong nation-state, Roca implemented compulsory military service in 1901 and signed a treaty to settle a border dispute with Chile in 1902.

Given the national concern to consolidate the army as an integral part of modernization, it is easy to imagine that Argentina was eager to learn about Japan's military success on the far side of the globe. In fact, Argentina's interest in Japan's military power began earlier with the Sino-Japanese War. In 1894, *La Nación*, one of the leading newspapers in the country, published an article about the conflict in the Far East. Only a few days after war had been declared, the article on August 2 titled "China y Japón: La declaración de guerra" (China and Japan: The declaration of war) gives the reader a general assessment of the situation. It refers to Japan as "the one that takes the initiative, the one that is ready for great revolutions."[24] The writer's sympathy becomes palpable when he argues that Japan "sacrifices itself for a civilizing purpose," while China "is going to employ its forces to maintain its static situation, its backwardness."[25] The depiction of Japan in terms of its "civilizing purpose" indicates that the Argentine newspaper saw the potential of this rising power even before their actual triumph in April of 1895.

When the Russo-Japanese War broke out a decade later, the Argentine public once again paid careful and consistent attention to the conflict, as did the rest of the world.[26] It is also worth remembering that Argentina offered direct support to Japan during the war by selling two battleships in 1903: the *Rivadavia*, renamed the *Nisshin* in Japanese, and the *Moreno*, re-baptized in Japan as the *Kasuga*. Today the Ministry of Foreign Affairs of Japan still acknowledges on their website that these cruisers "played a key role in the decisive May 1905 Battle of Tsushima, which sealed Japan's victory."[27] For Marcelo Higa, the significance of this military assistance lies in strengthening the diplomatic relationship between Japan and Argentina, which had already been established in 1898.[28]

In the early twentieth century, Argentina's major newspapers covered the Russo-Japanese War on several occasions, either directly through personal accounts or indirectly through what other countries were reporting.[29] In particular, *La Nación* published various articles on this topic between 1904 and 1905.[30] While these newspaper articles address different aspects of the war, what they have in common is a highly positive view of Japan's military forces. Similar to how the Japanese saw themselves as the "saviors" of the Western world against the "uncivilized" Russians, Argentine media also internalized this imperial discourse, perhaps not unrelated to their own sense of exceptionalism. For example, in an article from April 2, 1904, titled "Guerra Ruso-japonesa: Notas militares y navales" (Russo-Japanese war: Military and naval notes), the author celebrates how the Japanese generals received education in the military academies in Germany and France and thus held strong ties to Western technology. Another article from May 9, 1904, titled "El imperio del sol levante: Progresos sorprendentes" (The empire of the rising sun: Amazing progress), discusses Japan's strong army in relation to the country's sophisticated hygiene culture. According to this article, "If Japan has succeeded in such a short time in being a first-class military power, it is not only due to the organization of its combat units, but also to that of the auxiliary services of the army and especially that of sanity."[31] When Japan's victory was almost certain toward the end of the war, *La Nación* highlighted how the Japanese model could provide some useful lessons for Argentina. The article from June 20, 1905, titled "La 'nación' en el imperio del sol naciente" (The 'nation' in the empire of the rising sun) claims that the war clearly revealed the transformative power of Japan: "that old country, renovated, that suddenly emerges with a virile and ardent youth, suitable for warrior triumphs and for the conquests of civilization."[32] The essay goes on to suggest that Argentina should learn from Japan's experience:

> We, as a community that is still looking for its path and that still has a lot to initiate and learn, are extremely interested in everything that refers to the *palpitating example* of what good organization and a clear and logical plan can do for the future development and greatness of nations.[33]

In this passage we see a direct link between what was regarded as Japan's "palpitating example" and Argentina's own efforts to create a modern nation-state. This connection became more apparent when the young army general Juan Domingo Perón, who would later serve as the country's president twice, taught an academic course on the Russo-Japanese War at the Escuela Superior de Guerra in 1933. This class led to the publication of his two volumes under the title *Apuntes de historia militar: Guerra Ruso-Japonesa de 1904–1905* (Notes on military history: Russo-Japanese war of 1904–1905). Perón not only describes the Japanese as "a hardworking and civilized people," but also argues how "with the results obtained in the war it was easy to foresee . . . the importance that Japan would assume among the greatest world powers."[34] Although Japan was geographically a non-Western country, the consequences of the war made it clear to the Argentine public that it was a successful modern nation that demonstrated desirable attributes for their own country. This alternative model of transpacific modernity is based on Japan's growing geopolitical power and influence. In the pages that follow, I will examine in detail how the military aspiration for transpacific modernity was envisioned by two intellectuals in the early-twentieth-century Argentina.

Manuel Domecq García and the Russo-Japanese War

During the Russo-Japanese War, the government of Japan invited Argentina to send a navy official to witness the combat, and the captain Manuel Domecq García was chosen to serve in the role. As an observer, Domecq García studied the operations, the tactical skills, and the philosophy of the Japanese navy, which he compared to his own naval forces.[35] During his two years of stay in the Asian nation, he visited military sites and became close friends with Admiral Tōgō Heihachirō, Commander-in-Chief of the Japanese navy. When Tōgō defeated Russia at the Battle of Tsushima, Domecq García was also present on the flagship, the *Mikasa*. After returning to Argentina, he maintained close contact with the Japanese immigrant community, serving as president of the Japanese Argentine Cultural Institute and contributing to the promotion of Japanese tradition and culture.

In his book *Guerra Ruso-Japonesa 1904–1905: Estudio sobre la preparación y eficiencia de la Marina Japonesa*, written in 1917, Domecq García discusses his observations of the Japanese imperial navy in addition to his general impressions of the country.[36] Unlike Wilde and Rohde, Domecq García came to Japan without any previous knowledge of the country's traditions. When he saw Mount Fuji upon his arrival, he wrote, "I consider that greeting by Japan's sacred mountain a fine omen of arrival in a country that is completely unknown to me, its customs, its language and its peoples, etc."[37]

He was, however, keenly aware of the effectiveness of the military tactics used by the Japanese forces. For Domecq García, Japan's triumph in the war was not a surprise, as many had claimed, but an inevitable result of the dedicated preparation by its people. In his book, he argues that Europe was astonished only because of its ignorance of the reality of the Asian nation:

> I have heard many times, especially during and after the last war, that Japan had surprised Europe with its triumphs given that no one expected or imagined them. But I say that Europe was surprised because it wanted to, because it listened to writers who lacked in authority, and because it has been indifferent and simple.[38]

As he points out, the problem was the Western perspective that refused to consider Japan's power seriously. He insists that "Europe did not realize nor believe that Japan could march ahead in the way it had adopted; Europe still did not take Japan seriously, believing that that country of men with fans and skirts living in paper houses could never become anything other than a simple joke."[39] According to him, the perfect example of this ignorance was the Russian Empire itself, which he referred to as a country blindly believing itself to be invincible and protected by divine will. Echoing the positive notions about Japan that we saw earlier in the newspaper articles, the Argentine veteran soldier imagined "civilized" Japanese as opposed to "ignorant" Russians. He concludes that had the world carefully studied the organization of the Japanese navy, everyone would have easily foreseen their victory.[40]

Domecq García's critique of the European perspective on Japan can be compared to the vision of Wilde and Rohde that I discussed in Chapter 1. However, the Argentine admiral offers a different view, owing to his firsthand experience with the navy and his insistence on the aggressive, combative nature of the Japanese people. During his time in the island nation, he often visited the Navy school and interacted with the students. According to his assessment, the Japanese navy was among the most gifted and powerful fighting forces in the world: "I believe that it is difficult to find people like the Japanese who possess great aptitudes to be a soldier and especially to be a marine."[41] He suggests that these people have what he calls "an eminently combative spirit." As he puts it, "the military sentiment is developed in them [the Japanese] in an extraordinary way, and the warrior life has always attracted them the most."[42] While Wilde and Rohde highlighted the laudable model of Japanese society in terms of their hygiene practice, aesthetics, and spirituality, Domecq García saw an example of collective aggressiveness and advanced technologies in Japanese militarism.[43]

Guerra Ruso-Japonesa 1904–1905 carefully analyzes the organization and the structure of the Japanese navy. First, the Argentine author describes the efficiency and the perseverance with which the people prepared themselves for the war: "In the creation and organization of an efficient force like the naval force, they impose perseverance, method and, above all, reserve in what is done regarding naval matters. Only by following this system were the Japanese able to develop their entire organization plan."[44] Similarly, Domecq García admired the work ethic of the people he met at the arsenal in Yokosuka, near Yokohama. In the book, he describes how they worked tirelessly without a break for the production of battleships. Of particular interest to him was the role of the discipline and the comradeship that led to Japan's historical victory: "in an effective way there existed two major qualities without which any organization or plan inevitably fails: discipline and comradeship or *esprit de corps*."[45]

Here Domecq García's celebration of the practice of self-discipline and the notion of collective devotion should be understood within the context of Japanese nationalism. When he wrote the introduction to *Guerra Ruso-Japonesa 1904–1905* in September of 1908, Japan was at the height of its imperial expansion in East Asia, which ended with the annexation of Korea in 1910. The fervor of national sentiment was therefore directly linked to the discourse of Japanese exceptionalism. It is in this aspect of military nationalism that Domecq García discovers the source of inspiration for his own country, with the Asian country representing an exemplary model of patriotic spirit. In one of his letters from 1904, he expresses admiration for the fanaticism and the idiosyncrasy of the Japanese people: "These people have a special education made of stoicism; they do not show feelings in the same way that we do and they believe that the one who dies for the homeland is the one who, without any formalities, truly reaches paradise or supreme happiness."[46] Like Rohde, Domecq García was deeply attracted to the value of spirituality. However, unlike the former's focus on Japanese religion (particularly Shintoism), the latter's interest in the spiritual aspect of Japan underlines connections between the practice of self-control and the military institution. In his personal notes, the admiral observes how everyone, from government officials to ordinary people in the streets, knew that they had to sacrifice their personal interests for the greater good of the Empire:

> Because the war with Russia was a fact known to all Japanese, it was considered something like an obligation everyone had done for the homeland.

... That patriotic sentiment was maintained by everyone with the greatest satisfaction, which means that it was embodied in the public spirit, this inescapable duty that every Japanese had to fulfill once the supreme moment of sacrifice had arrived. The people who profess these sentiments are invincible![47]

What is at the core of Domecq García's understanding of Japan is this shared sense of patriotism, the imperialist nationalism, that is embodied in the "public spirit." He describes people of Japan as "patriotically selfish" (patrióticamente egoístas) because their motto is "all for country."[48] As a veteran soldier, who served as the Minister of the Navy under President Marcelo T. de Alvear, he saw benefits of introducing such a nationalistic spirit to his own people. To make Argentina "invincible," he seems to propose, it would be beneficial to adopt Japan's "patriotic sentiment."

Domecq García states that one of the purposes of writing *Guerra Ruso-Japonesa 1904–1905* was to study the Japanese model in order to apply its teachings to Argentina: he wants to analyze "some conclusions or principles that can serve to formulate convenient plans for our own navy."[49] In fact, he declares that his book can provide practical knowledge about successful warfare: "I have no doubt that considering with certain attention the observations and the notes that this report contains, one can learn some lessons from them and find useful data to formulate a plan for the organization of war and defense that any navy or any cautious country should obtain."[50] On the one hand, his numerous visits to the arsenal ships in Japan allowed him to obtain first-hand knowledge about the country's military methodologies and techniques. On the other hand, his ambition was to translate Japanese patriotism into Argentine nationalism. He states that "my school has been the Great Empire of Japan," implying that Japanese imperialism can present useful ideas of progress to his country.[51] In a celebratory tone, he puts an emphasis on Japan's superb example: "What a great example this race has given us, a people whom until recently we considered inferior to us! So much knowledge we can gain from them, even though there are people of our own race who have not been able to constitute and form themselves as they [the Japanese] have done."[52] Here, the Japanese are depicted as a superior race to other groups, including "people of our own race." Similar to what we saw earlier in *La Nación*, the characterization of Japan as an alternative model of civilization is once again indisputable. With his knowledge of Japan's military strategies, its spirit of self-sacrifice, and its collective sentiment of nationalism, Domecq García proposes that Argentina should eagerly and quickly learn from the remote country in Asia. As I show in the next section, such conviction was also shared by Yoshio Shinya who became a kind of spokesperson for Imperial Japan when he immigrated to Latin America at the turn of the century.

Yoshio Shinya's Translation of Japanese Imperialism into Argentina

Yoshio Shinya was the first Japanese immigrant who arrived in Argentina through official means.[53] Originally from Saga in the western part of Japan, Shinya joined the navy ship *Sarmiento* as an assistant in 1899, when it reached the port of Nagasaki (the first time an Argentine ship docked in Japan). The sixteen-year-old Shinya followed the ship's captain Onofre Bedbeder around the world before arriving in Buenos Aires in 1900, becoming a pioneering member of the Japanese immigrant community in Argentina. He had a close relationship with Manuel Domecq García and, together, they created the Japanese Argentine Cultural Institute in 1933.[54] In his prologue to Shinya's book, Domecq García wrote that "Yoshio Shinya is an Argentine in spirit, he loves our country with true affection."[55] During his time in Argentina, Shinya dedicated himself wholeheartedly to the development of the commercial relationship between Japan and Argentina. He married an Argentine woman of European descent, Laura Hudson de Denholm, who was the niece of the famous writer and naturalist, Guillermo Enrique Hudson, also known as W. H. Hudson. Among their four children was Violeta Shinya, who is regarded as "the first Nikkei intellectual in Argentina."[56]

As a fervent nationalist, Shinya published several books about his native country for the Argentine readership, including *La verdad sobre la cuestión Manchuriana* (1933; Truth about the Manchuria question), *Imperio del sol naciente: Su maravillosa evolución moderna* (1934; Empire of the rising sun: Its marvelous modern evolution) and *Los ideales del Japón* (1939; The ideals of Japan). In addition, he served as a contributor to such national newspapers as *La Prensa*, *El Mundo*, *La Nación*, and *El Diario*, as well as a correspondent for some Japanese newspapers, including *Kokumin Shimbun*, *Tokyo Nichi Nichi Shimbun*, and *Tokyo Asahi Shimbun*. In his study, Facundo Garasino explains how Shinya incorporated the discourse of Japanese imperialism into the narrative of Argentine nationalism through cultural propaganda. According to Garasino, Shinya's experience is an example of how "migrant communities understood the expansion of the Japanese Empire and translated locally its cultural discourses from their double status of imperial subjects and migrant ethnic minority."[57] Garasino identifies three ways in which Shinya promoted the positive images of Japan in Argentine society: 1) by claiming the legitimacy of Japan's military actions against China, 2) by correcting misconceptions about Japanese culture in the West, and 3) by demonstrating the loyalty of the Japanese immigrants to the host country.[58] Moreover, Shinya's dual identity—promoter of imperial Japan and pioneer of Japanese immigration in Argentina—can be understood in line with Eiichiro Azuma's notion of "borderless settler colonialism," which, "not only functioned to shore up the backbone of Japan's empire building but also promoted the borderless quest of Japanese overseas development in accordance with the western precedent of frontier conquest and civilization building."[59]

Published in 1934, *Imperio del sol naciente* is Shinya's signature text because of its extensive coverage of the history of the Japanese Empire. In his prologue, Domecq García characterizes the book as the most important text about Japan in his country.[60] I would also argue that *Imperio del sol naciente* stands out as one of the first books about Japan in Argentina that was written by a Japanese immigrant. As such, one can suspect that Shinya's writing indicates a certain historical narrative about the collective "us" as opposed to works written by non-Japanese authors. Nevertheless, as I show in the following pages, a close analysis of his book reveals more similarities than differences between Shinya and other Argentine intellectuals (Wilde, Rohde, and Domecq García) in terms of their unapologetic celebration of modern Japan. What is notable, then, is Shinya's ability to self-identify as both one of "us" (Japan) and one of "them" (Argentina). Put differently, the dichotomy between "us" and "them" is not easily distinguishable in Shinya's discourse of nationalist-immigrant subjectivity. To use Joseph Tobin's words, it can be argued that Shinya creates his locus of enunciation through Japan's dual capacity involving "self-exoticization" (emulating the other) and "self-orientalization" (becoming the object of the other's imagination).[61]

Imperio del sol naciente explores both the ancient and the modern history of Japan, with topics ranging from politics, religion, and economy to education, arts, and culture. Similar to Domecq García's military report, the glorification of the Japanese Empire is unequivocal throughout the book. For example, Shinya refers to Japan as "a country of the Far East hitherto all but unknown, the Empire of the Rising Sun, which began its ascending march on the path of glory."[62] Japan's expansionist view is often reflected in his nationalist discourse, which argues that the country has the right to claim its legitimate role as one of the most powerful nations in the world: "Japan emerged from centuries of isolation from the rest of the world, confident in itself, *firmly resolved*, full of noble ambitions, radiant and impetuous like the bright morning star and *ready to conquer a dominant place on earth*."[63] In some way his language invokes a colonialist attitude that shows a firm determination to "conquer" the world. As Japan pursued imperial objectives on the Asian continent beginning in 1894, the country's ambition to claim a "dominant place" was felt everywhere by the 1930s. Not unlike the idea of America's "manifest destiny," Shinya's book suggests that modern Japan is "destined" to follow its "ascending path" (camino ascendente) in the sociopolitical and economic spheres.[64] In a sense, his commitment to defending his country of origin reflects a larger narrative of Japanese immigrant experience in Latin America. As Daniel M. Masterson and Sayaka Funada-Classen point out, "More so than other immigrant groups in Latin America, the Japanese before World War II strove to maintain both ethnic and cultural conformity to their Japanese heritage. A central component of this was a staunch loyalty to their Japanese homeland."[65]

Of relevance to such a colonialist perspective is Shinya's theory suggesting the superior nature of the Japanese people. According to him, the modern development of Japan, especially in the aftermath of the Russo-Japanese War, reveals how the Japanese can challenge the traditional, Eurocentric understanding of race relations: "The contemporary evolution of the Japanese people has served to forever disavow the theory of racial psychology based on the physiological characteristics of races."[66] At first sight, Shinya's proposal seems to indicate an attempt to destabilize the dominance of the European race. However, it must be highlighted that his discourse is built on the assumption that the Japanese race is superior to other Asian groups, as well as to the country's indigenous Ainu people, whom he calls a "primitive race."[67] Similar to how some intellectuals of the Meiji era defined the presumed "whiteness" of the Japanese in opposition to their neighbors, Shinya imagined a racial hierarchy between his people and other Asians.

In his earlier work, *La verdad sobre la cuestión Manchuria* (1933), Shinya had already defended Japan's military actions in Manchuria. He argued that the imperial army was protecting their "special interests" in northern China and that those interests were rightfully acquired through international treaties. According to him, it was thanks to the presence of the Japanese soldiers that the region was able to resist violent forces by local warlords. In

Imperio del sol naciente, Shinya further continues this argument and sustains that the people of Manchuria have made considerable progress under the administration of the Japanese army:

> The workers of Manchuria are peaceable; and since Japan began to administer the South Manchurian Railroad under its direction, it has prospered rapidly, thanks to the custody of the Japanese army garrison that maintains order. Faced with the threat of new regional disturbances, they requested Japan's support and, based on its advice, successfully became an organized and stable state. For its part, Japan guaranteed and continues to guarantee their stability because the tranquility of that territory is vital to the future development of the Empire, politically and economically speaking.[68]

His defense of Japan's control of China is based on the assumption that the colonial administration has managed to maintain order and to improve the political and economic aspects of the region. In his view, the imperial government benefited not only Manchurians but also all those who desired peace and stability in East Asia. Indeed, the self-representation of such a "friendly," "peaceful," and even "benevolent" process of colonization was used by the Empire to endorse its nationalist policy. According to Azuma, "The pursuit of overseas development frequently came with an advocacy of 'peaceful expansion(ism)'"—an associated ideology that enabled Japanese settler colonialism to present itself as something different from state-led military aggression."[69]

From this perspective, it comes as no surprise that Shinya also seeks to defend Japan's occupation of Korea as a necessary and productive enterprise. He writes that Korea has made significant advancement under the protection of the Japanese Empire, particularly in the areas of education and economy: "The Japanese administration in Chosen [Korea] is considered an exemplary colonial government. The natives have the same rights as the Japanese, and peace and order reign in every corner of the territory since it has been annexed to Japan."[70] Once again, the ideology of "peaceful expansion" through education and industrialization is meant to purposefully obfuscate the coercive nature of conquest and colonization. Interestingly, Shinya's nationalist discourse supporting Japan's expansion in China and Korea seems to echo the narrative used by Argentine politicians of the time to discriminate against people of African and indigenous descent. Just as "indios" and "negros" were forcefully incorporated into Argentina's sociopolitical structure in order to modernize the country, Chinese and

Koreans were relegated into marginalized subjects under Imperial Japan. In both cases, the success of territorial expansion lay in the fabricated idea of racial homogeneity. As Ignacio Aguiló reminds us, "[a]long with *criollos*, free and enslaved blacks, assimilated Amerindians (particularly in the northeast), *mestizos* and other mixed people constituted a highly heterogeneous and fragmented popular sector that needed to be homogenized."[71] For Shinya, an emphasis on the homogenous nature of "Yamato" or the Japanese race is palpable: "the perfect *homogeneity of the 'Yamato' race* is important."[72] Ironically, it is through the historical interconnectedness between Japan and its neighbors that a homogenous race can be conceptualized. Both Argentina and Japan turn to the invention of racial homogeneity as an integral part of political consolidation as well as the suppression of topographical differences.

Moreover, Shinya goes a step further to connect the exceptional nature of the Japanese race to their ability to adapt different cultural and social norms.[73] While Domecq García admires the Japanese for their advanced military techniques and their collective sense of patriotism, Shinya emphasizes his countrymen's malleable characteristics. For example, he discusses the long history of Chinese/continental influence on Japan: "the Japanese people knew how to benefit from the culture, the art and the religion of the continent without jeopardizing their moral independence. They were able to nationalize all the exotic elements that entered their territory."[74] Although he acknowledges that China brought important cultural, artistic and religious influences to Japan, he makes it clear that this process was not passive reception but active simulation and adaptation. As he explains, "[t]he introduction of Chinese civilization to Japan was not a simple act of adaptation. It was an act of selection and assimilation. Then, as in the nineteenth century, the country was not a mere imitator, since it improved what it received from abroad."[75] His allusion to the culture of synthesis reminds us of Rohde's perspective we studied earlier. For both Shinya and Rohde, Japan achieved the integration of foreign influences without losing its original traditions. In particular, Shinya mentions Buddhism, which was initially introduced to Japan from China via Korea: "The greatest part of *the conquest of the continental civilization* was that which corresponded to Buddhism. . . . But even this conquest was only partial, since Japanese Buddhism is a very different product from all the forms of this Asian religion. The religion was able to prosper in Japan only because of its Japanization."[76] Different from Rohde, Shinya uses a more aggressive colonialist language when referring to "the conquest of the continental civilization." This is noteworthy because it underscores the author's allegiance to Japan's imperialist agency that wants to "conquer" the foreign religion through the process of "Japanization." Lurking beneath Shinya's celebration of Japan's adaptability is the assumption that his country is entitled to appropriate the foreign Other through strategic transculturation. According to this view, Japan's strength is precisely its capacity to adopt external influences without losing sight of its own essence. In other words, Shinya's Japan represents what Michael Taussig calls "mimetic faculty" through which to appropriate the character and the power of the original (China). According to Taussig, "[m]imetic faculty is the nature that culture uses to create second nature, the faculty to copy, imitate, make models, explore difference, yield into and become Other."[77] Through "mimetic faculty," Japan seeks to nativize ideas and practices of other countries as a way to develop its own culture.

Furthermore, Shinya also turns his attention to Japan's history of sociopolitical transformations following the Meiji Restoration, whereby the country incorporated Western models. For him, Japan's exceptional characteristic is based on its place as "the natural leader of the Oriental races in adopting Occidental ways and thoughts."[78] With Japan's strong desire for modernization and Westernization in mind, he advocates his country as a new model for civilization: "The Japanese influence had the gift of putting a halt to the dominating politics of the Western powers in the Far East, showcasing at the same time, with the facts, the possibility of harmonic fusion between the two great civilizations of the East and the West, once considered absolutely irreconcilable."[79] Of course, the allusion to an imaginary fusion between the Orient/East and the Occident/West is not a new topic in Latin American literature. As Julia Kushigian has shown, such orientalist writers as Octavio Paz, Jorge Luis Borges, and Severo Sarduy addressed this literary mixture in a number of ways.[80] What is unique about Shinya is his specific locus of enunciation as a Japanese immigrant in Latin America. Considering that his intended audience was Argentine, his depiction of Japan as a country of "fusion" can be understood as a deliberate move toward promoting the positive image of his native land. He suggests that Japan presents a desirable form of civilization to Argentina, not only owing to its rich history of cultural synthesis but also, perhaps more importantly, because of its widespread Western influence. In this regard, he once again makes a clear distinction between Japan and its neighboring countries: "While Japan found itself eagerly caught up in organizing its institutions according to the Western model by embracing important innovations of modern civilization, its two neighbors—Korea and China—remained stubbornly attached to the old routine. They disregarded foreign customs and hated to enter into relations of exchange with interested powers."[81] Here Shinya seems to propose that Japanese people can bring a new kind of modernity to Argentina based on their successful integration of Western characteristics, unlike Chinese and Koreans who are incapable of adapting foreign traditions. Nevertheless, it must be recognized that his allusion to Japan's "harmonic fusion" does not mean that this East-West binary is placed in equal terms. To him, Western modernization is clearly preferable to Eastern "backwardness." In the lecture he delivered at the Japanese Argentine Cultural Institute in 1941, Shinya emphasized the prevalent influence of the West in his country. As he puts it, "Western civilization in what is useful and beneficial for life and the scientific-mechanical application of human knowledge ... today reaches all corners of the Empire."[82] In short, he considers Japan the most "Western" nation in East Asia.

Finally, Shinya's role as an active member of the Japanese Argentine Cultural Institute deserves further discussion. The Institute was first established in 1933 with Manuel Domecq García serving as president and Shinya as secretary. Among its objectives was to promote Japan through public conferences, presentations, and various cultural events. The Institute invited many speakers from both the Japanese immigrant community and the local Argentine society, creating a productive space for intercultural dialogue.[83] What is notable is the Institute's affiliation with the Argentine Social Museum (Museo Social Argentino), a leading organization that was meant to advance public debates on sociopolitical issues of the time, including hygiene, disease control, immigration, and eugenics.[84] Domecq García was a personal friend of the director of the Museum, Guillermo Garbarini Islas, who was himself personally interested in Japanese culture. There was mutual respect and admiration between members of the Japanese community and the Argentine technocrats associated with the Museum. According to Norma Yokohama, her father Kenkichi Yokohama and Shinya—both of them pioneers of Japanese immigration in Argentina—had periodic meetings with Domecq García and Garbarini Islas between 1933 and 1940.[85] The Museum also hosted courses on Japanese language, literature and culture such as *ikebana*. Through their close association with the Museum, Shinya and other leaders of the Institute tried to advocate their country's civic and moral virtues for the betterment of Argentina (interestingly, their activity reminds us of Wilde's interest in introducing Japan's hygiene practice to Argentina). Such reception of Japan in the Museum during the 1930s is noteworthy because other leaders of the Museum clearly advocated

European immigration. In a survey conducted by the Museum in 1939, Pablo Calatayud addressed concerns about what he called "exotic races":

> Restrict the immigration of exotic races, allowing only minimal quotas. Very large quotas should be allowed for the northern European countries, Scandinavians, English, Danish, Dutch, Belgians, which are the countries of peace and progress. The quotas for other European countries could be more controlled, studying the abilities of adaptation to our soil. ... *The immigration of Orientals should be very restricted.*[86]

Given the amicable relationship between the Japanese Argentine Cultural Institute and the Social Museum, we can argue that the above-mentioned quote reveals the exceptional, "non-Oriental" characteristic of Japanese immigrants in Argentina. As Graciela Karina Torales wrote on the centenary of the Argentine Social Museum, the history of their relationship to the Japanese Argentine Cultural Institute has not been forgotten: the inaugural speech delivered by Garbarini Islas a century ago underscored the meaningful engagement between the Museum and the Institute, not only for Japanese immigrants but also for "all members of society interested in participating."[87]

By addressing Japan as a modern Asian country with prominent Western features, Shinya joined Wilde and others in supporting Japanese immigration to Argentina.[88] The Japanese, he claims, are not only civilized but also loyal to the authority, which would make them ideal candidates for immigration. His book even claims, without evidence, that there are no criminals in the Japanese immigrant community: "[t]he Japanese people are among those who best know how to respect laws and authorities. In Argentina, where more than 4,000 live, there are no Japanese prisoners in the jails."[89] Like his associate Domecq García who was among the most sympathetic supporters of the relationship between Japan and Argentina, Shinya displayed loyalty to both his country of origin and his adopted country. His commitment to making a better Argentina is evident in the article he published in 1934, titled "Call on the Youth" (Llamamiento a la juventud). As he declares, "I aspire to collaborate with the Argentine youth to make this land a great nation, because I am convinced that here, on the banks of the Plata, a model people must be formed for the civilized world, since no other country has the elements and conditions that the providence granted to us."[90] As both a fervent nationalist and the first Japanese immigrant, Shinya skillfully fused together the discourse of imperialism and the narrative of assimilation. He never hesitated to celebrate the glory of the Japanese empire, and some members of Argentina's elite class were drawn to these images based on their own vision of exceptionalism. Consequently, his writings made no small contributions to the myth of the "model minority" for early Japanese immigration. It would take many years before such a romanticized depiction of Japan would be challenged through a new kind of immigrant literature in Argentina.

PART II
NIKKEI LITERATURE AS COUNTER-NARRATIVE

CHAPTER 3

Hybrid Nikkei Identity

Héctor Dai Sugimura's Buscadores en mis últimas vidas *and* Maximiliano Matayoshi's Gaijin

In Part I, I examined how positive images of Japan were constructed by Argentine intellectuals of mostly European descent (except for Shinya) from the late nineteenth century to the early twentieth century. Each of these writers celebrated different aspects of Japan by focusing on its hygiene culture, its aesthetic and spiritual tradition, or its imperial trajectory. Nevertheless, they shared the same agenda that uncritically portrayed Japan as a superior, "white" country in Asia that could serve as an alternative model of transpacific modernity for Argentina.

Part II will discuss how contemporary writers of Japanese descent have been challenging such an essentialized notion of Japan since the end of the twentieth century. Unlike Brazil or Peru, Argentina does not have a long history of Nikkei literary and cultural production. It goes without saying that the main reason for this absence is the small size of the population. While Brazil and Peru are known to have the largest Japanese communities outside the country, there is a significantly smaller group in Argentina. As I mentioned in the introduction, this contrast can be highlighted further if we look at recent scholarship. While there is an increasing number of studies investigating the cultural and sociopolitical contributions of the Nikkei communities in Brazil and Peru, the influence of the Japanese diaspora in Argentina has received little critical attention from scholars. The most important study is *Historia del inmigrante japonés en la Argentina* (2004–2005), published in both Spanish and Japanese by the Federación de Asociaciones Nikkei en la Argentina. While this excellent two-volume project minutely traces the history of Japanese immigration from sociological and anthropological perspectives, my study hereafter emphasizes the cultural production of the Japanese immigrants, especially in literature. Other notable historical studies include Rodríguez Goicoa's *Japón en la Argentina* (1938), James Lawrence Tigner's "The Ryukyuans in Argentina" (1967), Isabel Laumonier's "Japoneses: Esa otra inmigración" (1989), Zaia Okinawa Kenjin Rengokai's *Aruzenchin no Uchinanchu Hachiju-nenshi* (1994), Marcelo Higa's "Desarrollo histórico de la inmigración japonesa en la Argentina hasta la Segunda Guerra Mundial" (1995), and Silvina Gómez and Cecilia Onaha's "Asociaciones voluntarias e identidad étnica de inmigrantes japoneses y sus descendientes en Argentina" (2008).[1] One of my goals is to analyze the literature and culture that explore the presence of Japanese immigrants in Argentina. My central concern is to show how the emerging group of Nikkei writers can shed new light on the meaning of national identity in contemporary Argentina.[2]

Chapter 3 studies the representation of hybrid identity in two of the pioneering works of Nikkei literature in Argentina, namely Héctor Dai Sugimura's *Buscadores en mis últimas vidas* (1995) and Maximiliano Matayoshi's *Gaijin* (2003). These novels are significant because they are among the first literary works that address the formation of what can be characterized as a Japanese Argentine identity.[3] As Marcelo Higa highlights, "in the Argentine context, there did not even exist a descriptive term such as 'Japanese-Argentine': one was 'Argentine,' a term that could be softened occasionally by adding the clarification 'descended from Japanese.'"[4] Nevertheless, the term "Japanese-Argentine" is suggestive insofar as it reveals both the possibility and the limit of the hyphenated immigrant identity. My argument is in line with Trinh Minh-ha's discussion that underlines the challenge of the hyphenated space between Asia (Vietnam) and America: "It is in having to confront and defy hegemonic values on an everyday basis, in other words, in assuming the between-world dilemma, that one understands both the predicament and the potency of the hyphen."[5] I argue that both Sugimura and Matayoshi provide us with useful tools that allow us to not only decipher what it means to be a person of Japanese descent, but also to reframe the very definition of what it means to be Argentine in contemporary times.

Contemporary History of Japanese Immigration in Argentina

To fully understand the significance of Nikkei literature in Argentina, I will return to the history of Japanese immigration. As shown by the brief historical account in the introduction, most Japanese immigrants enjoyed comfortable social status in Argentina because they did not experience the kind of epistemic violence that happened elsewhere in the region. Other countries in Latin America have publicly persecuted Japanese and other Asians: some examples include the so-called "coolie trade" in nineteenth-century Cuba and Peru, the anti-Chinese propaganda in Mexico in the 1930s, the 1940 riots in Lima, the terrorist group known as Shindō Renmei in Brazil in 1940s, and the deportation and internment of Japanese nationals and Nikkei Latin Americans (mostly Peruvians) during World War II.

In Argentina, on the other hand, the Japanese have generally received better treatment, even though this does not mean that they were totally exempt from racism and discrimination. Higa describes this history as "the peaceful insertion of the Japanese in Argentine society."[6] The early moment of sporadic immigration dates back to the late nineteenth century. Even though today Brazil and Peru represent the largest Japanese diaspora communities in the region, Argentina is said to be the first Latin American country to receive a Japanese sailor, named Kinzo Makino, in 1886. According to the national census of 1902, there was at the time a total of ten Japanese residents registered in Argentina.[7] However, Japanese immigration did not officially begin until 1908-1909.[8] As elsewhere in the region, the majority of the first immigrants came from Okinawa, also known as the Ryukyu Islands. Unlike in other countries, however, those who settled in Argentina usually did not arrive directly from Asia, but from neighboring countries. As Daniel M. Masterson and Sayaka Funada-Classen point out, "they were refugees from the poor conditions on the sugar plantations of these two nations [Brazil and Peru], and many of the Japanese pioneers in Argentina entered the country covertly."[9] The first wave of Japanese immigration (until World War I) can thus be characterized as an indirect "transmigration" or "remigration."[10] According to Gary Y. Okihiro, sixty-eight Okinawans from Brazil and seven from Peru arrived to Argentina in 1910, making the total number of Japanese immigrants to be approximately three hundred.[11]

In a sense, the experience of these newcomers was uniquely defined at the initial moment of settlement: they viewed Japan as the origin, Brazil or Peru as the transition, and Argentina as the new home. Put differently, Argentina was considered an alternative not only to their native land, but also to other Latin American nations. After 1914, the transmigration movement was replaced by the so-called "calling" procedure (known as *yobiyose*) as the principal mode of entry to Argentina. Between 1914 and 1930, the Argentine government allowed its Japanese residents to call their relatives and friends in their homeland to join them. However, from 1930 to 1941, calling was limited to immediate families, such as spouses and first cousins.[12]

Although the majority of Japanese immigrants settled in the city of Buenos Aires, some left the capital and moved to other cities, such as Rosario, Córdoba, Mendoza, Tucumán, Salta, Jujuy, Resistencia, Santa Fe, and Corrientes. While many made their living through agriculture, others found jobs in iron foundries, sugar refineries, as well as in the areas of transportation, gardening, stevedoring, and carpentry.[13] Some families developed successful businesses in horticulture and floriculture, as we will see in Héctor Dai Sugimura's book. Beginning in the 1920s, most Japanese immigrants left wage-earning domestic jobs for independent employment, including bars, cafés, and taxis.[14] The formation of *kenjin-kai* or prefectural association contributed to the success of these independent businesses.[15]

Following World War II, Argentina implemented a five-year plan in 1947 under president Juan Domingo Perón in order to bring more immigrants to the country. Although the primary targets were Europeans, Perón's plan benefited Japanese immigrants as well. As Okihiro explains, "Japan was a key source, because of favorable attitudes toward the Japanese among Argentina's political leadership and because of redevelopment and population pressures in postwar Japan and Okinawa."[16] In fact, the friendly relationship between Japan and Argentina cannot be discussed without mentioning Perón, especially during his first regime between 1946 and 1955. According to Masterson and Funada-Classen, "Perón continued to maintain very good relations with the Japanese community in Argentina throughout his years in power."[17] He and his wife, Eva (Evita) Perón, supported the Nikkei community in Argentina by sending emergency supplies to their homeland as part of postwar reconstruction and by providing humanitarian aid to their distant families following the deadly North Kyushu flood of 1953. In some way, Japanese immigrants were seen as equal to the famous *descamisados* (literally meaning "shirtless"), the loyal Argentine workers who supported Perón's nationalist politics. As Evita told members of the Japanese community in 1949, "I want you to find in me not only an ally but also a friend."[18] For his part, Perón had long been interested in Japan and its history; as mentioned earlier, he published his impressions about the Russo-Japanese War in *Apuntes de historia militar*. In his speech delivered in 1949, he suggested not only the idea of coexistence between Japanese and Argentines but also of mutual respect between the two nations: "This Japanese community that through unity honors itself and honors us with their coexistence should have the most absolute feeling that for us, in this land, its members are as Argentine as ourselves, that they have the same respect as our men, and that *there is no difference between a Japanese man and an Argentine man.*"[19] These remarks about "coexistence" can certainly be interpreted as a political campaign through which to celebrate the country's purported racial diversity. At the same time, his discourse reveals the unique positionality of Japanese immigrants in society. By blurring the difference between a "Japanese man" and an "Argentine man," the Argentine president bestows Japanese immigrants a certain privilege. As far as the Nikkei community was concerned, their loyalty to Perón was also consistent and unquestionable. Kagashi Sugawara, the president of the Japanese Argentine Association, once declared that their community looked upon Perón "as if he were our self-sacrificing father and the immortal Evita our tender mother, to both of whom we promise to be honest and obedient children."[20] The way Perón's government treated the Japanese can be compared to how they perceived other ethnic minorities in Argentina, such as Jews and Arabs. As Raanan Rein, Aya Udagawa, and Pablo Adrián Vázquez point out, "Peronism went beyond the legal entitlement given to Jews, Arabs or Japanese as Argentine citizens, and offered them political entitlement as well."[21] The online newspaper *Anticipos* even goes so far as to suggest that Peronism is "national, popular, and Japanese," referring to a number of loyal Nikkei representatives who served in Perón's government.[22] Among them was Ángel Kiyoshi Gashu, who was named Director of the Secretary of Technical Affairs in 1952, as well as the head of the National Directorate of Statistics and Census. In 1954, Gashu became the first Nikkei to be elected as a deputy of the National Congress and participated in the foreign relations committee.[23]

A half-century later, the perception of Japanese immigrants and their descendants took a new turn at the beginning of the twenty-first century. It has been argued that the 2001 economic crisis was a wake-up call for Argentina in terms of its redefinition of national identity.[24] In the contemporary politics of ethno-racial diversity, Asian immigrants, especially the Japanese, played a special role. In her article, Chisu Teresa Ko refers to Japanese Argentines as "ideal champions of multiculturalism because of a presumed foreignness that distinguishes them from the local *negros*, and their positive cultural and racial meanings vis à vis other Asians."[25] Ko's study points to Argentina's recent efforts to reinvent itself from a homogenous, white nation to a more heterogeneous, multicultural one. In her view, Japanese immigrants contribute to an alternative paradigm of racial politics through their ability to reveal the possibilities as well as the limits of Argentine multiculturalism.[26] In this sense, we can argue that the construction of a Japanese Argentine identity is deeply rooted in the idea of Argentina's nationhood. For Argentina, a self-proclaimed melting pot of racial and ethnic blending, using Japanese immigrants as instrumental symbols of diversity can be both convenient and practical. Similar to how the Japanese community was celebrated by Perón and his government in the mid-twentieth century, the relative visibility of Nikkei Argentines continues to serve Argentine's society as a way to underline the notion of diversity and multiculturalism.

Hybrid Identity in Héctor Dai Sugimura's Buscadores en mis últimas vidas

The foregoing overview of the contemporary history of Japanese immigration allows us to contextualize the Nikkei literary works I will be examining in the following pages. One of the guiding themes that I want to address is the notion of hybridity. In his essay "Cultural Identity and Diaspora," Stuart Hall famously theorizes the notion of "cultural identity" in two ways. First, he captures its collective nature by referring to "one, shared culture, a sort of collective 'one true self,' hiding inside the many other, more superficial or artificially imposed 'selves,' which people with a shared history and ancestry hold in common."[27] Hall's second definition involves not only the fact of "being," but also the process of "becoming": "Cultural identities come from somewhere, have histories. But, like everything which is historical, they undergo constant transformation. Far from being externally fixed in some essentialized past, they are subject to the continuous 'play' of history, culture, and power."[28] For Hall, this fluid nature of cultural identity is most evident in an immigrant or a wandering subject of insider/outsider who readily transgresses geopolitical boundaries. As a result, a diaspora is constructed and reproduced through constant negotiations between multiple languages, traditions, and histories. Hall defines the diaspora experience "not by essence of purity, but by the recognition of a necessary heterogeneity and diversity; by a conception of 'identity' which lives with and through, not despite, difference; by *hybridity*."[29]

Homi Bhabha takes a different approach to the idea of hybridity, which he describes as "a problematic of colonial representation and individuation that reverses the effects of the colonialist disavowal, so that other 'defined' knowledges enter upon the dominant discourse and estrange the basis of its authority."[30] Unlike Hall, Bhabha invokes hybridity as a way to contest colonial domination and to turn marginalized others into subjects of their own historicity. In this sense, hybridity creates resistance against cultural hegemony. Bhabha identifies the location of hybridity as the "third space" wherein cultural differences between colonizer and colonized are transfigured into a productive contact zone for the subaltern subject. In his words, this "in-between" space represents "the terrain for elaborating strategies of selfhood—singular or communal—that initiate new signs of identity, and innovative sites of collaboration, and contestation, in the act of defining the idea of society itself."[31] This "third space" of hybridity is both disruptive and subversive because it "challenges our sense of the historical identity of culture as a homogenizing, unifying force."[32]

These postcolonial approaches to the concept of hybridity give us the framework through which to analyze the Japanese Argentine identity in Héctor Dai Sugimura's *Buscadores en mis últimas vidas*. Sugimura is one of the first published authors who contributed to the creation of Argentina's contemporary Nikkei literature written in Spanish. He was born in 1969 to Japanese parents who lived in Escobar in the province of Buenos Aires. From an early age, Sugimura was interested in writing fiction and art, especially painting. Even though he ended up studying law at the University of Buenos Aires, his passion for literature was never impaired. In 1994, his story "Para no retroceder" (To not retreat) won the first prize for the First National Competition for Short Stories organized by the Asociación Universitaria Nikkei. The jury, which included the two renowned authors María Elena Walsh and Mempo Giardinelli, described his story as a subtle and weirdly charming plot that borders on the fantastical and the mystic, showcasing an attractive air that is representative of Japanese culture. The connection between fantasy and reality is also what captivated the journalist Cristián Trouvé: "The fundamental questions, the bizarre conclusions, the fantastical situations that come true through the verisimilitude of the story are characteristics of Sugimura's writing."[33]

Published in 1995, *Buscadores en mis últimas vidas* is Sugimura's first and only novella that I have found to this date.[34] The story revolves around a young law student, "Dai Hombre" (Dai Human), who is mysteriously transformed into a cat, "Dai Gato" (Dai Cat). Confused about the reality of man's consciousness in a cat's body, the narrator-protagonist embarks on a journey to discover the reason behind this unanticipated transformation. During the process of self-discovery, Dai Gato receives help from many characters, including other cats (especially a cat named Shiro who will become his teacher), other humans (especially Yuriko, a young girl he falls in love with), and magical creatures such as the "Luciérnaga Conciencia" (Consciousness Firefly) and the "Maestro Divino" (Divine Master). These interactions lead Dai to spiritual contemplation in which he learns that life is a series of "circles" that constantly open and close (in the novella he goes through three lives in different times before reaching the state of "eternity"). He also realizes that his initial search for the mystery is, in reality, a search for "anhelos eternos" (eternal longings). Toward the end of the book, Dai and his cat-teacher Shiro wage a war against the "Insensible" in order to protect the people and the animals they call "buscadores de anhelos eternos" (seekers of eternal longings).

Sugimura's novella reminds us of Franz Kafka's "The Metamorphosis" (1915), in which the protagonist wakes up one day to find himself transformed into a "monstrous vermin." Like Kafka's story, *Buscadores en mis últimas vidas* depicts a fantasy world where humans and animals live side by side, often in conflict with each other. Unlike the German-speaking Jewish author, however, the Japanese Argentine writer creates a protagonist who is able to embrace the meaning of his unexpected metamorphosis in the end. In *Buscadores en mis últimas vidas*, different Japanese elements are manifested in Dai and other characters. First, we can detect certain autobiographical aspects, including how the story is set in Escobar (where Sugimura was born), how the protagonist's name derives from the author's own, and how Dai Human studies law (Sugimura became a lawyer at age twenty-three before publishing his book). A Japanese Argentine identity is also shown through the protagonist's early life in the book. In the first chapter called "The crucial trip" ("El viaje crucial"), Dai Human describes the forty-eight-hour trip he made from Argentina to Japan when he was eight. At age twelve, he won the speech contest in the Japanese language.[35] In addition, the narrator explains how his parents owned a farm for plants and flowers in Escobar, a city known as the National Capital of Flowers. As mentioned earlier, the cultivation of flowers was an important business for many Japanese immigrants in Argentina in the early twentieth century. Moreover, most of the names in the novella appear to be Japanese, including that of the protagonist, "Dai," which means "big" or "great" in Japanese.

This name is given by Yuriko Tanaka who adopts Dai Cat and tells him, "I named you Dai because you were going to be a cat, a great cat."[36] The book describes Dai as a hero and a savior of both humanity and the animal world. When he saves the life of another cat, the veterinarian calls him a "great hero" who is among the "saviors" committed to helping others.[37]

The multiple references to Japanese culture in *Buscadores en mis últimas vidas* suggest an original narrative about Nikkei experience in Argentina. When Dai Human suddenly becomes Dai Cat, he finds himself in an "Oriental community": "Apparently it was an Oriental community. Those faces and customs were very familiar to me, which gave me the impression that I was probably a member of that society."[38] This reflection of the presumed image of the Japanese Argentine society is significant because it is included in the chapter titled "The new world" (El nuevo mundo). At first glance, the newness of the situation seems to be related to the human world viewed through cat's eyes. However, I argue that the title can be also interpreted as a new country for people coming from abroad. Hence Dai Cat's experience in "the new world" can be understood as a metaphor for the larger narrative of Japanese immigration in Argentina. From this perspective, it is worth mentioning that the book is dedicated "to those who did not lose the magic of believing in the incredible, nor the sensitivity to perceive the credible and, especially, to those who have lost them."[39] Considering the myriad of challenges immigrants had to face upon their arrival to a new country, it is not difficult to imagine that this passage alludes to the history of Japanese people and their families who experience the sense of *extraviado* or being lost in Argentina. Therefore, in my view, one of the central narrative themes in the novella is the immigrant's struggle for existence in the host country.

It is in this context that we can critically analyze the way in which Dai Cat is treated within the local Japanese community in Argentina. When he looks for food at the fish market owned by the Kitayama family, people yell at him by saying "Get away from me, you dirty cat!" or "Don't bother me, I'm busy!"[40] After enduring such insults, Dai shares a personal reflection: "What is wrong with the people from this new world? I understand I'm not a very attractive animal, but I haven't done anything to be treated this way."[41] Such an episode underlines the tension that can exist within the Nikkei community. Here the mistreatment of a young Japanese immigrant (represented by Dai Cat) by another family (the Kitayama) shows that not everything about the story of Japanese immigration was harmonious. Unlike the idealized picture of Japan celebrated by the authors I studied in the previous chapters, Sugimura offers a more nuanced narrative that reveals the multifaceted, sometimes painful reality of Japanese immigrants in Argentina.

Moreover, another notable aspect in the novella is the emphasis on education for immigrant parents. It can be said that the Tanakas represent a typical Japanese family, "the type of family that everyone would envy."[42] Mr. Tanaka, the father, is depicted as "a cold man who doesn't talk much," while his wife is "an active woman [who] did two or three things at the same time."[43] Their daughter Yuriko is the one who saves Dai at the earlier-mentioned fish market scene and brings him to the family. The book shows how Yuriko wants to pursue a career in music, but she knows that her parents would never approve of her dream because they want her to study economics at the University of Tokyo, the most prestigious university in Japan. Her mother is especially concerned about the education of Yuriko and her brother Masato: "She cared that they studied more, so that they could get into a respectable university in the future."[44] The value of education emphasized by her parents, who are Issei, or the first generation of Japanese immigrants, is contrasted with the interests of Yuriko, Nisei, or the second generation. These are different generations of immigrants trying to define their own ethics, values, and lifestyles. Later in the book Yuriko unexpectedly becomes pregnant with her boyfriend Taro, who tells her to give up the baby. She feels devastated and abandoned, but there is no way she can break the news to her conservative parents. Ultimately, she tries to commit suicide by throwing herself at a moving train, only to be saved by Dai and other cats. For Christiane Kazue Nagao, this relationship between Yuriko and her parents indicates a critique of traditional Japanese values. As she puts it, "[t]he narrator tells us these facts with great irony. There is a deep critique of the bourgeois ideals of social advancement, of the industriousness of Japanese people, and of the emphasis placed on university education as a mark of prestige."[45] We can argue that the novella problematizes the essentialized discourse of Japanese immigration by illustrating the generational gap between Issei and Nisei. As R. Radhakrishnan reminds us, the first and the second generations of immigrants have "different starting points and different givens" when it comes to the definition of "home."[46] Similar to Dai's negative experience within the Nikkei community, Yuriko's conflict with her family underscores a complicated reality of immigration that cannot be reduced to a single narrative. As a result, *Buscadores en mis últimas vidas* turns to a hybrid Japanese Argentine identity that goes against what Bhabha calls "a homogenizing, unifying force."[47]

If Dai is the novella's protagonist and hero, Yuriko is the heroine who leads him to discover the meaning of life. When Dai meets Yuriko, he realizes instantly that nothing matters more to him than his romantic relationship with her: "I fell in love from the first moment I saw her. Her way of challenging me, of looking at me, of hugging me. Her hair, her eyes, her angelic complexion, her small and warm breasts."[48] While the originality of Sugimura's protagonist stems from his Japanese Argentine features, Dai's language about the female body—"her small and warm breasts"—still indicates the objectification of women like what we saw in Chapter 1.

At any rate, love plays a critical role during Dai's journey of self-discovery, through which he becomes a "seeker of eternal longings."[49] Interestingly, the book juxtaposes the idea of "eternal longing" (anhelo eterno) to that of "ephemeral longing" (anhelo efímero). According to Dai's cat-master Shiro, "eternal longing" is related to the process of self-reflection, which he describes as "a constant attitude of searching."[50] However, if we understand Dai's experience as a metaphor for a larger narrative of Japanese immigration in Argentina, the notion of "constant searching" reveals a broader significance. More than a search for love and eternity, it can imply an immigrant's search for belonging in the new country. Although we must recognize diverse experiences of assimilation and integration, one of the common denominators among all immigrant stories is the anxiety surrounding the question of where to belong. Trapped between the country of origin and the host country, the Nikkei immigrant is in constant search for some form of fixed subjectivity. We may ask ourselves, what does the hyphen refer to when discussing the hyphenated "Japanese-Argentine" identity? Can the hyphen speak for itself without implying discrepancy between Japanese and Argentine elements? It is worth remembering that, for Trinh Minh-ha, the hybrid space between Asia and America reveals how "the challenge of the hyphenated reality lies in the hyphen itself . . . the realm in-between, where predetermined rules cannot fully apply."[51] Thus, it is safe to argue that for Dai, the symbol of Japanese Argentine subjectivity, the "longing" for belonging is indeed "eternal." To use Stuart Hall's words, his search for a new cultural identity is subject to "the continuous 'play' of history, culture, and power."[52]

Nostalgia, Discrimination, and Multiculturalism in Maximiliano Matayoshi's *Gaijini*

While the history of Japanese immigration is a subtext told by a cat-human character in *Buscadores en mis últimas vidas*, this topic takes center stage in Maximiliano Matayoshi's novel *Gaijin* (2003), which means "foreigner" or "outsider" in Japanese. Like Sugimura, Matayoshi is a second-generation Japanese Argentine. He won the prestigious Premio Primera Novela UNAM/Alfaguara in 2002, which made him the first Nikkei writer in Argentina to receive international recognition. According to Mercedes Giuffré, *Gaijin* "[r]econstructs the inner and linguistic metamorphosis of this individual and, as a corollary, comes to install in our imaginary in plain revision the memory of that group of people who came from a land so far away and whose descendants today are a very rich and little explored part of our Argentine identity."[53] As Matayoshi described in an interview, his novel is based on the true story of his father.[54] The story begins with the journey of a thirteen-year-old protagonist, Kitaro (we only learn his name toward the end of the book), who leaves his family in postwar Okinawa to find a better life in Argentina. During the ocean trip, Kitaro and other passengers make stops at numerous port cities, including Hong Kong, Manila, Singapore, Lorenzo Marquez (Mozambique), and Cape Town (South Africa), before reaching Buenos Aires. Upon arrival, Kitaro is sent to a separate room because he has no family in Argentina. However, his best friend from the trip, Kei Arakaki, and his uncle end up "adopting" him in the Arakaki family. Together with Kei, Kitaro starts working at the Arakaki family's *tintorería*, while learning Spanish and gradually assimilating to the new country. His experience as a Japanese immigrant is depicted through the first-person narrative, unfolding different episodes of friendship, love, nostalgia, and discrimination. After completing a degree in medicine in Mendoza, Kitaro decides to visit his family in Japan for two months. At the end of the story, we find him anxious to return to Argentina to be reunited with his girlfriend Julieta, one of the daughters of the Arakaki family.[55]

In the novel, Kitaro strives to preserve emotional ties to his homeland. After living in Argentina for several years, he still refers to Japanese as "my language" and Japan as "my country."[56] One of the cultural values that Kitaro embraces is the practice of silence, which is described as an essential mode of communication among Japanese and Japanese Argentine characters. For these characters, silence does not simply imply the absence of words or feelings. On the contrary, it represents a productive space through which to express different kinds of emotions, including joy, anger, frustration, and love. In particular, silence plays a key role in the relationship between Kitaro and his girlfriend Julieta. As the protagonist explains, "with Julieta silence did not bother me."[57] When he returns from Mendoza to Buenos Aires, he still feels comfortable communicating with her in silence: "It was still very easy to talk to her because silence was not uncomfortable and we did not need so many words to understand each other."⁵⁸ In a way, their romantic relationship is nurtured quietly rather than through dialogue. As we shall see in the next chapter, silence is also celebrated as an important value of Japanese culture in Anna Kazumi Stahl's *Flores de un solo día*.

Moreover, Kitaro also uses silence to communicate with his father who had died during the war. He frequently refers to memories of his father through flashbacks. Gazing at the night sky on the ship deck, the protagonist quietly remembers the story his father told him about shooting stars: "The story Dad told was much better: the shooting stars were the souls of kind-hearted people who at night saw everyone they loved and then returned to the other stars."⁵⁹ Even though his father was already dead by the time Kitaro left Japan, memories of his father constantly emerge throughout the book. In one scene, Kitaro recalls the day in his youth when a war general came to his school to teach them about the "cruelty" of the Chinese: "He told us about Chinese men who killed their children and beat their wives, about children who beat their parents and teachers, and about grandparents who had to work all day without a break."⁶⁰ When his father heard about this incident, he sat down with Kitaro with a stern look and reminded him that they had a neighbor, Mr. Chow, who was a friendly toymaker. The father asked Kitaro if he believed that Mr. Chow too was hurting his wife or mistreating his family, to which Kitaro could not respond.⁶¹ Here the way in which Kitaro is led to question the "official" narrative of war is noteworthy because it offers a different view of Chinese people than Wilde's illustration of the "barbaric" China (Chapter 1) or Shinya's defense of Japan's imperial mission in Manchuria (Chapter 2). In the case of Matayoshi, Kitaro's memory of his father focuses more on empathy and understanding than on the conflict-ridden relationship between Japan and China.

Another example of Kitaro's Japaneseness is manifested when he breaks up with Nenina, who is Argentine-born and the daughter of his Spanish teacher, Ms. Hoffman. When they first meet at church, Kitaro immediately falls in love with Nenina and begins to attend mass regularly. His friend Kei tells him that she would never be interested in him because she is a "gaijin" or foreigner.⁶² Nevertheless, the two become good friends and even entertain the idea of semi-romance, until one day Ms. Hoffman and Nenina leave the town without bidding farewell to Kitaro. Heartbroken, he regrets having left Japan: "What was I doing in that house? I had traveled thousands of kilometers for months only to iron clothes for the rest of my life. I should have stayed in Japan."⁶³ Later, while living in Mendoza,

Kitaro experiences a failed romance again with Lara, another Argentine girl. Although Lara develops a closer relationship with him, they too end up going separate ways, and she eventually marries a man who resembles him. These two episodes can be interpreted as instances of racial "Othering," in which the Japanese protagonist is seen as an uninvited foreign "Other" who is not to be mixed with Argentines of European descent. By underscoring the impossibility of mixed-race relationship, the novel makes a subtle critique of the essentializing narrative of whiteness in Argentina.

With regard to the notion of Otherness, it must also be noted that *Gaijin* makes explicit references to the racial discrimination experienced by Japanese immigrants. First, the novel describes Julieta's frustration when people call her "Chinese" and make fun of her at church.[64] Later, Kitaro experiences the same kind of racism when he moves to Mendoza: "some kids who were playing soccer let the ball escape, which stopped near me. 'Hey, Chinese, pass me the ball.' I kicked it but somehow it did not go where I wanted. 'You dumb Chinese, go back to China, *chin chu lin*,' they yelled and I stopped listening to other insults."[65] According to Matayoshi, this scene was based on a real-life experience, which initially led him to resist his Japanese identity.[66] As I explained earlier, the Japanese in Argentina did not endure state-sponsored racism. Nevertheless, neither Kitaro nor Matayoshi seem able to escape the reality of xenophobia. Their experience is, of course, nothing new. It is well-known that Asians—almost always referred to as "chinos" regardless of one's specific origin—are relegated to the margins of history in Argentina and elsewhere. Through the derogatory language such as "dumb Chinese" and "chin chu lin," Matayoshi implicitly criticizes racial stigmatization against Asians in general. In this sense, he is more explicit than Sugimura in his denunciation of the casual injustices committed against Japanese and other Asian communities in Argentina.

While the elements of Japaneseness have left their stamp on Kitaro, his Argentineness also becomes evident as the new country begins to assume prominent place in his immigrant identity. By the time he returns to Japan, he has already been so integrated into Argentine society that he has difficulty remembering the faces of his mother and his sister. Instead, his family in Mendoza has replaced those in Japan as the people he feels closest to. It is at this point that Kitaro realizes that Argentina has become his new "home": "Thirteen years ago, I had embarked on crossing all oceans in order to return home one day. And to achieve this I learned to iron, learned a language and also learned that there exist lands where you cannot even imagine the sea. I crossed those lands and now I was ready to cross oceans again."⁶⁷ The stereotypical image of an Issei is someone who is reluctant to accept the host country, always yearning to go back to his homeland. However, Kitaro seems to represent the opposite: for him, Argentina is the place he ultimately belongs to. At the same time, it is also important to recognize that neither country is able to offer him the kind of security he seeks. In other words, his "home" is not exclusively Japan nor Argentina. Japan is not a home in a geographical sense and yet his cultural associations are strong enough to constantly remind him of his roots. Argentina, on the other hand, is physically closer, but not safe enough to prevent the experience of discrimination. Caught between the two countries and not feeling "at home" in either of them, Kitaro finds intimacy through the people he comes to love. As Svetlana Boym reminds us, "To feel at home is to know that things are in their places and so are you; it is a state of mind that doesn't depend on an actual location. The object of longing, then, is not really a place called home but this sense of intimacy in the world."⁶⁸ To put it differently, Matayoshi's immigrant character, like Sugiyama's, resides in what Bhabha calls the "third space" or the in-between location of hybridity.

Of particular relevance to this capricious concept of home is the ambiguity of the term "gaijin" in the novel. The Japanese passengers on the ship use this idea to refer to Westerners (Americans, Dutch, and Argentines with European heritage), but not to other non-Japanese people, such as the Chinese ("three gaijin and one Chinese").⁶⁹ The word is also mentioned to depict the white colonizers who exploit black slaves in Lorenzo Márquez ("gaijin with whips in his hand").⁷⁰ However, as an immigrant, we know that the real "gaijin" in Argentina is Kitaro himself, the racialized foreigner who is trying to be integrated into society. In Mendoza, Kitaro expresses a strange sense of detachment: "So now I had a surname that was not mine. I lived in a country to which I did not belong and with a family which I was not a part of."⁷¹ By applying multiple meanings to the idea of foreignness, the novel underscores how the notion of "gaijin" can be applied to both the white and the non-native, while demarcating the shifting boundary between insider and outsider.

Furthermore, the unique characteristic of his "gaijin-ness" goes beyond the simple binary between Japan and Argentina. Before leaving Japan, Kitaro imagines the country in South America to be "better" than the United States. As he recalls, "I knew some guys who had left and others who said that it was like America, but better: Argentines didn't kill Japanese."⁷² This image of Argentina as an alternative country to the violent US also appears earlier during the war: "I tried to think of something else, like how Argentina would be without tanks, without American soldiers and without death."[73] As mentioned before, history has shown that Argentina maintained a neutral position during World War II, and its opposition to the Nikkei community was minimal. Unlike the US—Japan's enemy country—Argentina is viewed in the novel as a protective asylum for the Japanese protagonist. In this regard, Kitaro's illustration of the Arakaki family's house has a symbolic meaning. According to him, "It always seemed to me that the house functioned as a refuge for all the Japanese who, like me, were beginning a new life in Argentina."[74] In the early twentieth century, many of the first wave of Japanese immigrants came to Argentina covertly from Brazil and Peru to escape the poor conditions on the sugar plantations. In a similar vein, Kitaro demonstrates a positive attitude toward Argentina as an alternative to the US. However, we must emphasize that his view is not a blind celebration of diversity and inclusion, as evidenced by his earlier experience of racism. Rather than reinforcing the utopian image of Argentina, *Gaijin* presents a more critical understanding of multiculturalism in the country.

In terms of Kitaro's hybrid, transnational identity, it is also worth mentioning that he manages to learn English in addition to Spanish, which indicates that there is more than a simple juxtaposition between two languages. On the ship, he picks up English from his friend, Kiyoshi, who had previously attended a bilingual school in Japan. Because of his English lesson, Kitaro's first foreign phrase is not in Spanish, but "good afternoon" in English.[75] He also learns a song in English without understanding the meaning of the lyrics. As a result, the conversation between Kitaro and Kiyoshi turns multilingual: "*Good afternoon, how are you?*, he said in Spanish. *Very good*, I replied and couldn't help laughing."[76] Given that the rest of the dialogue takes place in their native language, this linguistic play involves English, Spanish, and Japanese. It is the tension that stems from the confluence of these three languages that Kitaro finds amusing. Later, Kiyoshi's English lesson turns out to be useful for Kitaro when he finds a job as a translator in Mendoza. This occurs in 1964 when Tokyo hosts the Summer Olympics, and his job entails listening to various radio stations overseas and writing reports on the Olympic games in Spanish. The task requires not only the knowledge of Japanese and Spanish, but also that of English since some stations were only transmitted in English. Kitaro recognizes his gratitude to his friend: "When I managed to find a radio broadcasting in English, I thanked Kiyoshi's classes and wrote what was missing from the report."[77] This episode once again highlights how the triple linguistic and cultural codes comprise Kitaro's immigrant identity. His worldview is defined through the negotiations between three languages, countries, and cultures. These negotiations then allow the protagonist to contest the traditional dichotomy that views Latin America's Japanese diaspora exclusively in terms of the confrontation between two countries. Consequently, it can be argued that Kitaro's multicultural identity suggests an alternative notion of selfhood and sensitivity. As we will see in the next chapter, American identity also plays an important role for one of the main characters in *Flores de un solo día*.

Read together, my analyses of *Buscadores en mis últimas vidas* and *Gaijin* shows how the new generation of Nikkei writers has been challenging the conventional depictions of Japan and the Japanese since the beginning of the twenty-first century. While Sugimura's magical cat-human can be interpreted in symbolic terms as the representation of a larger narrative of Japanese immigration, Matayoshi's protagonist deals more directly with his own experience as a racialized foreigner in Argentina, revealing instances of nostalgia, assimilation, and discrimination. Despite their different narrative approaches, both authors are pioneers in creating characters who find themselves trying to define their own Japanese Argentine identities. Through the idea of hybridity manifested in their immigrant characters, the two novels articulate different modes of Japaneseness than the ones set forth by Wilde, Rohde, Domecq García, and Shinya. At the same time, the emphasis on the fluid nature of multicultural identity in both texts indicates a critical approach to Argentina's historical discourse of whiteness. Rather than adhering to the idealized vision of Japan viewed through the lens of whiteness, Sugimura and Matayoshi present a more nuanced and reflective perspective on the country of their ancestors.

CHAPTER 4

Gendering Orientalism and Female Agency

Anna Kazumi Stahl's Flores de un solo día *and Alejandra Kamiya's* Los árboles caídos también son el bosque

Whereas Chapter 3 centered on the representation of Japanese Argentine identity in two novels written by men, this chapter turns to the female Nikkei voices created by Anna Kazumi Stahl and Alejandra Kamiya. Rather than focusing on the female body (Sugimura) or assigning women a secondary role as romantic partners (Matayoshi), Stahl and Kamiya write about women protagonists who defy conventional norms of gender dynamics. Their characters are capable of imagining a shared sense of solidarity against male-dominated (and often white-dominated) society. My analysis of Stahl's novel *Flores de un solo día* and Kamiya's short stories in *Los árboles caídos también son el bosque* will illustrate how the two writers seek to contest the fetishized notions of women and offer alternative viewpoints on Nikkei cultural identity in contemporary Argentina.

Gendering Orientalism

Before moving on to the analysis of Stahl's novel and Kamiya's short stories, it is useful to highlight the current debate about Latin American/Argentine Orientalism. Building on Edward Said's *Orientalism*, scholars have developed various approaches to the study of Orientalism in Latin American literature in the last three decades.[1] Some of the pioneers in this field, such as Julia Kushigian and Araceli Tinajero, agree that Latin American Orientalism differs from the traditional European Orientalism in that it explores points of comparison and interconnectivity rather than relations of imperial hierarchy. In more contemporary times, Mabel Moraña characterizes Orientalism through the process of what she calls "discursive hybridization and pluralization" in Latin American literature.[2] Most recently, in her insightful study of Mexican Orientalism, Laura Torres-Rodríguez investigates how the notion of the Orient serves to shed new light on the (re)production of the Mexican imagination and institutions of knowledge.[3]

In the case of Argentina, Francine Masiello has argued that Orientalism represents a challenge to both modernity and *modernismo*. She claims that the Orientalist paradigm in Argentine literature is "a metaphor for marginality" for it "signals the failure of an overarching national ethic to produce a language of communal expression."[4] She further refers to how "the Oriental trope is a challenge to modernismo itself, to the entrenched privilege accorded to Latin American writers of that last fin de siglo."[5] From a different viewpoint, Christina Civantos analyzes the literary depictions of the Middle East in such writers as Domingo Faustino Sarmiento and Leopoldo Lugones. She examines how the Orient was imagined and experienced by Arab and non-Arab writers in the formation of Argentina's national identity.[6] In a similar vein, Axel Gasquet explores a wide range of Orientalist writers, arguing that the study of Argentine Orientalism reveals a non-Eurocentric perspective in at least two levels: the ability to resist the cultural and ideological hegemony of "hispanidad" and the possibility of cultural dialogue between two regions that are considered peripheral from the Western point of view.[7]

In dialogue with these previous studies, I seek to contribute to the ongoing conversation about Argentine Orientalism by focusing on Nikkei literary production. As Lisa Lowe has shown, the idea of Orientalism has often been oversimplified and reduced to "a monolithic, developmental discourse that uniformly constructs the Orient as the Other of the Occident."[8] According to her, Orientalist discourse is inherently versatile, elusive, and malleable. Therefore, it is constantly redefined by a myriad of interests, including those prompted by differences in gender, race, and class.[9] Lowe's study points to the fact that Orientalism is a complex and multifarious field that requires careful attention to historical specificity and national traditions.

In Chapter 3, I discussed how two male Nikkei writers have come to challenge Argentina's conventional narrative about Japan through their own hybrid stories of immigration. In this chapter, I will focus on the feminine gaze that is often overlooked within the masculine vision of Orientalism, thereby shedding light on the so-called "gendering orientalism."[10] Beginning with Gayatri Spivak's classic text "Can the Subaltern Speak?" (1985), many scholars have explored the relationship between Orientalism, imperialism, race, and gender.[11] My following analysis of Stahl and Kamiya underlines the possibility of female agency that was absent in Sugimura and Matayoshi. As we noted in the previous chapter, both *Buscadores en mis última vidas* and *Gaijin* portray female characters in stereotypical manners, defining their subjectivity only in terms of their romantic relationship to male characters. Thinking about a more critical, gendering paradigm of Orientalism that goes beyond dominant masculinity, we can also refer to the feminist scholar Sara Ahmed's understanding of otherness as "a form of extension." As she explains, "[r]ather than othering being simply a form of negation, it can also be described *as a form of extension*. The body extends its reach by taking in that which is 'not' it, where the 'not' involves the acquisition of new capacities and directions—becoming, in other words, 'not' simply what I am 'not' but what I can 'have' and 'do.'"[12] At the same time, my emphasis on the female-centered narrative follows what Anne Cheng calls the theory of "ornamentalism": "Simultaneously consecrated and desecrated as an inherently aesthetic object, the yellow woman calls for a theorization of persons and things that considers a human ontology inextricable from synthetic extensions, art, and commodity."[13] In the following pages, I will show how Stahl and Kamiya create an alternative form of Argentine Orientalism through their production of female agency, thereby resisting the facile essentialization and commodification of Asian and Nikkei women.

Female Agency and Ternary Identity in Anna Kazumi Stahl's *Flores de un solo día*

Like Sugimura and Matayoshi, Anna Kazumi Stahl is Nisei (second generation), but she is a North American author of Japanese descent who writes in Spanish and resides in Argentina. A daughter of a Japanese mother and an American father, Stahl spent her childhood and early adulthood in New Orleans. She studied in Argentina as a university student and later decided to settle permanently in Buenos Aires. Even at the biographical level, it is easy to see how her identity embodies the multicultural immigrant life in contemporary Argentina. As Francine Masiello observes, "Claiming various national belongings, Stahl engages the crisis of identity that besets a translator and marginal observer who is forced to wear the mask of immigrant identity and speak through the screen of several languages not readily her own."[14]

Published in 2002, *Flores de un solo día* is Stahl's first novel, which was selected as a finalist for the Rómulo Gallegos Prize for new Latin American fiction. Several critics have written essays about the novel, and my analysis is necessarily in dialogue with them.[15] In his analysis of *Flores de un solo día*, alongside two other books of fiction dealing with Asians in Latin America (Karen Tei Yamashita's *Brazil-Maru* and Cristina García's *Monkey Hunting*), Gustavo Geirola mentions that these works "destabilize the idea of an identity conceived in terms of a binary opposition, which in English is translated as *hyphenated-identity*."[16] For me, Stahl's novel shows how an immigrant identity can be defined not only through conventional hyphenation and biculturalism, but via the mingling of three different cultural contexts, including Japan, Argentina, and the United States. Put differently, the novel articulates Nikkei subjectivity in terms of what can be called a "ternary identity," which challenges the traditional structure characterized by a simple opposition, or a Hegelian dialectic. From this perspective, I argue that *Flores de un solo día* calls into question the conventional postcolonial notion of "diaspora" determined exclusively through thesis and antithesis, whether between colonizer and colonized, Occident and Orient, center and periphery, or self and other. Chisu Teresa Ko also pays attention to the intersection among the three points of cultural and national references. For Ko, the key concepts to understand Stahl's novel are "self-Orientalism" and "inter-imperiality." She argues that the book skillfully uncovers the histories of multiple empires "by tracing Orientalism's trajectories—from Japan to the United States and Argentina—and by weaving together the lingering and connected effects of imperialism from before Columbus to the present."[17]

In *Flores de un solo día*, the main characters are women: Aimée Levrier, a second-generation Japanese American, and her mother Hanako, who is mute because of a brain disease she suffered during her childhood. They live in New Orleans until the death of Hanako's husband, Henri, at which time they are sent to Buenos Aires by Aimée's grandfather, Francisco Oleary or

"El Argentino." Aimée is only eight and has no knowledge of Spanish when they arrive in South America. Years later, we find Aimée fully integrated into society, living with her Argentine husband, Fernando Marconi, and running a small flower shop where Hanako specializes in the art of *ikebana* (Japanese flower arrangement). However, their comfortable life is abruptly interrupted by the arrival of a mysterious letter informing Aimée that her grandmother has passed away in New Orleans and that she is the only heir to an estate that is worth $750,000. Despite the fear of confronting the forgotten past, Aimée decides to return to the United States. During her brief journey, she discovers a complex web of family secrets that reveals not only the history of Hanako and herself in Japan and the US, but also the real reason why the two were sent to Argentina.

First, the novel's Japanese elements are demonstrated through Hanako, the only character with a Japanese name, meaning "flower girl." With her reticence and gracefulness, she is the quintessential symbol of Japanese femininity: "If Aimée is pretty, the mother is much prettier, with Japanese features that, by their harmony, express a universal beauty."[18] In addition to her muteness, Hanako is unable to leave the house because of her agoraphobia, fear of being outside, which is a disorder she developed after witnessing the atomic bombs in Japan during World War II. Besides being signs of a physical impediment, her muteness and agoraphobia can also be understood in symbolic terms: while muteness represents the experience of Japanese immigrants' inability to speak Spanish upon their arrival in Latin America, agoraphobia indicates the difficulty of leaving one's comfort zone in a foreign country. For Hanako, the small apartment in Buenos Aires is the only place where she feels safe and protected. The familiar faces of Aimée and Fernando not only guarantee a predictable daily life but also promise her emotional stability. As the narrator comments, their faces "let her live in a known and predictable universe. They allow her to be happy; she is almost always happy, quiet but without anxiety, without an air of mental illness."[19] Hanako's speech disorder also reflects the quiet environment in their apartment, which reminds us of the reference to silence in *Gaijin*. Similar to what we saw in Kitaro, silence is an important mode of communication for the Japanese characters in *Flores de un solo día*, especially between the mother and the daughter. For Hanako and Aimée, it is far from "an empty silence" for it symbolizes "a warm and easy space, which opened between two people and was filled not with words but with the things they did together."[20] Hanako displays her feelings through subtle gestures, including the almost imperceptible sound or melody she makes, the delicate expression on her face, and the firm posture of her body. Of particular importance is the way in which she interacts with others through her gaze: "She always spoke with her eyes: she looked at people—those she knew—and could express a million things in an instant, directly to the mind and the heart of the other person."[21] Despite her disabilities, Hanako's language transcends muteness as her eyes can clearly communicate her thoughts. Indeed, it is her extraordinary gaze—"an open gaze, almost smiling" (una mirada abierta, casi risueña)—that defines the relationship between Hanako and Aimée.[22] Here the silent gaze shared by the two female protagonists creates the condition of possibility for resistance against male characters, such as Fernando Marconi and Javier Nakamura, who are unable to penetrate into their shared space of femininity. Fernando feels frustrated because he cannot comprehend Hanako's expressions: "He finds it hard not being able to communicate with Aimée's mother. He does not know what she thinks, what she wants or needs."[23]

In addition, Hanako also turns to the art of *ikebana* to display her emotions. It is well-known that *ikebana* is a traditional art of flower arrangement that has been practiced in Japan since the fifteenth century, although its origin can be traced as far back as the sixth century.[24] In *ikebana*, a variety of natural elements, ranging from flowers and branches to leaves and seeds, are used creatively to compose a multicolored work of visual art. Although this tradition is often associated with home decoration, it is more than a mere style of ornamentation, given that it encompasses various philosophical and spiritual values. For instance, one of the fundamental principles of *ikebana* is the inseparability between humans and nature or between one's internal thoughts and one's external environment. Based on this idea, the basic structure of flower arrangement is a scalene triangle created by three main points. It is usually understood that these points are embodiments of Heaven, Earth, and Humankind.[25]

In *Flores de un solo día*, Hanako is an adept *ikebana* artist, as evidenced by the fact that her customers use "hanako" and "ikebana" interchangeably: rather than request a specific floral design, they only ask for a "hanako-style." According to the narrator, she has a direct and immediate relationship with the flowers she works with: "Hanako gives flowers shape, height and air, definition; and she receives from them color and warmth or coldness, the curve or the severe angle. And through that relationship in the long run what emerges is an expression, a suggestion (almost more complete than what could be done through words) of a feeling, posture or attitude."[26] By communicating through or with flowers, Hanako is able to establish her own way of thinking, feeling, and living. As both practitioner and guardian of the *ikebana* tradition, she embodies Japan's original culture and spirituality. As Ko notes, "Hanako's mastery of ikebana seems instinctive, natural to her Japaneseness and undeterred by her disabilities."[27]

Her daughter Aimée also displays certain Japanese elements (for example, in her "Oriental eyes"), but her identity is not easily definable through a single country or language. Unlike her mother, Aimée represents a more complex multicultural subjectivity. When she arrives in Buenos Aires, the eight-year-old Aimée is depicted as a mature and independent girl whose task is to take care of her disabled mother. Here, the traditional roles of mother and daughter seem to be reversed. During their trip, Hanako keeps her eyes closed out of fear, while Aimée bravely protects her: "The daughter guided her, a feminine hand with small bones inside the other, smaller but chubby, soft, hand of a girl."[28] At first the narrator characterizes Aimée as "a talkative and energetic little person who only lacked the language to get by."[29] Indeed she quickly learns Spanish and finds herself successfully assimilated into society. Aimée's new identity in the host country is most clearly shown through her marriage with Fernando, a native-born Argentine of Sicilian descent, who selflessly supports her when her tranquil life is disrupted by the mysterious letter from Louisiana. Perplexed by the meaning of the letter, she discovers peace in her husband's voice: "The voice of that man and the dense soundness of his body give her strength, because they confirm belonging, the idea that she is where she should be, that this is *her* place."[30] For Aimée, there is no doubt that Fernando's Argentina is the familiar home—"*her* place"—where the life is insulated from unusualness and uncertainty.

Although Hanako and Aimée take different approaches to the reality of immigrant life in Argentina, they share indivisible connections, which can be understood as female alliance against male-dominated society. The novel characterizes Hanako and Aimée's relationship in terms of a unity that is based not only on their family ties but also on their shared femininity. As characterized by the narrator, "They were like two drops of water thrown into the oil; beyond their similarity and their union, they faced the remote foreign land together and lived a slow transition together."[31] When Aimée was young, she completed all schoolwork while physically close to her mother, perceiving her affectionate gaze and feeling the warmth of her hands. Their physical proximity and spiritual union are what enable the mother and the daughter to survive in a foreign country. The role of silence is once again critical in this relationship, as they have a better understanding of each other through silence than through words: "They both have the same figure; they walk at the same time; their movements share fluid movements of delicate arms and slender legs. They prepare the food together and share silence, which is not cold, but warm and continent, like an environment in itself."[32] As mentioned earlier, the inseparable union between the female protagonists is not accessible to male characters like Fernando. Hanako and Aimée create a sense of female solidarity through their shared struggles, which is incomprehensible to the white male character of European descent. Even though there are stereotypical images of Japanese women (quietness, beauty, *ikebana*, etc.), those same qualities are precisely what make them independent and resilient. That is, Stahl employs a discourse of gendering Orientalism to create female characters who are no longer passive subjects under masculine control. Rather, they are active participants of knowledge production through which they gain access to a thriving business and a comfortable middle-class life in Argentina.

Moreover, we can detect another instance of female alliance between Aimée and Bess Tibbets, the black servant in their house in New Orleans where Aimée and Hanako lived before arriving to Buenos Aires. Since Aimée was still young and Hanako was unable to take care of her daughter, Bess gave both women the protection they needed. Her role was especially critical for Aimée. If Hanako was Aimée's biological mother, Bess was her spiritual mother, always providing her with "the support, the floor, the walls and the ceiling, the stability of the world."[33] At the same time, Bess was an extraordinary teacher for Aimée, who had many questions about the world, such as how school functioned or why her parents did not sleep together like other parents. Aimée trusted the black servant more than anyone else in the house, seeing in her "a model of an adult woman."[34] Consequently, as an adult searching for her origins, we find Aimée constantly remembering her second mother during the trip in New Orleans.

Bess's influence in Aimée cannot be underestimated. First, it gives an important American influence to Aimée's transnational, ternary identity. Bess comes from a poor neighborhood where violence and crime occur frequently. With her African roots and her voodoo practice, she embodies the racial and religious diversity of New Orleans. It is interesting that the novel describes this US port city as different from the rest of the country: "Everything would start later than in other cities, at least Anglo-Saxon ones."[35] In fact, the reference to the less Anglo-Saxon characteristic of New Orleans is already noticeable in Stahl's previous collection of short stories, *Catástrofes naturales* (Natural disasters), published in 1997.[36] Perhaps we can go so far as to say that the city of "The Big Easy" is itself a central character for the author, who herself is a Louisiana native. According to Debra Castillo, *Flores de un solo día* is among the few contemporary novels that portray New Orleans as "a placeholder to anchor a theory and practice of writing that goes beyond the thematic in transcending national boundaries."[37] As Castillo observes, there are many Latin American features in New Orleans, which can be defined as "a border city between the US and Latin America, as well as a city that has long been seen as an exotic outpost in the US urban imaginary."[38] For Aimée, therefore, the American influence represented by Bess has a specific regional connotation, grounded in the dynamic cross-cultural nature of New Orleans.

Another aspect of Bess's America is the racism that Aimée and Hanako experience before moving to Argentina. In the previous chapter, we saw how Matayoshi's *Gaijin* portrays Argentina as a kind of shelter for Japanese immigrants. Similarly, *Flores de un solo día* creates an image of hospitable Argentina in contrast to that of a racist American South. In the novel, Hanako faces discrimination in her community in New Orleans during "a time of racism still unpunished" and "the era of racist segregation."[39] She is even mistreated by her stepmother, Marie Levrier, who employs the racist rhetoric of the time to annul the marriage between Hanako and her husband, Henri, referring to the infamous Louisiana state law that prohibited mixed marriages.[40] Marie eventually gains custody of Aimée by making a false accusation against Hanako. Out of fear of losing the girl to the manipulative Marie, her supposed husband, Francisco Oleary, sends both Hanako and Aimée off to his sister in Argentina. Unlike the hostile circumstances of the xenophobic community in Louisiana, Argentina provides Hanako with a place of security where she can safely practice her *ikebana*. In addition, it is the small apartment in Buenos Aires that allows Hanako and Aimée to develop the female alliance I discussed earlier.

Marie's mistreatment of Hanako is one of the many secrets Aimée uncovers during her sojourn in the US. In addition, she learns that her biological father is not Henri but her putative grandfather Francisco, "El Argentino." As it turns out, Henri and other American soldiers killed Hanako's father during the war in Japan, leaving the eight-year-old girl orphaned. Tormented by his fervent Christian faith, Henri brought Hanako to the US and married ("adopted") her in order to "protect her from evil."[41] However, it was Francisco whom Hanako actually fell in love with. Despite her speech disorder and agoraphobia, Francisco was one of the few people she opened up to and the only person she wanted to see outside the house.

Although "El Argentino" was married to Marie, their marriage was based solely on a contract he had with Marie's father, Claude Lavrier, who had asked Francisco to spy on her because he was afraid of her obsession with power and control. As a reward, Francisco received a property in West Feliciana, where he would later meet with Hanako clandestinely. In the end, he decided not to reveal the truth to his daughter Aimée before his death, knowing that it would destroy her familiar world, especially her relationship with Hanako and Henri.[42] When Aimée arrives in New Orleans, she visits Francisco's house and discovers the poems and letters that he had written for her and Hanako. One of the poems reads, "You are the truth that I hide / I love you without being seen / I wish to make myself worthy / Of seeing you, my daughter, grow" ("Sos la verdad que oculto / Te amo sin que me veas / Quisiera hacerme valer / De verte, mi hija, crecer").[43] After recovering the bittersweet history of her family, Aimée is finally able to obtain closure with the past and returns to Buenos Aires where Hanako and Fernando are awaiting.

Hence Aimée's biological roots actually consist of Argentina (Francisco) and Japan (Hanako), which makes her a Nikkei individual. However, her identity transcends the simple binary of Japan-Argentina, as evidenced by her close ties to the United States through Bess. In the novel, we find Aimée struggling to articulate her thoughts in multiple languages. The letter from New Orleans forces her to confront the forgotten past, and it is at this time that Aimée realizes that she no longer feels capable of reading in English, which she had essentially abandoned twenty-five years ago.[44] While she has difficulty deciphering the language, she sees an image of her eight-year-old self. The blending of English and Spanish, of childhood and adulthood, takes center stage in her narrative as she examines the documents:

> She looks over some of them [letters]—*we duly notify, the express agreement, the holder, the owner, not by marriage or blood relation*—and suddenly, like lightning, a little voice appears in her mind saying: '*I am eight, and I . . . this is my . . . her name is . . . just for a little . . . because then . . . to take us back to . . .*' Is that her own voice? From when? Who is she saying all this to?
>
> Revisa algunas de ellas—*we duly notify, the express agreement, the holder, the owner, not by marriage or blood relation*—y de repente, como un rayo, se le aparece una vocecita en la mente que dice: '*I am eight, and I . . . this is my . . . her name is . . . just for a little . . . because then . . . to take us back to . . .*' ¿Es ésa su propia voz? ¿De cuándo? ¿A quién está diciendo todo eso?[45]

The confluence of Spanish and English in this passage is indicative of what Ottmar Ette calls "translingual praxis," which denotes "an unending process of the constant intersection of languages."[46] Multiple languages do not necessarily create different meanings in the text. Instead, they "mutually permeate one another, such that new translingual formulations arise."[47] Moreover, Aimée's translingual reflection is made possible thanks to her Japanese mother who silently encourages her to confront the family history. It is Hanako's quiet expression that gives Aimée ultimate security and assurance: "Her expression showed the gentle security that is characteristic of her, the opposite of doubt."[48] It is clear that Aimée is not really interested in the property in New Orleans. Rather than beginning a new life or remembering an old life, she wishes to find closure from the past in order to return to the comfortable life she has established in Buenos Aires. However, uncovering her connections to the US is an inevitable process toward the making of her ternary subjectivity. As a result, the novel creates a multicultural space in which to negotiate distinct meanings involving Japanese, Argentine, and American features. *Flores de un solo día* delineates the Nikkei identity beyond the conventional notion of Japanese Argentineness, providing alternative forms of enunciation from the female perspective. It is through the flux of cross-cultural exchange that Stahl articulates a dynamic relationship transgressing boundaries—both physical and metaphoric—across the Pacific.

Japanese Heritage and Femininity in Alejandra Kamiya's
Los árboles caídos también son el bosque

Similar to Stahl's novel, women play central roles in Alejandra Kamiya's short stories. However, whereas Stahl describes her immigrant characters based on three points of cultural reference, Kamiya places more emphasis on how the legacy of the Japanese heritage is translated into the Argentine context. Consequently, the past (Japan) and the present (Argentina) are deeply intertwined with each other in Kamiya's stories. As Laura Galarza observes, "[t]he familiar and the unknown, the close and the strange, something that could be a misunderstanding ends up being the birth of something new."[49] Kamiya's literary career began in 2007 when she attended the writing workshops by Inés Fernández Moreno and Abelardo Castillo. For the next decades, her fame as a talented writer of short stories came to be recognized both within and outside of Argentina. Her many awards include

Premio Universidad Católica Argentina-SUTERH (2007), Premio Feria del Libro de Buenos Aires (2008), Premio Fondo Nacional de las Artes (2009), Premio Fundación Victoria Ocampo (2012), Premio Internacional de Cuentos Max Aub (Spain, 2011), Premio Horacio Quiroga (Uruguay, 2012) and Premio Unicaja (Spain, 2014).

In this section, I will analyze three stories from *Los árboles caídos también son el bosque* that are directly related to Japanese heritage. The first story, "Desayuno perfecto" (Perfect breakfast), is set in contemporary Japan. It follows second-person narration representing the inner voice of a Japanese female protagonist who is instructed to prepare a "perfect breakfast" for her husband and son. The narrative voice commands methodically and almost militaristically that the protagonist must wake up before sunrise: "You won't wait for the light to come in through the window."[50] The family lives in Tokyo, not far from the famous Tsukiji fish market, where the protagonist is supposed to look for a "perfect mackerel." The fish has to be absolutely fresh because "a perfect breakfast requires perfect fish and the freshest fish is in the vicinity of the Tsukiji market."[51] For the most part, the story details the mundane life of a typical Japanese family who sleeps on tatami and kneels down to eat traditional food. Kamiya's text incorporates numerous Japanese words, such as *miso shiru* (miso soup), *natto* (fermented soybeans), *nori* (seaweed), and *ohashi* (chopsticks). The female protagonist is also depicted in terms of conventional Japanese femininity, as evidenced by her silent obedience and selfless dedication to the men in the household. However, the simple repetition of ordinary life abruptly comes to an end: after seeing off her husband and son, the protagonist commits suicide by placing her head in the oven. As the narrative voice instructs, "You are going to turn on the switch and put your head on the oven door as if it were a pillow on which you are going to rest."[52] At the end, the only thing we find is "the apology note" left on the kitchen table.[53]

Several themes stand out in this story. First, Kamiya employs concise words to carefully describe a universal, everyday task: the ritual of preparing a breakfast. In this task, the idea of "perfection" is rooted in the values of discipline and modesty that are respected in Japanese society. For example, the protagonist is instructed to bring home a "perfect mackerel" as soon as possible because any delay would cause the fish to lose its freshness. According to the narrative voice, a failure to follow the command would be "a crack in the smoothness of your plan."[54] Upon returning to the kitchen, the female character must prepare all the food in a flawless manner because "no angle should be out of tune, no color should clash or fade."[55] When her husband and her son compliment her by saying how the breakfast is "oishi" (delicious), she does nothing but appreciate them "smiling more with eyes than with lips that do not detach."[56] Finally, before her unanticipated death, the inner voice tells her to clean the house impeccably, for it would be a "lack of humility" otherwise.

At first sight, it can be argued that the story portrays the female protagonist as a "perfect woman" whose honor must be preserved even at the cost of her life. However, the surprise ending of the story can also be interpreted as a symbol of defiance against the notions of "peacefulness" and "obedience" that are often attributed to Japanese women. I argue that by illustrating the self-destruction of a Japanese woman, Kamiya calls attention to one of the most serious and unspoken social issues in contemporary Japan. According to a recent report by Japan's Ministry of Health, Labor and Welfare, there are more than one thousand housewives who commit suicide each year. In 2018, for instance, more housewives (totaling 1,163) killed themselves than the unemployed (872) and students (771).[57] While the problem of juvenile suicide has received much public attention in recent years, the reality of wives and mothers who commit suicide each year has rarely been a topic of conversation in Japanese media, much less outside the country.[58] In this regard, Kamiya's story sheds light on the hidden life of Japanese women, thereby creating a much more complex image of femininity than the one described by Sugimura and Matayoshi. At the same time, the protagonist's death by her own hand can also be interpreted as the ultimate form of resistance to patriarchy. As a "perfect" wife and mother, she completes all the domestic tasks assigned to her without any complaints. Faithfully following traditions and customs, she always serves men in the household with a smile. Despite her silent gesture, however, she is not a voiceless character as her behavior is compared to a flower that is placed on the kitchen table, "the flower, open like a mouth that screams" (la flor, abierta como una boca que grita).[59] Like the screaming flower, her suicide is more than a simple act of submission. Instead, it can be interpreted as a moment of self-determination as well as an example of resistance against Japan's pervasive culture of patriarchy.

Unlike the previous story, Kamiya's "Arroz" (Rice) is more autobiographical and based on the life of Japanese immigrants in Argentina. The story describes an unnamed protagonist and narrator, a Nikkei woman in Buenos Aires, who goes to lunch with her father at a restaurant in San Telmo, the oldest and most traditionally Hispanic part of the city. Like *Flores de un solo día*, the theme of silence permeates the story. The reader learns that neither the protagonist nor her father is talkative and that they often communicate with each other without words. They share a kind of "comfortable silence, light like the air of which it is made, and in which the flavor of what we eat is better expressed."[60] The female protagonist explains that she can gain deeper understanding of her father through intuitions: "I know many things about him like this, without knowing them, just sensing them."[61] Just like how Hanako and Aimée prefer to interact with each other through quiet gestures, the daughter-father relationship in this story also demonstrates silence as an essential mode of communication.

In "Arroz," the Japanese father refers to Argentina as "a child country" because it only has two hundred years of existence, compared to Japan's millennial history.[62] He explains that he had experienced war and poverty in his native land before coming to Argentina during the 1970s. Upon arrival, he faced difficulties adjusting to the new country and still carries around a dictionary to look up words in Spanish. The daughter refers to how different generations of Nikkei Argentines deal with the linguistic aspect of their immigrant lives: "For myself, who was born and raised in Argentina, I am too lazy to look up words in the dictionary. He is not. My Japanese father's Spanish is vaster and more concrete than mine."[63] In general, Nisei children are usually described as the ones who speak better Spanish than their Issei parents. However, Kamiya rewrites this stereotype by having the narrator admire her father's Spanish as being "vaster and more concrete" than her own. In this way, the author pays homage to the efforts and sacrifices made by early immigrants to survive in the new country.

In this story, the past and the present are interrelated through the lives of the father and the daughter. What connects the two characters is the knowledge of how to clean rice and the image of rice fields in Japan. The protagonist claims that "[b]y seeing my father's gestures, I can reach the past, Japan, or my father's story, which is also mine."[64] Although she has many questions about his immigrant life in Argentina, they do not have much time left because he appears to be seriously ill. When the father says that his doctor ordered a biopsy for him, she suddenly becomes aware of his imminent death: "I feel what is lurking, and a certainty akin to the one of day being succeeded by night, a kind of vertigo."[65] Toward the end of the story, she is able to ask him one last question about how to prepare rice. According to her, "Now I see clearly, I can almost touch, the grains of rice coming off."[66] Even though their brief conversation takes place at the center of Buenos Aires, their imagination travels across the ocean and reaches rice fields in Japan. Now the daughter is not only the heir of a family secret (how to prepare rice) but is also the guardian of Japanese food culture in Argentina.

Similar to "Arroz," the final story "Partir" (Departing) also has autobiographical elements and deals with the history of Nikkei Argentines from a female point of view. Told by a female first-person narrator, the main plot describes her experience of childbirth or "parto," which she defines as "the act of coming to life" (el acto de llegar a la vida).[67] At the same time, the Spanish word "partir"—"to leave" or "to depart"—also implies other meanings with regard to immigration. The narrator refers to how her father, dressed in a kimono, came to Argentina to start a new life: "He left not when he departed from Japan but when he decided to stay in Argentina."[68] While the father discovered a sense of permanence when he decided to settle in South America, the daughter had a difficult time avoiding racism at school:

> The other boys would point with their index fingers and call me "Chinese." I'd tell them I was Japanese but they said it was the same thing. I wouldn't answer them. I couldn't understand why they'd say that, or many other things. They yelled at me, pushed me and some of them hit me. They all seemed very angry at me.[69]

This scene reminds us of Kitaro's similar experience of discrimination in *Gaijin*. However, Kamiya's female character presents a distinct story of foreignness that goes beyond the Nikkei history in Argentina. Like the injustice she endures as a "foreigner" in Argentina, her experience as an outsider in Japan is equally distressing. She explains that another meaning of "partir" is "make halves" (hacer mitades), and that is exactly how she is perceived during her visit to Japan: as "half," meaning "half-Japanese" or a child of mixed race.[70] As she states, "I am Japanese in Argentina and Argentine in Japan, with lowercase letters for me and capital letters for the country."[71] The unidentifiable characteristic of a Nikkei woman is such that she is literally "partida" or "divided" between Argentina and Japan, unable to claim her wholeness in any culture.

Although she is not accepted in either country, she comes to realize that one can be complementary to the other. For her, there is no need to reject her Japaneseness in order to embrace her Argentineness, and vice versa. Similar to the way in which the past/Japan and the present/Argentina are interlaced in "Arroz," the former constitutes an integral part of the latter in "Partir." The narrator makes a reference to how in some forest in Southern

Argentina (perhaps in Bariloche), "trees that fall are not removed but are left to form part of the landscape."[72] This story, from which the book takes its title, can be interpreted as a metaphor for the lives of many Nikkei Argentines. The fallen trees symbolize the history of Issei, who experience not only the war in Japan but also the difficulties of assimilation in Argentina. Some of them have literally "fallen" or lost their lives while helping to build reputations for the Japanese community in Argentina. Later generations, such as Nisei and Sansei (third generation), are symbolized by the image of "the landscape." In this setting, the new generation is able to thrive in today's society thanks to the sacrifices and the contributions of their parents and grandparents.

Of particular note is the cultural legacy that can be transmitted by women in their immigrant families. In "Partir," the female character gives birth to a baby boy called Kenta. His name, if written as 健太 in Japanese characters, can mean "strength," "vigor," or "good health." In the story, his name actually comes from the protagonist's grandmother Katsu (カツ or 勝つ), which can be translated as "to win." Even though the protagonist never had a chance to meet her grandmother who stayed in Japan after the war, she feels that there are strong connections between them. People say that the two women look alike, and she recognizes the characteristics of a powerful, independent woman in her grandmother: "I did not know her except for stories my father told and a picture I once saw where I looked for the strong woman who supported her family and her husband's family alone, losing everything several times during the war."[73] Her grandmother's life inspired her in such a way that she still feels connected to her, especially as she goes through childbirth alone in her forties. It is through her memory of Katsu that the protagonist comes up with the name Kenta for her own son. Both names indicate the idea of being strong and victorious, which is also related to the legacy of female solidarity between two Japanese women. As the protagonist describes toward the end of the story, "I feel like I am part of something much bigger. Something that started on the other side of the world, where people arrange their shoes when they take them off. And it is still here, where people leave them the way they want."[74] Transcending temporal and spatial boundaries, the symbolic relationship between grandmother and granddaughter brings Japan closer to Argentina, linking the past to the present. Kamiya's protagonist readily embraces the fact that she is neither totally Japanese nor Argentine; instead, she incorporates elements of both in order to become part of "something much bigger" than a limited framework of nation-state.

Through their narratives of gendering Orientalism, both Stahl and Kamiya make unique contributions to the history of Nikkei literature in Argentina. Their characters embody instances of female solidarity and critiques of patriarchal values, as opposed to the women figures in Sugimura and Matayoshi who are relegated to being objects of masculine desire. Based on their own personal and sociohistorical circumstances, the female protagonists in Stahl's novel and Kamiya's short stories defy the conventional narrative of what it means to be Japanese or Nikkei women in Argentina. Unlike the romanticized vision of Japan depicted by men, the Japaneseness illustrated in these writings is more complicated and multifaceted. As both women and people of Asian descent, Stahl and Kamiya create a discourse of counter-modernity in twofold: against the system of patriarchy one the one hand, and the ideology of whiteness on the other. Hence, their works paint an alternative picture of the literary and cultural canon in twenty-first-century Argentina.

CHAPTER 5

Visual Representations of Japan in Contemporary Argentine Cinema

In this chapter, I will examine the representation of Japanese immigrants and their descendants in three contemporary Argentine films, which I compare with another film dealing with the experience of Chinese immigrants. Like the recent history of Nikkei literature, the participation of Japanese and other Asian actors in Argentine cinema is a relatively new phenomenon. As Lucía Rud notes, "although immigrants from these Asian countries were present in the country's political and social scene during the twentieth century . . . they did not form part of the cinematographic representations of Argentine cinema until the last years of the 1990s."[1] As we will see, most of the films I analyze in this chapter are from the twenty-first century. According to Joanna Page, Argentina's cinematographic scene went through a crucial transformation following the 2001 economic crisis: "the Crisis delivered a hefty blow to Argentina's First World aspirations, reinforcing at the same time the specificity of national experience."[2] Films, she argues, provided the national audience with a tool for "self-reflexivity," which allowed them to reconfigure their cultural and social identities.[3] As a result, there was a renewed interest in portraying different immigrant groups through such movies as *Bolivia* (2002) and *Vladimir en Buenos Aires*

(2002).[4] In this sense, the fictional and non-fictional films studied in this chapter lead us to a new understanding of Argentina's national imaginary that is seeking more racial diversity and inclusivity.

The first film I examine is Clara Zappettini's documentary *La otra tierra: Japoneses en Argentina* (1986). As one of the earliest visual manifestations of the Nikkei experience in Argentina, the film intends to shed light on the struggles of Japanese immigrants and their descendants in the country. Some of the themes I discussed in Chapters 3 and 4 will reappear in this documentary, including the conflict between Japanese and Argentine identities as well as generational differences within the Nikkei community. This chapter will then compare two fictional movies from the 2010s: Gaspar Scheuer's *Samurai* (2013) and Sebastián Borensztein's *Un cuento chino* (2011).[5] While these films similarly present Asian immigrants as constituents of Argentina's multicultural society, they also show how the Japanese are portrayed in a more positive light than their Chinese counterparts. I argue that the Japanese protagonist in *Samurai* is a contemporary representation of transpacific modernity that is fully expected to contribute to Argentina's future. By contrast, the Chinese immigrant character in *Un cuento chino* is reduced to a dehumanized object that plays no significant role in the making of a new Argentina. A comparative analysis of the two films reveals the continued relevance of the discourse of transpacific modernity in the twenty-first century. Lastly, in order to understand the legacy of the Nikkei community in Argentina, I examine the documentary *Silencio roto: 16 Nikkeis* (2015), directed by Pablo Moyano. This film narrates, for the first time, the story of Nikkei Argentines who lost their family members during Argentina's military dictatorship in the late 1970s. In dialogue with the topic of silence that I discussed in the previous chapters, my analysis will highlight several meanings of silence in the film and their broader implications for Argentina's Nikkei society today and beyond. As shown in this chapter, the study of visual representations can complement the earlier analysis of literary work because they both seek to redefine the traditional narratives of modernity, nation-building, and immigrant identity.

Fallen Angels: Analysis of Nikkei Voices in La otra tierra: Japoneses en Argentina

The documentary *La otra tierra: Japoneses en Argentina* was directed by Clara Zappettini and produced by Argentina Televisora Color (ATC).[6] It features interviews that focus on different ways in which Nikkei Argentines have participated in society. Although the film was not created by members of the Nikkei community in Argentina, its emphasis on personal stories suggests that the experiences told via the screen denote a certain historical authenticity. Technically, it is not what Yosefa Loshitzky calls a "diasporic film," that is, a film produced within the diaspora and represents "a form of otherness that poses cultural and political challenges to the hegemony and homogeneity claimed by the nation state."[7] Nevertheless, I argue that *La otra tierra* provides examples of diasporic narrative, even though it does not escape from reinforcing stereotypes about people of Japanese descent.

The documentary begins with a brief introduction by the well-known tango singer and composer Guillermo Fernández, who explains the popularity of tango among the Japanese whom he describes as "a sensational and marvelous race." The film opens with mysterious smoke accompanied by traditional Japanese music. The audience can also hear the sound of the ocean and a vessel, which reflects the experience of transoceanic voyage from Japan to Latin America. The positive perceptions of the Japanese that we examined in Chapters 1 and 2 are once again apparent in *La otra tierra*. Members of the film crew ask ordinary people on the streets of Buenos Aires about their impressions of Japanese Argentines (notably, all the interviewees were people of European descent). There is a shared sense of respect when asked the question, "what image do you have of the Japanese who live in Argentina?" For example, a middle-aged man talks about how the Japanese "form a great community and they work a lot; they have come to have a special life within our society, perhaps not very integrated, but they gave us a good example." Similarly, in another interview, an elderly woman tells the reporter, "I think they are peaceful people, working people, very educated, very respectful." It is clear that the video shows stereotypes about Japanese immigrants, and words such as "peaceful," "respectful," and "hardworking" remind us of Wilde's and Rohde's celebrations of Japan in the early twentieth century.[8]

However, these perceptions are counteracted by other interviews that tell more intimate, multifaceted stories about the Nikkei experience in Argentina. One of the first interviews within the Japanese Argentine community involves seventy-four-year-old Kame de Migasato who came from Okinawa in 1934 to follow her then-boyfriend. Together with other women from Okinawa, Migasato later published the book, *Okinawa imin joseishi* (Immigration History of Okinawan Women), in 1979. As she recalls, the life was not easy for her and her family because of the language barrier:

"we suffered a lot to survive, there was a lot of difficulty." Against the singular narrative associated with Japanese immigrants, her experience as Issei focuses on the challenging process of survival and adaptation in the host country. Moreover, the documentary illustrates the heterogenous nature of the labor force represented by the Nikkei community. Through multiple conversations, the viewer learns not only about the popular business of dry cleaning (interview with Carlos Migasato), but also about other fields, such as art (Kazu Takeda), floriculture (Kenichiro Sawatani and his wife Emiko), and martial arts (Masafumi Sakanashi).

In my view, one of the highlights of the documentary is the story of Nisei Miguel Ángel Ganiko, who discusses the struggles of being a Nikkei actor in Argentine society. In the interview, he recognizes his identity as Argentine and yet he always returns to the question, "what are my possibilities and limitations as an Oriental person in an Occidental country?" Ganiko has a blunt response to the reality of stereotypes and clichés:

> At this moment I am thinking, what can I do in this medium [theater]? I still don't know, but I feel like I am the tip of a spear. I feel like I will have to experiment, to see what happens in this medium, to see the reception toward actors who have Oriental features. What is difficult is breaking with the clichés, breaking with the image of the Japanese. In general, when people see me and ask me what I do, I say, well, I'm an actor, and people have that image of Japanese as being good and hardworking; someone who can be any professional like an engineer or a doctor. But being an actor and seriously studying for the acting career seems very strange to them. I want them to not categorize me in this idea of "become Japanese" because, before playing Japanese, I can be an actor and other characters.

His interview reveals the limited framework that is available to him as a Nikkei actor. The essentialized image of "Japanese" and the attributes associated with the myth of the "model minority" do not allow him to freely exercise his artistic skills. As a result, he has to constantly grapple with prejudice and societal expectations. His urgent call for the need to reject categorization suggests that he is seen first and foremost as "Japanese" no matter how much he claims his Argentineness.

Moreover, Ganiko's struggles against essentialization are also shared by others from his generation. The topic of generational differences comes into focus toward the end of the documentary when the narrator interviews three young Nikkei Argentines, namely Yoshio Takashima, Nelida Higasiyosihama, and Cecilia Onaha. When asked if he perceives any conflict with his parents, Takashima, who is Nisei, responds, "Yes, there is a conflict-ridden relationship. As I see it, they [my parents] are very traditional. ... In my case, I am very integrated into Argentine society. ... Compared to the Italian and Spanish communities, the Japanese community is the one that most instills traditions in their children." Similar to the generation gap we observed in *Buscadores en mis última vidas*, Takashima's experience embodies the contentious relationship between Issei parents and their Nisei children. Interestingly, we can also detect disagreements between Nisei and Sansei (third generation). For Takashima, the cultural heritage preserved by his parents' generation is an undesirable burden he has to deal with: "I say that it is a burden because, if I am Argentine, I think I have to dedicate myself to my country. So, the fact that my parents condition me to a certain type of things, I take it as a burden." On the contrary, Cecilia Onaha, who is Sansei, argues that "From my point of view and from my generation, we save those [Japanese] traditions and the culture because we consider it a valuable part of us as Argentines. Now, it is a project into the future like a bridge so that we can contribute to Argentina through our heritage in a better way." Moving beyond the generational conflict between Issei and Nisei, the documentary highlights how Sanseis are more respectful and appreciative of what their grandparents had brought from their homeland. To quote Onaha, they are inclined to "save" Japan's cultural traditions and are willing to serve as a "bridge" to help create a better future for Argentina. The ways in which different generations of Nikkeijin represent themselves as protagonists of their own histories demonstrate the multi-layered narratives of immigrant experience. Perhaps the only common denominator among them is the image of "fallen angels." As one of the narrated voices explains in *La otra tierra*, "I think that those of us who are born here with such different blood—one that belongs to the Orient and another to Occident—or those who somehow carry these two worlds within them, are like fallen angels; we are on neither one nor the other side." It becomes clear that there is no homogenizing story of assimilation, integration, identity-formation, or even discrimination among Japanese immigrants and their descendants. By means of the documentary, we can learn about how these "fallen angels" are able to (re)claim their diverse voices in contemporary Argentina.

Samurai-Turned-Gaucho: Contemporary Discourse of Transpacific Modernity in Gaspar Scheuer's *Samurai*

While *La otra tierra* traces the real history of Japanese immigration in Argentina, Gaspar Scheuer's *Samurai* portrays a fictionalized version of the historical-cultural relationship between Japan and Argentina.[9] Loosely based in history, *Samurai* is set in late-nineteenth-century Argentina with a mythical storyline: an elderly Japanese immigrant tells his grandson that a famous samurai, Saigō Takamori (1828–77), has secretly escaped to Argentina after his failed rebellion against the Meiji government. Known as the "last samurai," Saigō is one of the most well-known samurais in Japan's modern history. His life spanned from the late Edo period to the early Meiji era. Always faithful to the virtues of old feudal powers, he organized the Satsuma Rebellion in 1877 against the newly established Meiji government, which led to his eventual death. Today he remains a beloved historical figure throughout Japan and beyond. As described in the beginning of the film, "Legends began to circulate immediately saying that Saigō had not died. That he had fled far, far away, to rebuild his army and restore the lost order." According to the old Japanese immigrant, Saigō's fateful mission is to recover the "lost order" and create "a new Japan" in rural Argentina. When his grandson, named Takeo (played by Nicolás Nakayama), decides to look for the legendary samurai, he comes across an armless gaucho, Poncho Negro (played by Alejandro Awada). Together they embark on a quixotic journey across the Pampas. Their search for Saigō and their collective efforts to reestablish the nostalgic order represent an attempt to simultaneously preserve traditions and resist modernity.

According to the director, a central theme of the movie is what he calls a "historical dialogue" between Japan and Argentina. In an interview for *Revista Sake*, Scheuer mentions his interest in the parallel history from the nineteenth century:

> That political change so marked in Japan that reestablished power to the Emperor, but with American ships in the port; that historical contradiction connected in parallel to a moment here [Argentina]. I felt like there was a great possibility of historical dialogue about what was happening in one place and in the other. At the same time, I felt like there could be a strong movie in the iconic way. The gaucho [and] the samurai, two figures that one would never connect and yet that could dialogue based on the situation of being figures in their decline, their dying days.[10]

His notion of "historical dialogue" is related to how Argentina looked toward Japan as a model of transpacific modernity in the past. As I discussed in Chapters 1 and 2, some Argentine intellectuals were deeply inspired by Japanese culture and tradition. In the same way, *Samurai* depicts a nineteenth-century military officer who is thrilled to meet Takeo in the Pampas (he shows particular interest in Takeo's *katana* or Japanese sword). Familiar with the history of Saigō's rebellion, the colonel says he is fascinated with "the radiance of a millennial civilization." On the contrary, his dismay with Argentina's underdevelopment becomes clear when he says, "here the only thing that grows are weeds." The way both the director and the fictionalized colonel express their fascination with Japan in this contemporary film illustrates how the narrative of transpacific modernity still remains relevant in today's Argentine culture.

The movie plot revolves around the friendship between Takeo and Poncho Negro, the samurai and the gaucho. At first, they are suspicious of each other, with Poncho Negro introducing Takeo to others merely as "my friend Japan" ("mi amigo Japón"). The failure of the Argentine gaucho to recognize Takeo's name reveals a familiar instance of Orientalization in which the specificity of the Japanese character is ignored. Nevertheless, the two protagonists soon begin to trust each other while traveling through rural Argentina. Takeo provides food during the journey and feeds the armless gaucho with his own spoon. For his part, Poncho Negro helps Takeo navigate through Argentina's mountainsides, often speaking Spanish to the locals on his behalf. In symbolic terms, the friendship between them can be understood as a metaphor for the historically amicable relationship between Japan and Argentina. At the same time, it must be noted that the two men establish a strong bond because they both belong to marginalized groups in a country dominated by white, European immigrants. Neither the Japanese immigrant nor the gaucho would constitute the mainstream heritage of Argentine populations. Rather, as Scheuer states in the quoted interview, they share "the situation of being figures in their decline, their dying days." In this sense, Poncho Negro's selfless dedication to assisting Takeo in search of Saigō cannot be taken lightly, especially given that Poncho Negro is killed by his enemies during the trip. On the one hand, we can argue that the gaucho sees the reflection of his own marginality in the life of the Asian immigrant. At the same time, the film describes Argentina as a kind of utopia where the old Japanese values dismantled by the Meiji Restoration can be restored. Even though Takeo and Poncho Negro's shared dream of restoring the tradition eventually fails against the force of modernity, the supposed alliance between the two characters is never tarnished throughout the film.

The close relationship between the samurai and the gaucho can be compared to other cultural symbols in Latin America. For instance, the Nikkei community in Peru imagined a shared heritage between the Inca and the Yamato, while in Brazil there was a similar attempt to connect the indigenous Tupí tribes to the original Japanese people.[11] With regard to samurai and gaucho, they equally represent allegories of traditional values, including honor, devotion, hard work, and loyalty. As Inazō Nitobe famously wrote in *Bushidō: The Soul of Japan* (1899), the way of the samurai has long been a source of Japan's moral principles rooted in Buddhism, Shintoism, and Confucianism.[12] In Argentina, the gaucho has been an important national symbol since the publication of José Hernández's epic poem *Martín Fierro* in 1872. In opposition to Sarmiento, who ascribed to the gaucho negative traits such as laziness and ignorance, Hernández re-imagined the gaucho as a hero of the Argentine nation and thus initiated the long tradition of the so-called gaucho literature.[13]

Contrary to the heroism embodied by Hernández's protagonist, Poncho Negro is far from the national symbol of Argentina. It is true that he is a veteran of the Paraguayan War (1864-1870) who received medals of honor because he lost both arms during the battle. However, his extreme poverty forces him to sell those medals for survival. The disabled gaucho is so desperate that he initially deceives Takeo by lying about Saigō's whereabouts in the Pampas in order to receive the care he needs. As an atypical gaucho who is unable to symbolize heroism, his ultimate death can be interpreted as a rejection of the conventional narrative of Argentine nationalism and modernity. In other words, a gaucho *without arms* represents a country *without promise*, a country that has failed to modernize itself.[14]

Interestingly, the film seems to suggest that Argentina's future depends on the unexpected character from the other side of the Pacific. While the older Poncho Negro meets his inevitable death, the younger Takeo becomes a central figure in the making of a new Argentine nation. As an immigrant, he undergoes the common experience of marginalization and Orientalization. His family tries to preserve Japanese culture by speaking the language, eating rice with chopsticks, wearing traditional kimono, practicing *kenjutsu* or the art of the sword and, most importantly, looking for Saigō in order to restore the "lost order." As expected, there are different ways in which members of his family experience the process of immigration in Argentina. Takeo's grandfather firmly believes in the values of old Japan and never stops believing that the legendary samurai is hiding in the Pampas. Before his death, he passes on his *katana* to Takeo as a symbol of family honor. On the other hand, Sachiro, Takeo's father, speaks Spanish at home (which infuriates his father), wears Western clothes, and is even recruited to the Argentine military. Caught between the past (his grandfather) and the present (his father), Takeo makes his own journey of self-discovery in rural Argentina assisted by Poncho Negro. When he tries to rescue his father in the army camp, the latter refuses to leave the military, saying that his service will help support the family financially. Sachiro admits that he made a mistake by leaving Japan but tells his son to save his life and to "follow his dream."

Takeo's journey of self-discovery is noteworthy because it shows how a naïve Japanese immigrant with no Spanish-language abilities is transformed into a skilled gaucho, whom Poncho Negro proudly calls a "strange little gaucho, but like a son" (gauchito raro, pero como un hijo). While looking for the legendary samurai in the Pampas, Poncho Negro becomes a kind of master who teaches his disciple the skills and the knowledge that are necessary to navigate through the hostile environment in the mountains. As someone who embodies the attributes associated with the samurai culture, Takeo can be understood as a contemporary symbol of transpacific modernity. Moreover, the fact that he is also acknowledged as a "little gaucho" indicates that he embraces both Japanese and Argentine characteristics. Following the death of his master, Takeo arrives at the seashore alone at the end of the film. There are several implications in this final scene. First, the fact that he is standing in front of the ocean means that he is either visualizing his grandfather's transoceanic voyage or imagining the actual land of his ancestors. The bright sunlight in the last scene can indeed be interpreted as the representation of Japan, famously known as the land of "the rising sun." Nevertheless, it is clear that Takeo does not intend to travel all the way across the sea. Instead, he climbs into a small canoe and says "Vamos" (Let's go) in perfect Spanish to the fishermen who immediately accept him as if he was one of their own. Takeo has now fully become a local Argentine with his newly acquired identity as a "little gaucho." The fact that the movie suggests a possible union between Takeo and Poncho Negro's criolla daughter is another example of his Argentineness. In short, it is not the deceased Poncho Negro but his successor Takeo who is destined to form an integral part of Argentina's future. As the samurai-turned-gaucho, the Japanese immigrant character is portrayed as the ultimate protagonist in the development of a new multicultural nation.

History of Discrimination and the Depiction of a Chinese "Package" in Sebastián Borensztein's Un cuento chino

Although Takeo successfully finds himself integrated into Argentina by becoming a legitimate "gauchito," it is important to note that his story does not reflect the experience of other Asian immigrants. In the following pages, I will study how the visual representation of Japan in *Samurai* differs from that of China in another contemporary film, *Un cuento chino*, directed by Sebastián Borensztein.[15] My argument hinges on differing sociocultural perceptions of Asian groups in Argentina. It is well-known that in Latin America Asian people are almost always relegated to the collective category of "chino" regardless of one's ethnic origin (except for Brazil where all Asians are called "japonês"). However, I argue that there exists a certain hierarchy between Japanese and other Asian groups in terms of how they are perceived in Argentine media. Therefore, not unlike the way in which Wilde characterized Japan as "civilization" and China as "barbarism" in the beginning of the twentieth century, the contrasting view concerning these two countries continues to have an effect in today's society.

In order to examine the role of the Chinese character in *Un cuento chino*, I will first turn to the history of Chinese and Korean immigration in Argentina. As I discussed previously, Japanese immigrants have generally enjoyed a non-conflicting status in the country based on the idea of "positive prejudice." While it is necessary to note that they have faced their own share of racism and discrimination, it is equally significant to highlight that other Asians have received much harsher treatment. In general, we can say that the majority of Japanese immigrants arrived in Argentina during the first half of the twentieth century, while most Koreans settled in the second half of the century. Although some Chinese people began immigrating at the beginning of the last century, the largest wave of their immigration took place in the twenty-first century (today they constitute one of the fastest-growing communities in Argentina). It is also worth mentioning that the most popular business among the Japanese was dry-cleaning, whereas Koreans are mostly dedicated to the textile industry and Chinese currently own many of the grocery stores throughout the country.[16]

In a pioneering study on the Korean diaspora in Argentina, Corina Courtis argues that Korean immigrants were often portrayed as "invaders" by the Argentine media during the 1980s and 1990s. She claims that newspapers and magazines produced the essentialized image of *barrio coreano* or Koreatown, where "dangerous" Koreans were "stealing jobs" from the residents of Buenos Aires.¹⁷ Some Korean immigrants were even accused of exploiting other Latin American immigrants, such as Bolivians and Paraguayans. Similarly, in the twenty-first century, Chinese immigrants are also seen as a threat to the country's economy and safety. The Argentine media frequently portrays them in derogative terms, like an organized crime group conducting illegal businesses. As Junyoung Verónica Kim reminds us, "[t]he recent discourse on Chinese immigrants in Argentina follows a similar logic to that of Korean immigrants. If the Korean immigrant's labor is racialized in the sphere of clothing manufacturing, the Chinese immigrant's labor is racially embodied in the trope of *los supermercados chinos* (Chinese supermarkets)."¹⁸

It is evident that racist attitudes toward Koreans and Chinese continue to permeate contemporary Argentina. Sociologists Dan Adaszko and Ana Lía Kornblit conducted a national survey in 2006 to examine the attitudes of xenophobia and racism among adolescents across the country. According to their survey, some of the most stigmatized racial and ethnic groups in the national imaginary include Jews, Chinese, and Koreans (notably, the Japanese are excluded from the list). Their study shows how Argentine youth tends to homogenize the image of Asians (Chinese/Koreans) and construct their opinions based on misconceptions.¹⁹ The study also indicates that 52 percent of the surveyed students explicitly rejected these Asian people, while only 15 percent accepted them.²⁰ As Adaszko and Kornblit explain, "In the case of Chinese and the Koreans, discrimination responds to a xenophobia that is understood in the most classic sense of the term—as rejection of the foreigner—which in this group is reinforced by physical traits (with which xenophobia adopts racist patterns). This rejection has been accentuated by the immigration waves of the last 20 years."²¹

The disparaging perceptions of Chinese immigrants outlined above provide an important context through which we can study Borensztein's *Un cuento chino*. Translated as *Chinese Take-Away* in English, this dramatic comedy was so successful in 2011 that it became Argentina's biggest box office hit among non-US movies. The story revolves around Roberto (played by the famous actor Ricardo Darín), a middle-aged owner of a small hardware store in Buenos Aires. He is obsessed with daily routine and control, which is manifested in his habit of counting every screw and filing complaints to the supplier if anything is missing. As a pessimistic loner, Roberto believes that everyone is a scammer trying to take advantage of him. In his spare time, he collects newspaper articles about unusual, catastrophic events from around the world. One day, he encounters the most unexpected scene on the street of Buenos Aires: a young Chinese man, Jun (played by Ignacio Huang), appears out of nowhere and asks him for assistance looking for a relative. Despite their linguistic incommunicability (neither character speaks the other's language), Roberto unwillingly brings Jun to his house, and the cohabitation eventually allows the two men to help each other in their respective lives. By illustrating "funny" moments of cultural clash and misunderstanding, *Un cuento chino* reflect the country's struggle to deal with the multiracial reality of the twenty-first century.

I believe that part of the success of the movie, which the film critic Paul Byrnes calls "a superb human comedy," can be attributed to the stereotypical images of Asians that are considered "amusing" in the Western world.[22] For example, at a dinner table, one of the characters voices a comment about Chinese culture through a language of exoticism: "There are millions of them. They eat whatever they can. [...] they eat scorpions, snails, ants." In the same way, Roberto, who is frustrated by the difficulty of communicating with Jun in Spanish, uses a racist slanted-eye gesture when ordering Chinese food. On another occasion, he makes fun of Jun's Spanish accent when he is unable to articulate the name "Roberto" properly, emphasizing the common stereotype about Asians who cannot pronounce the phoneme "r." The fact that these instances of Orientalization serve as the source of humor suggests that the movie reproduces the history of discrimination against Chinese immigrants that I described earlier.

The negative representation of China in *Un cuento chino* is in stark contrast with the positive depiction of Japan in *Samurai*. It is easy to compare the relationship between Roberto and Jun, on the one hand, and Poncho Negro and Takeo, on the other. The pairs in both films establish a kind of transcultural friendship, albeit in different ways. While Poncho Negro ends up treating Takeo "like a son," Roberto is a reluctant caretaker who decides to bring Jun to his house but tries to get rid of him through any means.[23] To be fair, Roberto does attempt to help Jun by calling the Chinese embassy and by taking him to the Chinatown section of Buenos Aires. However, Roberto's intention is never to welcome a stranger into his life but rather to throw him out quickly so he can return to his previous life of regularity and comfort. When the embassy calls him and says they have found, mistakenly, Jun's uncle, Roberto cannot help but show his excitement: "What was great for me was the part when the phone rang and a Chinese guy promised to come and pick up the 'package' tomorrow." In this scene Jun is reduced to a mere "package," an undesirable object waiting for immediate disposal. When a wrong family shows up the next day, Roberto is deeply frustrated and begs the family to take him anyway, a request they refuse pointedly.

Moreover, the dehumanization of the Chinese protagonist is related to how the film constantly infantilizes him in relation to other Argentine characters. Jun is portrayed as a weak, fragile, and even passive individual whose life completely depends on those around him. He follows Roberto's orders and accepts his decisions without any question or confrontation. Jun also imitates his caretaker's daily habit (e.g., preparing coffee and baguette for breakfast), but never actually learns any skills. In this sense, he is the opposite of Takeo who becomes a "little gaucho" thanks to his mentor Poncho Negro. In addition, it is important to note that Jun's spoken Chinese is never subtitled throughout the film. We can conclude, therefore, that he is made into a "voiceless" subject not only because of his incommunicability in Spanish, but also because of the inability of the audience to fully understand him speaking in his native language.[24]

It is through Roberto and his girlfriend Mari that Jun finds a modicum of purpose in his life. Mari is a country woman who visits her cousin in the city and who never hesitates to show her feelings for Roberto. In the movie, she is the only character who understands Jun's difficult situation and demonstrates sympathy toward him. As she puts it in one scene, "I imagined myself living in China. Alone. Lost. Without money, unable to speak the language." In order to help build the romantic relationship between Roberto and Mari, Jun plays a critical role by providing an opportunity for their (re)unification. Since Roberto is a loner who believes that the whole world is against him, he repeatedly rejects Mari in his life. It is thanks to his relationship with Jun that Roberto is able to move beyond his pessimism and finally decides to respond to Mari's affections. At the end of the film, we see Roberto desperately running to find Mari in her remote farmhouse, indicating that they have resolved previous conflicts and are now ready to start a new life together. As Hilary Chung and Luciano Bernadette point out, "At an intradiegetic level the figure of the Chinese migrant becomes an agent of transposition for Roberto, enabling his displacement from the obsessive meaninglessness of his narrow existence into his own fairytale happy ending with Mari."[25] If we consider the history of racism against Chinese immigrants, the way Jun offers a necessary piece in this possibility of a "happy ending" is worth noting. It means that he merely serves as an instrument that would enable the reunification of a local Argentine couple. In Ko's words, "The presence of Jun, in essence, allows Roberto and Mari to rehearse their given gendered roles as a couple and family."[26] Here, once again the comparison between Takeo and Jun proves relevant.

As we saw earlier, the Japanese protagonist in *Samurai* successfully adapts to Argentina by transforming into a "little gaucho." By contrast, the Chinese immigrant in *Un cuento chino* is only able to participate in Argentine society as a disposable object—a "package"—whose sole task consists of helping a promising couple restore their relationship. Consequently, although Jun is able to find his uncle in Mendoza at the end of the film, uncertainty remains regarding his own fate in the country. Unlike Takeo, he is portrayed as a perpetual outsider who plays no major role in shaping the future of Argentina. In other words, Japan has a place in the development of a new nation, but China is placed at the margin of history.

Understanding Multiple Meanings of Silence in Pablo Moyano's *Silencio roto: 16 Nikkeis*

Finally, the last film I will analyze in this chapter is Pablo Moyano's documentary, *Silencio roto: 16 Nikkeis*.[27] Unlike the images of Japan celebrated in *Samurai*, the immigrant experience depicted in this documentary is more tragic and sorrowful. It is well-known that the countries in the Southern Cone went through a tremulous period in the 1960s and 70s. In Argentina, state terrorism began with the establishment of the Argentine Anticommunist Alliance, known as the Triple A. The violence intensified after the military coup that led to the Dirty War (1976–83), causing more than 30,000 deaths and disappearances, the so-called *desaparecidos*. During this period, at least sixteen Nikkei Argentines were said to be kidnapped and tortured.[28] In general, it is said that the victims of this horrific violence were not determined by their race or ethnicity. In other words, Nikkei Argentines were not persecuted because of their ethnic origin, like the anti-Japanese campaigns that took place in Brazil and Peru during World War II. Nonetheless, we can argue that there were certain Japanese characteristics in the history of the Nikkei *desaparecidos*. In *Silencio roto*, Nikkei families are reluctant to talk about their disappeared siblings or children whose activism was considered an act of dishonor. In the following pages, I will examine different ways in which silence or silencing can be studied in the film. My contention is that *Silencio roto* presents a challenge to the narrative of transpacific modernity in two ways: by rewriting the history of Japanese immigrants in Argentina and by criticizing the government of Japan.

In Western societies, silence is often associated with the absence of speech or an empty space ready to be filled with words. It is thought that people must speak up in order to define their identity, to defend their rights, or to claim their visibility in society. Silence, on the contrary, is viewed as a passive state of submission, indifference, and complacency.[29] It goes without saying that being *silent* differs from being *silenced*: the former is usually deliberate, while the latter is always imposed. Nevertheless, both conditions equally refer to what Cheryl Glenn calls the "rhetoric of silence," which depends on "a power differential that exists in every rhetorical situation."[30] As the Slovenian philosopher Slavoj Žižek suggests, "the primordial fact is not Silence (waiting to be broken by the divine Word) but Noise ... it is not that silence is broken, but that silence itself breaks, interrupts the continuous murmur of the Real, thus opening up a space in which words can be spoken."[31] In Argentina, one of the loudest "noises" has been made by the Mothers and Grandmothers of the Plaza de Mayo, who have been searching for their loved ones for decades. Among them, Vera Jarach, whose daughter was kidnapped in 1976, said in a 2017 interview that "we never want silence again."[32]

In *Silencio roto*, the tradition of the Far East is described through the culture of silence. Unlike the West, Japan has long embraced and even institutionalized silence as an essential mode of communication. At the same time, silence is also regarded as a moral principle based on the Confucian ethics of obedience, hierarchy, and honor. During the early Meiji period, the philosopher Motoday Nagazane affirmed that the study of Confucius was fundamental to both Japanese morality and the understanding of the relations between ruler and subject.[33] According to Nagazane, the country had to adhere to the virtues of loyalty and filial piety, and the power of authority should never be questioned nor challenged.

Such a strict mentality of Japanese tradition was directly translated into the Nikkei experience in Argentina. *Silencio roto* tells the story of the Japanese Argentines who lost their family members during the dictatorship, a story that had never received public attention before. Like the other documentary, *La otra tierra*, this film is based on a series of interviews with members of the Nikkei community in Buenos Aires. In particular, *Silencio roto* focuses on the members of Familiares de los Desaparecidos de la Colectividad Japonesa (FDCJ), who share their memories of their disappeared siblings and children for the first time. Silence as a symbolic culture is perpetuated throughout the film, with quiet images of people's stern countenances expressing profound grief. For instance, the mother of Carlos Horacio Gushiken, one of the sixteen Nikkei *desaparecidos*, appears to be among the most affected. She suffered a great deal from depression and trauma after her son was taken away at age twenty-one, and the documentary shows how she struggles to even utter words to describe what happened. Her daughter explains the difficulty of discussing Horacio's militancy in the family because they considered his action "disgraceful." According to her, "having a son who was militant, no matter which side but to expose himself against the government that welcomed them, was a disgrace." Her statement is based on the idea that, as newcomers, the Japanese in Argentina ought to feel gratitude toward the host country. Confronting the government would be seen as an act of "dishonor" and "shame" to the entire family and community. Another interviewee, Jorge Nakamura's sister, refers to the culture of silence within the Nikkei society: "There was a total silence. [The Japanese idiosyncrasy that says that] if the authorities determine something, it is because the person acted wrongly." The idea of shame is related to the assumption that those arrested by the government were seen as "criminals," regardless of the reason. In the same vein, a friend of Norma Inés Matsuyama characterizes everyone's silence in terms of their obedient attitude: "I believe that the culture of submission, of Japanese people's obedience to the authority, in general, could have influenced the silence" (yo creo que la cuestión cultural de sumisión, de obediencia a la autoridad de los japoneses, en general, pudo haber influido en el silencio). The earlier-mentioned ethics of Confucianism seem to be at work for the collective silence of Japanese Argentines and their unwillingness to criticize or even question the government. *Silencio roto* suggests that Nikkei families did not speak up for thirty years as a result of their moral judgment, implying that their silence must be broken in order for truth to emerge and for justice to be served. As the director explains in a radio interview for *Japón Hoy*, "the title has to do with that process that led them to break the silence and unite as family members, to be present at the marches, and to recognize their siblings, their children and their uncles."[34] The fundamental significance of the film lies in revealing the Nikkei voices that had never been recognized before.

My purpose is not to diminish the importance of these emerging voices from the members of the FDCJ; instead, what I intend to highlight is how the meaning of silence should not be limited to a single narrative. It is certainly true that the ideas of honor and loyalty affected the collective consciousness of the Nikkei community. However, it is also important to acknowledge that there are multiple dimensions to the culture of silence. First, it is worth noting that the opinions of Nikkei *desaparecidos* were often rejected by their own family members. As shown in the documentary, most of the victims were Nisei who felt that their parents never really approved of their political views or their Argentine identities. As a result, it is possible to perceive some distance in the relationship between the disappeared victims and their families. For instance, Horacio Gushiken's sister describes how her brother's activism was driven by the reality of inequality in Argentina. According to her, his motivation was perhaps incomprehensible to those living in the sheltered environment of Nikkei society, especially among Issei. In her words, "he went out into society to fight for the ideals of the country where he was born as an Argentine, not a Japanese." Through their commitment to changing the country, Horacio and other activists sought to be associated with Argentina rather than with Japan, while their parents avoided anything political and even felt "ashamed" of their children's radicalism. In this sense, the silence of the Nikkei community reveals numerous conflicts between different generations as well as between diverse cultural identifications.

We can study another aspect of silence through the relationship between the Nikkei community and the Japanese embassy in Argentina. The film refers to how the families of the victims were abandoned by the Japanese government in their desperate search for truth. According to Julio Eduardo Gushiken's brother, the embassy refused to interfere because they claimed that the victims were "foreigners."[35] His frustration is shared by another member of the group, Elsa Oshiro, who remembers that "in the early days we must say that we encountered resistance in the Japanese government at interceding with the de facto authorities. They argued that these were Argentine or that they could not get involved in internal affairs."[36] Although the Japanese government insisted that they could not intervene in the domestic affairs of Argentina, in reality Nikkei *desaparecidos* included at least two dual citizens—Juan Carlos Higa and Oscar Oshiro—and one Japanese national, Katsuya Higa.[37] Moreover, as Diego Ardouin's study indicates, Japan's refusal to help their own citizens and Nikkeijin is in contrast to the readiness of other countries—such as France, Italy and Germany—to facilitate the escape of dissidents or petition a habeas corpus during the dictatorship.[38] Despite numerous demands for intervention, the Japanese government never provided support to the members of the FDCJ because they had created their own version of "truth." It was not until 2010 that the embassy acknowledged this tragic history and sponsored the first public event on Nikkei *desaparecidos*, called "Those who leave their mark do not disappear" (No desaparece quien deja huella).

By criticizing the government for their failure to protect members of the Nikkei community in Argentina, *Silencio roto* seeks to defy the "official" narrative in which the idea of race is disregarded and the marginalized voice is silenced. As I have argued in this book, the traditional images of Japan and the Japanese were often constructed by Argentines of European descent through the discourse of transpacific modernity. And those images were almost always uncritically stereotypical, which contributed to the myth of the model minority. It was only through the emergence of literary works from the Nikkei community itself that the representation of Japan became more nuanced and de-Orientalized. In other words, what Walter Mignolo calls "the decolonization of knowledge" allows Nikkei Argentines to resist the dominant discourse of nationalism and Eurocentric universalism. From this perspective, *Silencio roto* offers the possibility of counternarrative to Argentina's homogenizing identity by inserting the untold immigrant story into the nation's collective memory. As Chie Ishida argues, "The politics for the disappeared Japanese can be understood as a way of criticizing the national and community regime built over the elimination of individual political space and searching for an alternative society which would not totalize them under the name of Japanese."[39]

In the documentary, we learn about the history of Nikkei Argentines who courageously broke their silence after thirty years. At the same time, the culture of silence reveals more than a single narrative. There are different stories of silence/silencing in Argentina's Nikkei community, including the one created by generational differences and the one imposed by the Japanese government. For Juan Carlos Higa, one of the sixteen Nikkei *desaparecidos*, silence is deeply connected to the notion of truth.[40] His unpublished poem, entitled "poem of silence" and written in 1968, captures the power of silence in the following manner:

> Love is born in silence, it is realized in silence, it is remembered in silence. ... Justice is a song that the deaf do not hear ... and there is no deaf person worse than the one who does not want to hear the truth [that] is built in silence.
>
> El amor nace en silencio, se realiza en silencio, se recuerda en silencio. ... La justicia es un canto y los sordos no oyen ... y no hay peor sordo que el que no quiere oír más la verdad [que] se construye en silencio.[41]

Just like how love can be created quietly, truth can be reconstructed silently. For Higa, the condition of quietness does not translate into the absence of speech. Instead, as an unspoken voice, silence exposes different "truths" regarding the history of violence and trauma. Understanding the diverse characteristics of silence is a task that forces us to go beyond the official discourse of the nation-state and to rethink what it means to claim Nikkei identity in today's Argentina and beyond.

Conclusion

As I have demonstrated in this book, the representation of Japan in Argentine literature and culture has changed over time since the late nineteenth century. The historical parallels between the two countries begin to emerge through their shared process of modernization. While Japan sought to belong to the Western world following the Edo period, a similar push toward Westernization also became the engine for social changes in Argentina. Japan's rise as a global military power in the aftermath of the Russo-Japanese War meant that the country was seen as a strong nation, yet one capable of preserving ancient traditions. In the eyes of the Argentine elite class, this remote country in Asia offered a model of transpacific modernity not only through its aesthetic and spiritual values but also through its imperial ambitions. From this perspective, we can argue that Argentina's trade relationship with Japan and its neutrality during World War II were premised on a different form of modernization than liberal democracy.

Almost a century later, Nikkei writers are revising such a homogenizing vision of Japan. In their view, the country of their ancestors is a land of differences, even of contradictions. In his recent book *Una isla artificial: Crónicas sobre japoneses en Argentina* (An artificial island: Chronicles about Japanese in Argentina), the journalist and filmmaker Fernando Krapp writes about Japanese immigration as based on interviews and historical studies he conducted. According to him, "The children of the Japanese, and the Japanese who came to Argentina in their respective migratory phases throughout the twentieth century, have a different idea about what Japan is or was.

A diaspora becomes a question about identity, an identity that is in limbo between a promised land and a land that was lost."[1] The immigrant and diasporic narrative presented in Nikkei literature also puts into question the discourse of whiteness and multiculturalism in contemporary times. As hybrid subjects representing both countries but belonging to neither, Nikkei authors seek to capture the idea of in-betweenness in their texts. This way, they are redefining the notions of Japaneseness as well as Argentineness. As Alejandra Kamiya states in an interview for the online journal *Atletas*, this particular space of in-betweenness is precisely the source of her creativity: "I think the driving force for one's writing is discomfort. Somehow, I had to learn to feel comfortable there, in the 'between'; but it's a zone of discomfort."[2]

However, as I explained in Chapter 5, the narrative of transpacific modernity still remains relevant in today's Argentina as it continues to celebrate Japan and its symbolism, especially in comparison to other Asian countries. My analysis of contemporary films showed how Asians cannot be reduced to the single category of "chino" because each ethnic group manifests different experiences of assimilation, adaptation, xenophobia, and objectification. Put differently, one of the goals of my study was to de-essentialize and de-homogenize the very concept of Asianness in Argentina and Latin America.

While Nikkei voices contribute to Argentina's new immigrant literature in the twenty-first century, there has also been a different focus on Japanese culture as depicted by non-Nikkei writers. For instance, Paula Brecciaroli's *Otaku* (2015) revolves around the life of Gastón, a middle-aged *okaku* or aficionado of Japanese anime and manga. As Brecciaroli said in an interview, her protagonist embodies "prejudices, anecdotes, and superimpositions of many fans whom I met in my life"[3] In the story, this Argentine *otaku* has no real job, is still living with his father in a small apartment in Buenos Aires and dreaming about someday being famous in the world of fantasy. His father laments the situation by saying, "I look at you and find it hard to believe you're turning forty, son," while his sister launches an outright rejection, "when are you going to leave your world of fantasy and come down a little bit to reality?"[4] Despite their concerns, Gastón constantly finds himself nostalgic for past glories, remembering Argentina's first festival of Japanese anime that he organized in the 1990s. Importantly, the novel idealizes a modern Japan symbolized by technology and popular culture: as the protagonist declares, "they [are] always in the forefront."[5] By illustrating the popularity of anime and manga in today's Argentina, *Otaku* sheds light on the way in which a new generation of readers connect with Japanese culture.

En el hotel cápsula (2017; In the capsule hotel) is another example of non-Nikkei literary work that uses contemporary Japan as one of the central themes. Written by a well-known author and film director, Lucía Puenzo, the book is a collection of short stories about transnational tourism involving Japan, Thailand, and Cuba. The image of hypermodern Japan is evident in the title itself: a "capsule hotel," also known as "pod hotel," is a type of Japanese hotel in which many individual bed-sized rooms (called capsules) are offered for guests looking for basic, affordable accommodations. In Puenzo's title story, a female protagonist from Argentina stays at a capsule hotel in Tokyo, where people live in a permanent state of alienation and loneliness. As she observes, "[p]eople did not touch each other out in the streets; in fifteen days I had not seen a single couple walk hand in hand or kiss in public (unless they were foreigners); but in many public bathrooms there were vending machines that for five yens sold small, stridently colored plastic tubes, which inside hid thongs used by Japanese teenaged girls."[6] Despite the misconception (there are no such vending machines for five yens in Japan), the protagonist's perspective as a tourist offers an insight into the complex reality that exists between public and private life. Not unlike the chronicles written by Eduardo Wilde and Jorge Max Rohde in the early twentieth century, *En el hotel cápsula* presents a travel narrative that looks at the Asian country through the Orientalist lens of exoticism and stereotypes. When Puenzo's character travels to Kyoto and stays at a Buddhist temple, there is an image of ancient tradition and spirituality. The novel illustrates the lodging in terms of how "the centuries didn't seem to have passed on to the other side of the gate" and how "it looked more like a hostel for pilgrims suspended in time."[7] In this way, the relationship between the future and the past, represented by Tokyo and Kyoto respectively, continues to be a popular literary motif for some Argentine writers who have no Japanese heritage.[8]

Finally, the significance of Nikkei literature in Argentina that I have discussed in this book can be extended to a larger, global context. I propose that some of the themes about Japanese immigration analyzed in this study—differing degrees of assimilation and adaptation, generational conflicts, gender dynamics, and the power of silence—could lead to a future project on what can be called "Global Nikkei Literature." We may ask: How can we understand the transnational network of ideas concerning Nikkeijin? How do Nikkei authors seek to define their Japaneseness across the world? How do they negotiate with national identity vis-à-vis foreignness? How does the Nikkei voice represent a form of counternarrative to the dominant discourse? What can the Japanese diasporic narrative tell us about shared historical memories and traumas? For example, thinking about some specific authors, what are some of the similarities and differences among Karen Tei Yamashita (US), Doris Moromisato (Peru), and Alejandra Kamiya (Argentina)? Or how can we study comparatively the writings of Stewart David Ikeda (US), Ryoki Inoue (Brazil), and Fernando Iwasaki (Peru)? I believe that these questions could generate a productive conversation about the possibilities and limitations of examining Nikkei literature on a global scale. It is my hope that this book will make a small contribution to such a project in the future.

Notes

FOREWORD

1. It is important to note that the Greater East Asia Co-Prosperity Sphere was officially premised on pan-Asianism under Japanese political and cultural superiority rather than racial superiority as the Nazis had done in Europe or the US under Jim Crow.

INTRODUCTION

1. In this book, all translations are mine, unless otherwise noted. The original texts for primary sources are included in the footnotes. For example, Sirimarco's quote is the following: "Lindo es ver y admirar / Colectividades de países foráneos / Que se divierten y son felices / Como en el hogar patrio. / En esta tierra están contentos / Sin ignorar su patria querida / Que les dió ilusión y vida / Al ver la luz del mundo: / Sólo recuerdan madres y parientes / Que dejaron en tierra del Sol Naciente." Ángel Sirimarco, "Dedicada a la colectividad japonesa," 4.
2. In this book, I use the term "Nikkei" to describe Japanese who emigrated abroad and their descendants. Following the definition provided by the Association of Nikkei & Japanese Abroad, Nikkei refers to "Japanese people who have relocated overseas on a permanent basis, as well as their second, third and fourth generation descendants, irrespective of current nationality and degree of Japanese ethnicity." The Association of Nikkei and Japanese Abroad, "Who are 'Nikkei and Japanese Abroad'?" While *Nikkei* can be used as an adjective, *Nikkeijin* (people of Japanese descent) can only be used as a noun. In terms of the transnational characteristic of the Nikkei experience, I concur with Marcelo Higa who writes that "being Nikkei would become a way of globalizing the emigration experience to the Americas, in which the Japanese and their descendants had to face adaptation and assimilation into societies radically different from those from which they came." Marcelo Higa, "The Emigration of Argentines of Japanese Descent to Japan," 272. Moreover, Akemi Kikumura-Yano discusses the fluid nature of the term Nikkei: "The notion of transformations is central to the concept of Nikkei. Nikkei culture and identity is not a static entity that determines the behavior of its members at any given time. Rather, it is a symbolic social, historical, and political construction that involves a dynamic process of selection, reinterpretation, and synthesis of cultural elements set within the shifting and fluid contexts of contemporary realities and relationships." Akemi Kikumura-Yano, ed., *Encyclopedia of Japanese Descendants in the Americas*, 3.

3. See, for example, Lesser (2007), Tsurumi (2012), and López-Calvo (2013, 2019, 2022).
4. Important exceptions include Courtis (2000), Kim (2010, 2017) and Ko (2014, 2015, 2016).
5. My study is in dialogue with Axel Gasquet's book on Orientalism in Argentine literature, *Oriente al Sur: El orientalismo literario argentino de Esteban Echeverría a Roberto Arlt* (2007). While his book deals with a wide range of countries in the Orient, including the Middle East, my study specifically focuses on Japan and emphasizes the narratives of immigration.
6. According to Lesser and Rein, the New Ethnic Studies in Latin America goes beyond the traditional framework of the black-white-indigenous construction of social and racial identities in Latin America. See Jeffrey Lesser and Raanan Rein, "Challenging Particularity: Jews as a Lens on Latin American Ethnicity," 258.
7. My concept is inspired by Ko's 2016 essay, which discusses the possibilities and limits of a panethnic "Asian Argentine" identity in relation to the "Asian American" framework in the US. According to her, "if, in the United States, panethnicity was a way to contest explicit racial categorizations, in Argentina, panethnicity can be a way to contest a historical lack of recognition." Chisu Teresa Ko, "Toward Asian Argentine Studies," 273.
8. Junyoung Verónica Kim, "Asia-Latin America as Method: The Global South Project and the Dislocation of the West," 101.
9. Vicente L. Rafael and Mary Louise Pratt, "Introduction," 419.
10. Jeffrey Lesser, "In Search of the Hyphen: Nikkei and the Struggle over Brazilian National Identity," 39.
11. Lesser, "In Search of the Hyphen," 45.
12. It is worth noting that the Japanese in Brazil and the Japanese in Argentina also share certain commonalities in terms of their history of immigration (e.g., search for better economic conditions, nostalgia for home, conflict between a Japanese identity and the new sociocultural environment). Most notably, they equally belong to the space for the marginal "Other" as opposed to the European "self." Nevertheless, as I show in this book, the way in which the Japanese negotiated with this "otherness" in Argentina was different from the experience of Japanese immigrants in Brazil.
13. Ayumi Takenaka, "The Japanese in Peru: History of Immigration, Settlement, and Racialization," 93.
14. Ignacio López-Calvo, *The Affinity of the Eye: Writing Nikkei in Peru* 48. Also, a testimonial narrative that describes this history is Seiichi Higashide's *Adios to Tears: The Memoirs of a Japanese-Peruvian Internee in U.S. Concentration Camps* (2000).
15. Marcelo Higa, "Desarrollo histórico de la inmigración japonesa en la Argentina hasta la Segunda Guerra Mundial," 482.
16. Higa, "Desarrollo histórico de la inmigración japonesa," 488.
17. According to the data on "Japan-Argentina Relations" provided by the Ministry of Foreign Affairs of Japan, the number of Japanese nationals residing in Argentina was 11, 440 in 2020 and the estimated number of Japanese descendants was 65,000. See Ministry of Foreign Affairs of Japan, "Japan-Argentina Relations (Basic Data)."
18. James Lawrence Tigner, "The Ryukyuans in Argentina," 204.
19. Dale A. Olsen, *The Chrysanthemum and the Song: Music, Memory, and Identity in the South American Japanese Diaspora* 159.
20. Isabel Laumonier, "Japanese Argentine Historical Overview," 73.
21. Daniel M. Masterson and Sayaka Funada-Classen, *The Japanese in Latin America*, 92.
22. In other parts of Latin America, the Japanese community usually involved conflicts

between Okinawans and the Naichijin (people of mainland Japan), but those tensions were minimal in Argentina.
23. Marcelo Higa claims that one of the reasons why the Japanese were never considered a racial threat in Argentina was because they did not settle in ethnic neighborhoods, like the Koreans or Chinese. Higa, "Desarrollo histórico de la inmigración japonesa," 481.
24. Laumonier, "Japanese Argentine Historical Overview," 77.
25. Ignacio López-Calvo, *The Affinity of the Eye*, 6.
26. The Japanese Catholic Circle (Círculo Católico Japonés) was established in 1936.
27. Silvina Gómez and Cecilia Onaha, "Asociaciones voluntarias e identidad étnica de inmigrantes japoneses y sus descendientes en Argentina," 210–11.
28. Laumonier, "Japanese Argentine Historical Overview," 79.
29. Federación de Asociaciones Nikkei en la Argentina, *Historia del inmigrante japonés en la Argentina: Período de Preguerra (Tomo I)*, 297.
30. Gary Y Okihiro, "Turning Japanese Americans," 10.
31. Tigner, "The Ryukyuans in Argentina," 212.
32. As I discuss in Chapter 5, the experience of the Japanese can be contrasted to that of the Koreans, who struggled with racial discrimination, especially during the 1980s and the 1990s. Similarly, in the twenty-first century Argentina sees the growing number of the Chinese population as a threat to the national culture. As Francine Masiello observed in 2001, "the growth in Argentina of new Asian populations—mainly Korean and Chinese—is a source of preoccupation in a culture not especially tolerant of difference." Francine Masiello, *The Art of Transition: Latin American Culture and Neoliberal Crisis*, 144.
33. Higa, "Desarrollo histórico de la inmigración japonesa," 506.
34. Laumonier, "Japanese Argentine Historical Overview," 79–80.
35. For an excellent volume that discusses the redefinition of racial politics in Argentina, see *Rethinking Race in Modern Argentina* (2016), edited by Paulina Alberto and Eduardo Elena. Moreover, my theorization of Argentina's whiteness is in dialogue with Junyong Verónica Kim's notion of "white myth", which she employs to describe "a nation of white race and European culture." Junyoung Verónica Kim, "Desarticulando el 'mito blanco': Inmigración coreana en Buenos Aires e imaginarios nacionales," 170.
36. Julia Albarracín, *Making Immigrants in Modern Argentina*, 5.
37. Paulina L Alberto and Eduardo Elena, ed., *Rethinking Race in Modern Argentina*, 7.
38. European immigration was not the only factor that contributed to the whitening of Argentine society. For more information about the country's "hidden" racial diversity during the pre-immigration period, see Claudia Briones, "Mestizaje y blanqueamiento como coordenadas de aboriginalidad y nación en Argentina," 61–88.
39. George Reid Andrews, *The Afro-Argentines of Buenos Aires 1800–1900*, 93–112. In the last decades, scholars have investigated the important contributions of Jews and Afro-Argentines in the making of modern Argentina. Besides Andrews's book, other examples include Leonardo Senkman's *La identidad judía en la literatura argentina* (1983), Saúl Sosnowski's *La orilla inminente, escritores judíos argentinos* (1987), Marvin Lewis's *Afro-Argentine Discourse: Another Dimension of the Black Diaspora* (1996), Alejandro Solomianski *Identidades secretas: La negritud argentina* (2003), and David William Foster's *Latin American Jewish Cultural Production* (2009).
40. Aguiló's study focuses on cultural products created around the economic crisis of 2001 in order to examine how the ideas of race and national identity have been contested throughout Argentina's history.

41. Ignacio Aguiló, *The Darkening Nation: Race, Neoliberalism and Crisis in Argentina*, 7.
42. Aguiló, *The Darkening Nation*, 8.
43. The industrial workforce went from 430,000 in 1935 to more than 1 million in 1946. Jonathan C. Brown, *A Brief History of Argentina*, 198.
44. For an analysis of the relationship between Perón and *cabecita negra*, see Natalia Milanesio, "Peronists and Cabecitas, Stereotypes and Anxieties at the Peak of Social Change," 53–84.
45. See, for example, Lenton (2010), Adamovsky (2016), and Elena (2016).
46. In terms of the US history of whiteness and racial politics, Matthew Jacobson (1999) argues that racial categories and perceptions have required a continuous process of construction and reconstruction of a "white American" identity in relation to the diversity of European immigrant population. He claims that race in America lies in the contingencies of politics and culture, reflecting the power dynamics of a given historical period. More recently, David Roediger (2006) has written about how Italian immigrants, who were racialized outcasts when they arrived in the nineteenth century, became worthy of being ratified as "white Americans" during the twentieth century. Both Jacobson's and Roediger's analysis of the immigrant experiences and racial classifications point to the malleability of racial hierarchy in the United States.
47. Aguiló, *The Darkening Nation*, 48.
48. Aguiló, *The Darkening Nation*, 21.
49. I am aware that in the prewar era there was a corpus of materials in Japanese-language journals, such as *Shokumin Sekai*, *Kaigai* and *Shokumin*, that addressed questions of racial difference, whiteness, and alternative modernities. For a study of these questions in Brazil, see Seth Jacobowitz, "A Bitter Brew: Coffee and Labor in Japanese Brazilian Immigrant Literature," 13–30. Unlike Jacobowitz's study, my book concerns with Nikkei and non-Nikkei literature written in Spanish and does not analyze texts written in Japanese.
50. The term *ponja*, the reversal of Japón or Japan, is a popular but essentially pejorative slang used not only in Argentina but also in Peru and other parts of Latin America.
51. Mexico is another country in Latin America that has treated its Japanese immigrants fairly well compared to other Asians, although there was a moment of racialization during World War II through a forced relocation program. For more information, see López-Calvo's *The Mexican Transpacific: Nikkei Writing, Visual Arts, Performance*.
52. Yoshio Sakata and John Whitney Hall, "The Motivation of Political Leadership in the Meiji Restoration," 31.
53. It can be argued that the origin of Japanese Westernization is traced back to the sixteenth century when Christianity first arrived in Japan. Even during the Tokugawa period, there was the influence of *Rangaku* or the Dutch Learning in Nagasaki.
54. Gary D. Allinson, *The Columbia Guide to Modern Japanese History*, 9–36.
55. The Iwakura Mission (1871–73), a diplomatic expedition to the US and Europe, can also be understood as part of Japan's process of Westernization.
56. Fukuzawa introduced Western culture to Japan through many of his writings, including *Seiyo jijo* (1866; Conditions in the West), *Gakumon no susume* (1872; Encouragement of learning), and *Bunmeiron no gairyaku* (1875; An outline of a theory of civilization). While advocating for such Western ideals as freedom and progress, Fukuzawa also held nationalist-militarist tendencies and enthusiastically supported the Sino-Japanese War.
57. Eiichiro Azuma, *In Search of Our Frontier: Japanese America and Settler Colonialism in the Construction of Japan's Borderless Empire*, 2.

58. Azuma, *In Search of Our Frontier*, 2.
59. Richard F. Calichman, *What is Modernity?: Writing of Takeuchi Yoshimi*, xi.
60. Calichman, *What is Modernity?*, x. Notable contradictions abound in Takeuchi's assessment of Japan's imperial history when it comes to the Pacific War or the Greater East Asian War of 1941-1945. According to him, this conflict was both a culmination of Japan's imperial vision and an effort to liberate Asia from Western/American oppression. As Takeuchi puts it, "[t]he Greater East Asian War clearly contained a double structure, one that stemmed from modern Japan's tradition of war, beginning with the plan to invade Korea. This double structure involved the demand for leadership in East Asia on the one hand and a goal of world domination by driving out the West on the other." Yoshimi Takeuchi, "Overcoming Modernity," 125. What he calls a "double structure" of Japan's attitude toward Asia and the Western power must be underscored: while criticizing Japan's imperialist maneuvers in the region, he also defended Japan's leadership in the fight against Western colonialism.
61. Naoki Sakai, "Civilizational Difference and Criticism: On the Complicity of Globalization and Cultural Nationalism," 200. In his discussion of "the global index of whiteness," Sakai underlines how the historical mobility of whiteness created the condition of possibility whereby modern colonialism came to operate itself. In the contemporary world, he argues, the ideology of white supremacy has spread worldwide, including "the sudden xenophobic explosion against Koreans among the Japanese, the so-called 'whites' of Asia" (200). This reference to the racial discrimination against Koreans is, of course, indicative of how Japan's colonialist attitude remains a negative force in today's society. It goes without saying that the role of Japanese colonialism in East Asia continues to provoke fierce debate among politicians, scholars, and activists across the region. Recent contributions to this topic include Barak Kushner and Sherzod Muminov's *The Dismantling of Japan's Empire in East Asia: Deimperialization, Postwar Legitimation and Imperial Afterlife* (2016) and Christopher P. Hanscom and Dennis Washburn's *The Affect of Difference: Representations of Race in East Asian Empire* (2016).
62. To counter this traditional narrative of modernity, Walter Mignolo and other decolonial thinkers have proposed the arrival of Spanish colonizers to America in 1492 as the beginning of modernity. See Mignolo (2011).
63. Patrick Dove, *The Catastrophe of Modernity: Tragedy and the Nation in Latin American Literature*, 56.
64. Dove, *The Catastrophe of Modernity*, 56. Emphasis in original.
65. Arnd Schneider, "The Two Faces of Modernity: Concepts of the Melting Pot in Argentina," 174.
66. By focusing on a specific group of immigrants (Jews) in the country, Amy K. Kaminsky's recent book, *The Other/Argentina: Jews, Gender, and Sexuality in the Making of a Modern Nation* (2021), examines the influence of Jewish participation in the construction of Argentine modernity. She argues that Argentine modernity represents "a balance between unitary national identity and a mix of often-subdued internal differences that may trouble such unity but that also link the nation to a globalized cosmopolitanism." Kaminsky, *The Other/Argentina*, 2. For Kaminsky, Jewish authors seek to describe the project of modernity through a conflict between a collective sense of national belonging, on the one hand, and a diverse group of marginalized racial, gender and sexual identities, on the other.
67. Julia Albarracín, *Making Immigrants in Modern Argentina*, 8.
68. Beatriz Sarlo, *Una modernidad periférica: Buenos Aires 1920-1930*, 28.
69. Sarlo, *Una modernidad periférica*, 29.

70. My conceptualization of "transpacific modernity" owes a debt to Laura J Torres-Rodríguez's book *Orientaciones transpacíficas: La modernidad mexicana y el espectro de Asia* (2019). In her study, Torres-Rodríguez argues that Mexico's "orientations" toward different Asian countries (Japan, China, and India) constitute essential components in the cultural discourse of Mexican modernity, globality and singularity.
71. Jeffrey Lesser has shown that the "Japanese model" also existed in Brazil in the early twentieth century. As he states, "Since at least 1920, many in the Brazilian elite saw Japan, not Portugal, as a national model where traditional and economic modernization created international power." Jeffrey Lesser, *A Discontented Diaspora: Japanese Brazilians and the Meanings of Ethnic Militancy, 1960–1980*, xxii). Even though both Japanese Brazilians and Japanese Argentines symbolized the possibility of modernity in their respective countries, their experience was vastly different. While Japanese Brazilians represented a new race based on what Lesser calls "hypertradition and hypermodernity," the Japanese in Argentina were not even seen as a "race" because of the country's historical lack of recognition concerning non-Europeans. Lesser, *A Discontented Diaspora*, xxvii.
72. It is worth mentioning that the Argentine government offered assistance to Japan during the Russo-Japanese War by selling them battleships.
73. See Pardue (1994) for a study on Lugones and his interest in haiku. See Hagimoto (2015) on Borges and Japan.
74. Ignacio López-Calvo, "Worlding and Decolonizing the Literary World-System: Asian-Latin American Literature as an Alternative Type of Weltliteratur," 17.
75. For his discussion of "pluriversality," see Mignolo (2018).
76. My analysis of Nikkei literature is also inspired by Ottmar Ette's notion of "transarea studies," which he describes as a new way of studying South-South relations. As he puts it, "it is not about a *single* origin, but as many origins as possible, not about a *single* background, but as many backgrounds as possible, which try out, in the experimental space of the literatures of the world—and not a world literature centered upon Europe—futures that are new and perhaps not yet thought of." Ottmar Ette, *Transarea: A Literary History of Globalization*, 49.
77. It must be noted that Anna Kazumi Stahl is a US-born author who has been living in Argentina since 1995. She continues to write in Spanish and teaches creative writing at NYU Buenos Aires. While she is not a Japanese Argentine herself, I study her work as part of Nikkei literature in Argentina.

CHAPTER 1

1. It must be noted that both Wilde and Rohde were following the Western tradition of looking at modern Japan that was established by North American and European travel writers in the mid nineteenth century. For more information, see Benfey (2004).
2. Emphasis added. The original text reads, "practican la higiene del alma trabajando por mantener la placidez de su espíritu, como mantienen la de su cuerpo." Eduardo Wilde, *Por mares y por tierras*, 609. When I cite Wilde's writings in this chapter, I change his nineteenth-century Spanish to the modern style. For instance, I refer to "y" instead of "i" or "genuino" rather than "jenuino" as appeared in the original texts.
3. "Las condiciones higiénicas, públicas y privadas en China, son deplorables; la pobreza, la miseria, la abominable clase de alimentos, el desaseo y la humedad a par del excesivo

trabajo y la falta de abrigo, deberían ser causas de una disminución notable anual en la población." Wilde, *Por mares y por tierras*, 359.
4. For Wilde, China's representative symbol is "a great elephant without nerves" that is incapable of feeling anything even when his ear or foot is cut. Wilde, *Por mares y por tierras*, 390.
5. James Clifford and George Marcus, ed., *Writing Culture: The Poetics and Politics of Ethnography*, 8-13.
6. Mary Louise Pratt, *Imperial Eyes: Travel Writing and Transculturation*, 8.
7. Pratt, *Imperial Eyes*, 7.
8. Pratt, *Imperial Eyes*, 15.
9. Araceli Tinajero, *Orientalismo en el modernismo hispanoamericano*, 3.
10. While Gasquet mentions Wilde's and Rohde's general observations of Japan in his book, I analyze the two writers more systematically in the larger context of the representation of Japan and the Japanese immigrants in Argentina.
11. Gasquet, *Oriente al Sur*, 16.
12. Gasquet, *Oriente al Sur*, 291-92.
13. Gasquet, *Oriente al Sur*, 295.
14. It is worth remembering that, in his study of world history, Hegel characterizes both the Americas and Asia in derogatory terms as opposed to Europe, which he characterizes as the symbol of the "absolute spirit."
15. In 1878, he published *Curso de higiene pública* (Course on public hygiene) based on the classes he taught at the Colegio Nacional de Buenos Aires.
16. "el sedimento de mi corta estadía es una sensación de tristeza"; "París me ha parecido una ciudad aturdida, que no se da cuenta de lo que está pasando en el mundo." Eduardo Wilde, *Viajes y observaciones*, 18.
17. Lila Bujaldón de Esteves, "Eduardo Wilde and Japan," 463.
18. "todo cuanto veo es real y positivo, propio y genuino de este delicioso pedazo del globo que tanto deseaba conocer." Wilde, *Por mares y por tierras*, 437-8.
19. "asisto al acto de la transformación de un pueblo y llego en el momento supremo en que dos civilizaciones se tocan, para despedirse; la antigua sumergiéndose en los recuerdos del pasado, abriéndose paso la moderna con el asentimiento de los hijos de la tierra quienes, si no tuvieran más virtud que la de adaptarse a cambios tan radicales, esa sola bastaría para levantarlos ante los ojos de la humanidad entera y señalarlos como modelos." Wilde, *Por mares y por tierras*, 438.
20. Emphasis in original. "Fabrícanse en Europa millares de artículos análogos pero en casi todos ellos se ve la *factura* comercial no el *arte* divino. Un cabo de bastón en el viejo mundo occidental es un objeto vulgar, en el Japón es un ser vivo que habla, si representa una cabeza humana, y trina si remeda un pájaro." Wilde, *Por mares y por tierras*, 537-38).
21. "Y en el tren minúsculo, más pequeño, más ligero que un tranvía madrileño, el movimiento peculiar de toda llegada se inicia, pero no como en Europa, no con febriles impaciencias y curiosidades infantiles, no con ruido ni con alegría, sino grave y pausadamente." Enrique Gómez Carrillo, *El Japón heroico y galante*, 17.
22. Emphasis in original. "el artista ruso y yo, cambiamos nuestros trajes europeos por el nacional kimono, tan superior en *confort* y en elegancia." José Tablada, *En el país del sol (obra VIII)*, 130.
23. Tinajero, *Orientalismo en el modernismo hispanoamericano*, 16.

24. Beatriz González-Stephan, "The Teaching Machine for the Wild Citizen," 321.
25. Kristin Ruggiero, *Modernity in the Flesh: Medicine, Law, and Society in Turn-of-the-Century Argentina*, 91.
26. Beatriz González-Stephan, "Economías fundacionales: Diseño del cuerpo ciudadano," 40–41.
27. Alejandro Kohl, *Higienismo argentino. Historia de una utopía: la salud en el imaginario colectivo de una época*, 18. Moreover, Gabriela Nouzeilles (2000) points out how the discourse of medicine as well as the emphasis on hygiene culture played key roles in the creation of what she calls "somatic fictions" in nineteenth-century Argentina.
28. Kohl, *Higienismo argentino*, 63. Wilde dedicated himself to the country's sanitary problems through his work in the Comisión de Aguas Corrientes, Cloacas y Adoquinado in 1847, as well as in the Departamento de Higiene Nacional in 1880.
29. Ruggiero, *Modernity in the Flesh*, 87.
30. "instrucción, moralidad, buena alimentación, buen aire, precauciones sanitarias, asistencia pública, beneficencia pública, trabajo y hasta diversiones gratuitas; en fin, atención a todo lo que puede constituir una exigencia de parte cada uno y de todos los moradores de una comarca o de una ciudad." Eduardo Wilde, *Curso de higiene pública: Lecciones en el colegio nacional de Buenos Aires*, 9–10.
31. James Clifford and George Marcus, *Writing Culture*, 23–24.
32. "los chinos son ajenos a todos los elementos de civilización en el manejo de sus ciudades"; "las ciudades chinas son un laberinto de calles tortuosas, sucias y estrechas." Wilde, *Curso de higiene pública*, 276, 290.
33. Wilde, *Curso de higiene pública*, 287.
34. Wilde, *Curso de higiene pública*, 305.
35. "los microbios de la incuria habitual son más fuertes que los de las epidemias." Wilde, *Curso de higiene pública*, 305.
36. Ruggiero, *Modernity in the Flesh*, 2.
37. "Dejando al Daibutsu entramos en una casita japonesa de madera; es un juguete, un dije por su distribución y su limpieza." Wilde, *Curso de higiene pública*, 407.
38. Wilde, *Curso de higiene pública*, 600.
39. Wilde was so inspired during his visit to an elementary school in Tokyo that the fencing lesson in that place reminded him of the first years of his own schooling. Wilde, *Curso de higiene pública*, 464.
40. "Con elementos de educación trasmitidos de antepasados a descendientes y fomentados desde la cuna hasta el sepulcro, nada extraño tiene que se haya formado un pueblo afable, cortes, tolerante, sentimental, artístico y de gustos refinados; amantes de lo bello y de lo bueno, genuinamente honrado y estimable bajo todo punto de vista." Wilde, *Curso de higiene pública*, 606.
41. "El vizconde se ocupa en estos momentos de mandar inmigrantes a Brasil y a México. Yo lo incito a mandarlos también a la república argentina y le ofrezco remitirle las leyes y decretos relativas a la inmigración." Wilde, *Curso de higiene pública*, 473.
42. Wilde, *Curso de higiene pública*, 377.
43. According to Andrea Pappier, approximately 100,000 people of Chinese descent were living in different parts of Argentina in 2011. Pappier, "Inmigración china en Argentina," 1. With the dominant influence on food industries managed by Chinese families, as well as the cultural and educational activities that routinely take place in Chinatown in Buenos

Aires, the Chinese population has had a great success in integrating themselves within contemporary Argentine society.
44. "las japonesas jóvenes son casi todas bonitas, graciosas, alegres, afectuosas; lo más notable de sus atractivos físicos es el cuello, en seguida las manos y los pies." Wilde, *Curso de higiene pública*, 402.
45. "en todas partes la *musumé* [mujer joven] es encantadora, flor de aire libre y de refinamiento palatino, vibrante cigarra o áureo faisán." Tablada, *En el país del sol*, 193.
46. Wilde, *Curso de higiene pública*, 447.
47. "verdad es que quizá yo no encontraría tales calidades en un cuello separado de su cabeza y pecho correspondientes." Wilde, *Curso de higiene pública*, 447.
48. "muchas mujeres chinas proceden con sus maridos como europeas o americanas." Wilde, *Curso de higiene pública*, 281.
49. "los engañan, los ridiculizan, los estropean, los obligan a trabajar toda su vida, exigen todo de ellos y les pagan sus sacrificios con ingratitud, deslealtad y desconsideración." Wilde, *Curso de higiene pública*, 281–82).
50. "La mujer por su posición y por la estrechez del molde en que se desarrolla, no puede tener sentimientos tiernos, ni para sus padres, ni para sus hermanos, ni para los hombres a quienes no conoce." Wilde, *Curso de higiene pública*, 283.
51. Wilde, *Curso de higiene pública*, 310–14.
52. Wilde, *Curso de higiene pública*, 294.
53. Wilde, *Curso de higiene pública*, 333.
54. In her book *Ornamentalism* (2019), Cheng reconceptualizes race studies and feminist studies in order to propose a new understanding of Asianness through the figure of the "yellow woman." As she argues, "Instead of being pure capture or representing fugitive flight from the nominative biological or anatomical raced body, the yellow woman emerges as a 'body ornament' whose perihumanity demands that we approach ontology, fleshiness, and aliveness differently. By perihumanity, I mean to identify the peculiar in-and-out position, the peripherality and proximity of the Asiatic woman to the ideals of the human and the feminine. . . . And I offer a theoretical framework that I call *ornamentalism* in order to turn our focus to the peripheral and the supplemental and to explore the transitive properties of persons and things." Anne Anlin Cheng, *Ornamentalism*, 2–3.
55. Wilde, *Curso de higiene pública*, 412. Yoshiwara's district was officially approved by the Tokugawa shogun in 1617 under the specific conditions of isolation, enclosure, and confinement. Prostitution was not allowed outside of the *yukaku* (pleasure district), and the courtesans were not allowed to leave the area. According to some historians, at the end of the Edo period in 1868, between two and three thousand courtesans found themselves confined to this district. Hiromi Sone, "Prostitution and Public Authority in Early Modern Japan," 171. It is also worth noting that throughout modern Japanese history, Yoshiwara was popular among foreign visitors and served as an informal site of ostentatious diplomacy.
56. "Allí están las casas de las cortesanas con su mostruario semejante a una jaula, donde en lugar de pájaros hay mujeres jóvenes, bonitas las mas, bien vestidas todas, honestas en apariencia, sonriendo amablemente y sin hacer cosa alguna impropia." Wilde, *Curso de higiene pública*, 404.
57. Wilde also demonstrates his scientific interest when describing the bodies of Japanese prostitutes in detail: "even the ugly-faced ones have pretty eyes, fresh mouth, precious

teeth, healthy breath, a statuary body, well modeled, fine and well-cared-for skin, smooth, satin and delicate hands and exquisitely shaped small feet" (aun las feas de cara, tienen con raras excepciones ojos lindos, boca fresca, dientes preciosos, aliento sano, un cuerpo estatuario, bien modelado, piel fina y cuidada, suave, satinada, manos delicadas y pies pequeños de exquisita forma)." Wilde, *Curso de higiene pública*, 368.

58. "Las niñas que se prostituyen en sus casas no creen hacer mal; lo hacen con el consentimiento de sus padres." Wilde, *Curso de higiene pública*, 410.
59. Sone, "Prostitution and Public Authority," 171.
60. Sone, "Prostitution and Public Authority," 178.
61. Other Latin American travelers to Japan from the period such as Tablada, Gómez Carrillo, and Francisco Bulnes, all of whom visited Yoshiwara, also neglected the real situation of the Japanese courtesans.
62. "las casas de prostitución comunes, por lo tanto las genuinamente chinas, son miserables." Wilde, *Curso de higiene pública*, 367.
63. Wilde, *Curso de higiene pública*, 367.
64. "el sello de la pobreza, de la necesidad, de la costumbre, del abandono y la indolencia, del poco respeto diré, por el propio cuerpo." Wilde, *Curso de higiene pública*, 366.
65. Gasquet, *Oriente al Sur*, 191.
66. "A estar a mis informes debo decir que en el gran Yoshiwara de Tokio y en su símil de Yokohama, las habitaciones son grandes y aseadas, la comida de las pupilas sana y abundante y los vestidos a satisfacción de ellas." Wilde, *Curso de higiene pública*, 594.
67. Like Wilde, Rohde published some of his travel notes in the Argentine newspaper *La Prensa*.
68. "la ciudad inválida incorporóse virilmente para vestir un traje de íntegro corte americano." Jorge Max Rohde, *Viaje al Japón*, 57).
69. Rohde, *Viaje al Japón*, 58.
70. "el viejo Japón, con sus creencias y diferencias sociales, discurre bajo la careta europea que ofrece al ingenuo turista." Rohde, *Viaje al Japón*, 58.
71. "¡Qué menguado fruto engendra en este suelo la influencia occidental!" Rohde, *Viaje al Japón*, 115.
72. "¡Ojalá concluya la actual era con el renacimiento, y, por tanto, el predominio estético del espíritu indígena, pujante ya en la era de Nara, que abraza desde el año 645 hasta el año 780, en aquellas asombrosas pinturas y esculturas que atesora, especialmente, el santuario de Horyu-ji, hacia la época en que Europa espesa sombras en el cementerio donde yace la civilización latina!" Rohde, *Viaje al Japón*, 119.
73. Gasquet, *Oriente al Sur*, 256.
74. "Recuérdese que la incorporación foránea penetra en este suelo a mediados del siglo VI. Recuérdese que unos sacerdotes koreanos traen la buena nueva de la verdad, es decir, de la belleza, movidos, sin duda, por un designio trascendental ... Se cumple una jornada, la postrera jornada, del drama estético: la India infunde su conciencia, su lúcida conciencia a la China aletargada en el lomo del dragón mítico." Rohde, *Viaje al Japón*, 187–88.
75. On the spiritual ideals manifested in Japanese art, see Okakura Kakuzō's *Ideals of the East* (1903), which anticipated the historical justification for Japanese imperialism and cultural superiority.
76. "En la admiración que dejamos en el asombroso santuario perdura el concepto: lo universal y lo particular bautizan felizmente el nacimiento del arte japonés." Rohde, *Viaje al Japón*, 192.

77. For an analysis of Paz's relationship to India, see Hagimoto (2013).
78. It should be pointed out that Hearn neither spoke nor wrote in Japanese. In other words, he studied Japanese folk tales and traditions largely as an "interpreter" through the assistance of his wife and native informants.
79. Lila Bujaldón de Esteves, "Otro viajero argentino al Japón: Jorge Max Rohde (1892–1979)," 97. In the nineteenth century, Hearn's writings were popular not only in America and Europe but also in South America through translations.
80. Bujaldón de Esteves, "Otro viajero argentino al Japón," 101.
81. Rohde mentions several symbols of Western literature and culture. Besides Hearn, those references include Pierre Loti, François-René de Chateaubriand, Alphonse de Lamartine, H. H. Keyserling, Théophile Gautier, Gautier, Josiah Conder, and Claude Monet.
82. "la existencia del espíritu en los anales estéticos y del imperio." Rohde, *Viaje al Japón*, 101.
83. "Henos en el jardín de Lafcadio Hearn. Henos en el jardín de las piedras litúrgicas, de las lámparas que consagran a la estirpe, a la propia estirpe—en un sentido especial—en las numerosas existencias con que gustó encarnarse, a través del tiempo inmensurable, el espíritu que ahora penetra nuestra carne; de los árboles y las flores, cuyos matices y perfumes componen el difícil poema que leen claramente algunos monjes predestinados; de los hilos de agua que trasuntan el devenir perpetuo del cosmos, la eterna mudanza de la vida." Rohde, *Viaje al Japón*, 94.
84. Hephzibah Roskelly, "Cultural Translator: Lafcadio Hearn," 16.
85. "La japonesa es el dechado de la cultura; la japonesa es el triunfo armonioso de la civilización; la japonesa diviniza la humana materia con el misterio—inefable misterio—de la gracia. Por ella, especialmente por ella, el Japón es refugio—postrer refugio que le queda al universo—del nostálgico caminante." Rohde, *Viaje al Japón*, 217.
86. Cheng, *Ornamentalism*, 2–3.
87. "[n]uestras *geishas* recogen en sus fisonomías la suavidad dispersa por el mundo." Rohde, *Viaje al Japón*, 148.
88. Emphasis added. "Agradezcámoles la gracia de la farsa: por ellos el amor mercenario se purifica en el amor del arte; por ellos somos héroes del sueño en una noche de primavera." Rohde, *Viaje al Japón*, 152.
89. "el culto del arte en la religión de la belleza." Rohde, *Viaje al Japón*, 172.
90. "¿Alcanzará la influencia occidental hasta las mujeres japonesas? ¿Perdurarán, como heroínas del cuento azul, en la porcelana, el abanico y el biombo? ¿Entregarán a la generación que llega el mensaje de belleza que recibieron intacto de la generación anterior criada en las cortes feudales? Pensamos con nostalgia en el porvenir; pensamos que la gracia femenil que aun posee el mundo pueda oscurecerse con la sombra de un mundo que enterró, hace mucho tiempo, en la brega diaria de la vida, en la igualdad sexual de los derechos y las obligaciones, el secreto romántico de la gracia." Rohde, *Viaje al Japón*, 122.
91. Another evidence of his masculine view is the sheer lack of information on the Japanese feminist movement during the early twentieth century. For example, nowhere in his book does Rohde mention the New Women's Association (*Shin Fujin Kyokai*), the first organization founded by women in 1919 to fight for their rights in education and suffrage, among other fields.
92. "parécenos errónea la educación formal y especialmente europea que reciben las jóvenes, a quienes se obliga, por otra parte, a aceptar los prejuicios familiares de la añeja patria." Rohde, *Viaje al Japón*, 123.
93. Rohde, *Viaje al Japón*, 121.

94. "es fácil que la tradición—fuerza tremenda en la sociedad del imperio—choque con la vida diaria." Rohde, *Viaje al Japón*, 124.
95. "el imperio que en este lugar levantó la belleza es poderoso." Rohde, *Viaje al Japón*, 129.
96. "Ojalá el Japón sólo usufructúe de Occidente el arte de la técnica, en las ciencias y en las industrias, que hoy florece con extraordinario brío en el glorioso imperio." Rohde, *Viaje al Japón*, 119.
97. David Taylor, "Shaking the Buddhas: Lafcadio Hearn in Japan, 1890-1904," 177.
98. Gasquet, *Oriente al Sur*, 266.

CHAPTER 2

1. Joseph J. Tobin, "Introduction: Domesticating the West," 30. The process of westernization was strongly advocated by the group of educators and philosophers, called *Meirokusha*, which was founded by Mori Arinori in 1873 in order to promote "civilization and enlightenment" in Japan.
2. Isabella Lucy Bird, *Unbeaten Tracks in Japan: A Record of Travels in the Interior, Including Visits to the Aborigines of Yezo and the Shrines of Nikko and Ise*, vii.
3. For more information about the history of Shindō Renmei, see Fernando Morais's *Dirty Hearts* (2021).
4. Subodhana Wijeyeratne, "A Race to War: Japanese Public Intellectuals and Racial Explanations of the Russo-Japanese War," 1.
5. Naoko Shimazu, *Japanese Society at War: Death, Memory and the Russo-Japanese War*, 1.
6. Pankaj Mishra, *From the Ruins of Empire: The Revolt Against the West and the Remaking of Asia*, 2.
7. Leo Ching, "Yellow Skin, White Masks: Race, Class and Identification in Japanese Colonial Discourse," 72.
8. The term "Yellow Peril" was first introduced by Kaiser Wilhelm II of Germany in 1895 at the end of the Sino-Japanese War, also known as the "Yellow War." It was a racist notion that was meant to portray Asian people as a threat to the Western civilization. It must be noted that its legacy of racial discrimination continues to this day, as seen in Donald Trump's description of COVID-19 as the "Chinese virus" in early 2021.
9. Michael Keevak argues that the Western imagination of Asian yellowness was based on "numerous historical, scientific and cultural contingencies that had little to do with the 'real' Far East." Keevak, *Becoming Yellow: A Short History of Racial Thinking*, 100. In fact, it is worth mentioning that during the so-called "Age of Exploration," Europeans portrayed East Asians as "white" and never as "yellow" in their travel narratives and missionary writings. See Keevak's chapter 1.
10. Keevak, *Becoming Yellow*, 10.
11. Keevak, *Becoming Yellow*, 135.
12. Ching, "Yellow Skin, White Masks," 72.
13. Ching, "Yellow Skin, White Masks," 74.
14. In *Japan's Orient: Rendering Pasts into History* (1995), Stefan Tanaka makes a compelling argument about how Japanese historians in the late nineteenth and early twentieth century created a dominant narrative of "the Orient" or *toyo*, which helped legitimize Japan's expansionism in Asia.
15. Robert Eskildsen, "Of Civilization and Savages: The Mimetic Imperialism of Japan's 1874 Expedition to Taiwan," 389.

16. Eskildsen, "Of Civilization and Savages," 390.
17. Wijeyeratne, "A Race to War," 1.
18. Kan'ichi Asakawa, *The Russo-Japanese Conflict: Its Causes and Issues*, 55.
19. Asakawa, *The Russo-Japanese Conflict*, 81.
20. Shimazu, *Japanese Society at War*, 161.
21. In his analysis of the role of public intellectuals and their conceptions of race at the time of the Russo-Japanese War, Wijeyeratne concludes that the perception of whiteness remains influential in today's Japanese society. He concludes that "the deep-seated notion that that the Japanese are somehow more closely related—culturally, politically, biologically—to whites continues to find expression in contemporary Japanese society." Wijeyeratne, "A Race to War," 14.
22. Shimazu, *Japanese Society at War*, 164.
23. Brown, *A Brief History of Argentina*, 135.
24. "el que toma la iniciativa, el que se muestra dispuesto á las grandes revoluciones." "China y Japón: La declaración de guerra," *La Nación*, August 2, 1894.
25. "se sacrifica con un propósito civilizador"; "va á emplear sus fuerzas para mantener el estacionamiento, el atraso." "China y Japón," *La Nación*, August 2, 1894.
26. Across the world, people were eager to learn about the Russo-Japanese War, either through military accounts or journalistic venues. As David Schimmelpenninck Van der Oye notes, "military attachés, journalists, and other observers from Europe and North America flocked to the front. Already within months illustrated volumes began to appear to satisfy the public's appetite for news about the combat." Van der Oye, "Rewriting the Russo-Japanese War: A Centenary Retrospective," 81.
27. Ministry of Foreign Affairs of Japan, "Amigos Across the Ocean: Episodes in Japan-Latin America Relations."
28. Higa, "Desarrollo histórico de la inmigración japonesa," 477.
29. Keiko Imai (2006) investigates the depictions of Japan and its people in Argentine newspapers during the first half of the twentieth century, with a particular focus on the articles that appeared in *La Nación*, *La Prensa* and *El País*.
30. Some examples include the following: "Guerra Ruso-japonesa: Notas militares y navales" (Russo-Japanese war: Military and naval notes, April 2, 1904), "Nisshin y Kasuga: Su travesía al Japón" (Nisshin and Kasuga: Their voyage to Japan, April 11, 1904), "El imperio del sol levante: Progresos sorprendentes" (The empire of the rising sun: Amazing progress, May 9, 1904), "Las potencias y la guerra rusojaponesa" (The great powers and the Russo-Japanese war, June 6, 1904), "Morir por la patria: El heroísmo de los japoneses" (Dying for the motherland: The heroism of the Japanese, June 23, 1904), "Organismos viejos y jóvenes: Las guerras a grandes distancias" (Old and new organisms: Long-distance wars, June 3, 1904), "La táctica de los japoneses: Explicación de sus triunfos" (The Japanese tactic: An explanation of their triumphs, May 19, 1905), "La 'nación' en el imperio del sol naciente" (The 'nation' in the empire of the rising sun, June 20, 1905), and "La paz rusojaponesa: Las protestas del Japón" (The Russo-Japanese peace: Japan's protests, September 16, 1905).
31. "Si el Japón ha conseguido en tan poco tiempo ser una potencia militar de primer orden, no se debe sólo á la organización de sus unidades de combate, sino también á la de los servicios auxiliares del ejército y principalmente al de sanidad." "El imperio del sol levante: Progresos sorprendentes," *La Nación*, May 9, 1904.
32. "ese viejo país, renovado, que surge de pronto á otra viril y ardorosa juventud, apto para

los triunfos guerreros y para las conquistas de la civilización." "La 'nación' en el imperio del sol naciente," *La Nación*, June 20, 1905.

33. Emphasis added. "A nosotros, como colectividad que busca todavía su camino y que aun tiene tanto que iniciar y que aprender, nos interesa en grado sumo todo cuanto se refiere á ese ejemplo palpitante de lo que pueden una buena organización y un plan claro y lógico, para el desarrollo y engrandecimiento de las naciones." "La 'nación' en el imperio del sol naciente," *La Nación*, June 20, 1905.

34. "un pueblo trabajador y civilizado"; "con los resultados obtenidos en la guerra era fácil prever [...] la importancia que Japón asumiría entre las grandes potencias mundiales." Juan Domingo Perón, *Apuntes de historia militar: Guerra Ruso-Japonesa de 1904–1905*, 4–5.

35. Japan's Navy Academy was created in 1876, a few years after the establishment of Argentina's Escuela Naval Militar (Military Navy School) in 1872. Francesca Arena de Tejedor suggests that the two countries were contemporaries in their efforts to emerge as new international naval forces. Arena de Tejedor, *Argentina y Japón: Se conocieron en el violento amanecer del mundo moderno*, 42.

36. Of relevance to Domecq García's writing and the history of modern Japan is Juan Forn's novel *María Domecq* (2007).

37. "ese saludo del monte sagrado del Japón lo considero como buen augurio de llegada a un país que me es completamente desconocido, sus costumbres, su idioma, su pueblo, etc." Tejedor, *Argentina y Japón*, 90–91.

38. "He oído decir muchas veces, especialmente durante y después de la última guerra, de que el Japón había sorprendido a la Europa con sus triunfos que nadie los esperaba y que nadie se los hubiese imaginado. Pero yo digo que la Europa ha sido sorprendida porque ha querido, porque ha hecho caso a escritores sin seriedad, porque ha sido indiferente y simple." Manuel Domecq García, *Guerra Ruso-Japonesa 1904-1905: Estudio sobre la preparación y eficiencia de la Marina Japonesa*, 13.

39. "La Europa no se daba cuenta y no creía que pudiese marchar en la forma que había adoptado, seguía no tomándolo a lo serio, creía siempre que aquel país de hombres con abanicos y polleras y que vivían en casas de papel, no pasarían nunca de ser una simple chocarrería." Domecq García, *Guerra Ruso-Japonesa 1904-1905*, 12.

40. Domecq García, *Guerra Ruso-Japonesa 1904-1905*, 26.

41. "Creo que difícilmente puede encontrarse un pueblo como el japonés que posea mayores aptitudes para ser soldado y especialmente para ser marino." Domecq García, *Guerra Ruso-Japonesa 1904-1905*, 27.

42. "el sentimiento militar está desarrollado en él [el pueblo japonés] de una manera extraordinaria, y la vida guerrera una de las que más los atrajo siempre." Domecq García, *Guerra Ruso-Japonesa 1904-1905*, 27.

43. The emphasis on the combative spirit of the Japanese has often attracted Latin American writers since the nineteenth century. For example, Gómez Carrillo compares the Japanese *bushidō* to the Spanish cavalry. In his essay "El alma heroica" (1912), he refers to the historical samurai, Minamoto no Yorimitsu (948–1021), as "a bandit Don Quixote, bloodthirsty and ferocious." Gómez Carrillo, *El Japón heroico y galante*, 49. In Argentina, Jorge Luis Borges wrote a short story, "El incivil maestro de ceremonias Kotsuké no Suké" (1933), based on the legend of the 47 *rōnin* (lower-rank, masterless samurai). For an analysis of Borges's story, see Hagimoto (2015).

44. "En la creación y organización de una fuerza eficiente como debe ser la fuerza naval, se impone la perseverancia, el método y sobre todo la reserva en lo que se haga respecto a

asuntos navales, pues solo siguiendo ese sistema es que los japoneses consiguieron desarrollar todo su plan de organización." Interestingly, in one of his notes on the infantry, he describes how the Japanese spend a lot of time walking in the street. Domecq García, *Guerra Ruso-Japonesa 1904–1905*, 7, 21–22.

45. "existían de un modo efectivo las dos principales cualidades sin las cuales toda organización o todo plan fracasan irremisiblemente y que son: la disciplina y el compañerismo o espíritu de cuerpo." Domecq García, *Guerra Ruso-Japonesa 1904–1905*, 7.

46. "Este pueblo tiene una educación especial hecha al estoicismo; no demuestran el sentimiento en la forma que nosotros y conceptúan que el que muere por la patria es el que realmente llega sin más trámites al paraíso o a la suprema felicidad." Tejedor, *Argentina y Japón*, 94.

47. "La guerra pues con Rusia era un hecho conocido por todos los japoneses, se la consideraba algo así como una obligación que todos se habían impuesto con la patria ... Ese sentimiento patriótico lo mantenían todos con la mayor de las satisfacciones, lo que quiere decir que estaba encarnado en el espíritu público, este deber ineludible que todo japonés tenía que cumplir una vez llegado el momento supremo del sacrificio. ¡Los pueblos que profesan esos sentimientos son invencibles!" Domecq García, *Guerra Ruso-Japonesa 1904–1905*, 16.

48. Domecq García, *Guerra Ruso-Japonesa 1904–1905*, 19–20.

49. "algunas conclusiones o principios que puedan servir para formular ciertos planes convenientes para nuestra propia marina." Domecq García, *Guerra Ruso-Japonesa 1904–1905*, 3.

50. "No me cabe duda de que considerando con cierta atención las observaciones y los apuntes que este informe contiene, se puede sacar de ellos alguna enseñanza y obtener datos útiles para formular un plan de organización de guerra y de defensa que toda marina y todo país precavido deben tener." Domecq García, *Guerra Ruso-Japonesa 1904–1905*, 5.

51. Tejedor, *Argentina y Japón*, 94.

52. "¡Qué gran ejemplo es el que nos ha dado esa raza que hasta hace poco la considerábamos inferior a la nuestra! Cuánta enseñanza no podemos sacar de ella, al pensar que hay bastantes pueblos de nuestra propia raza que no han sido aún capaces de constituirse y formarse conforme lo que han hecho ellos." Domecq García, *Guerra Ruso-Japonesa 1904–1905*, 12.

53. Kinzo Makino settled in Argentina after being shipwrecked near La Plata in 1886, but he was not an immigrant in the traditional sense. Also, some scholars believe that the first Japanese to set foot in Argentina was a slave called "Francisco Japón," who was brought to Córdoba in the sixteenth century. For more information, see Assadourian (1965).

54. During his time on the navy ship, Shinya also became friends with Pedro Segundo Casal (1879–1957) who would serve as Argentina's Minister of the Navy between 1932 and 1933. Like Domecq García, Casal helped the expansion of the Japanese Argentine Cultural Institute.

55. Yoshio Shinya, *Imperio del sol naciente: Su maravillosa evolución moderna*, ii.

56. For more information on Violeta Shinya, see Martelli Giachino's article in *Alternativa Nikkei*.

57. Facundo Garasino, "Cultural Propaganda by Japanese Migrants in Buenos Aires: Experiencing Locally the Transnational Expansion of the Japanese Empire," (paper presented at the symposium Japanese Diaspora to the Americas: Literature, History, and Identity, Yale University, May 2019): 1.

58. Garasino further develops his argument about Shiya's role as a propagandist for Japanese

imperialism in Argentina in his forthcoming essay "Immigrant Propaganda: Translating Japanese Imperial Ideology into Argentine Nationalism" (2023). I want to thank Garasino for sharing his unpublished essay with me.

59. Eiichiro Azuma, *In Search of Our Frontier*, 3. Azuma's book examines the transnational history of Japanese immigrant settler colonialism as a way to highlight connections between Japanese America and Japan's colonial empire. For instance, he focuses on the histories of Ōtsuki Kōnosuke and Yokokawa Shōzō who became founders of the Japanese ethnic community in Hawai'i and California, respectively, in the late nineteenth century.
60. Shinya, iii.
61. Tobin, "Introduction," 30.
62. "un país del lejano oriente hasta entonces semi-ignorado, el Imperio del Sol Naciente, que iniciaba su marcha ascendente por el camino de la gloria." Shinya, *Imperio del sol naciente*, 17.
63. Emphasis added. "Salía el Japón de los siglos de aislamiento con el resto del mundo, confiado en sí mismo, firmemente resuelto, lleno de nobles ambiciones, radiante e impetuoso como el astro luminoso de la mañana y dispuesto a conquistar sobre la tierra un lugar preponderante." Shinya, *Imperio del sol naciente*, 17.
64. Shinya, *Imperio del sol naciente*, 96.
65. Masterson and Funada-Classen, *The Japanese in Latin America*, 286.
66. "La evolución contemporánea del pueblo japonés ha servido para desautorizar por siempre la teoría de la psicología racial basada en las características fisiológicas de las razas." Shinya, *Imperio del sol naciente*, 18.
67. "No profesando ninguna religión organizada, los Ainus, como toda raza primitiva, adoraban a los héroes." Shinya, *Imperio del sol naciente*, 47.
68. "El pueblo manchú que trabaja, es pacífico; y desde que el Japón tiene bajo su dirección la administración del Ferro Carril Sur Manchuriano, venía prosperando rápidamente, gracias a la custodia de la guarnición del ejército japonés que mantiene el orden. Ante la amenaza de nuevos disturbios regionales, solicitaron el apoyo del Japón y bajo su consejo, resolvieron constituirse en un Estado organizado y estable. El Japón, por su parte, le aseguró y le asegura la garantía de su estabilidad, ya que la tranquilidad de ese territorio es vital para el desenvolvimiento futuro del Imperio, política y económicamente hablando." Shinya, *Imperio del sol naciente*, 209.
69. Azuma, *In Search of Our Frontier*, 16.
70. "La administración japonesa de Chosen se considera un gobierno colonial modelo. Los nativos tienen los mismos derechos que los japoneses y reina paz y orden en todos los rincones del territorio desde que ha sido anexado al Japón." Shinya, *Imperio del sol naciente*, 204.
71. Aguiló, *The Darkening Nation*, 40.
72. Emphasis in original. "Tiene importancia . . . la perfecta *homogeneidad de la raza 'Yamato.'*" Shinya, *Imperio del sol naciente*, 15.
73. Scholars have studied Japan's ability to adapt foreign influences as one of the nation's most unique aspects. For instance, sociologist Roland Robertson discusses how "Japan exhibits a particular proclivity for adopting and adapting externally generated ideas for its own specific purposes." Robertson, *Globalization. Social Theory and Global Culture*, 93.
74. "Supo, así, el pueblo japonés, sacar provecho de la cultura, del arte, y la religión del continente sin poner peligro su independencia moral. Ha sabido nacionalizar a todos los elementos exóticos que entraron en su territorio." Shinya, *Imperio del sol naciente*, 47.

75. "[l]a introducción de la civilización china al Japón no fué un simple acto de adaptación. Ella fué una obra de selección y asimilación. Entonces como en el siglo XIX, no fué mero imitador, pues mejoró lo que recibió del exterior." Shinya, *Imperio del sol naciente*, 63.
76. Emphasis added. "La parte más grande de *la conquista de la civilización continental* fué la que correspondió al Budismo. . . . Pero aún esta conquista no fué sino parcial, pues el Budismo japonés es un producto bien distinto de todas las formas de esa religión del Asia. Esta pudo prosperar en el Japón solamente por su japonización." Shinya, *Imperio del sol naciente*, 63.
77. Michael Taussig, *Mimesis and Alterity: A Particular History of the Senses*, viii.
78. "el líder natural de las razas orientales en la adopción de los modos y pensamientos occidentales." Shinya, *Imperio del sol naciente*, 19.
79. "La influencia japonesa tuvo el don de detener la política dominadora de las potencias occidentales en el extremo oriente, demostrando al mismo tiempo, con los hechos, la posibilidad de la fusión armónica de las dos grandes civilizaciones del Oriente y el Occidente, otrora consideradas absolutamente inconfundibles." Shinya, *Imperio del sol naciente*, 17.
80. Julia A Kushigian, *Orientalism in the Hispanic Literary Tradition: In Dialogue with Borges, Paz, and Sarduy*, 1–18.
81. "Mientras el Japón se hallaba atareado en su afán de organizar sus instituciones de acuerdo con el modelo occidental, aceptando las importantes innovaciones de la civilización moderna, sus dos vecinos, Corea y China, seguían apegados obstinadamente a la antigua rutina, despreciando las costumbres extranjeras, y detestaban entablar relaciones de intercambio con las potencias interesadas." Shinya, *Imperio del sol naciente*, 98.
82. "la civilización occidental en lo que es útil y provechoso para la vida y la aplicación científico-mecánica del saber humano . . . alcanza hoy a todos los rincones del Imperio." *El Argentin Djijo*, "Conferencia de G. Yoshio Shinya: Pronunciada en el Instituto Cultural Argentino Japonés, el día jueves 26 de Junio de 1941."
83. For instance, Jorge Max Rhode gave a talk on "Estampas de la mujer japonesa" (Images of Japanese woman) in 1934, Albino Pugnalín offered a presentation on "La estética y heroísmo del alma japonesa" (The aesthetics and heroism of the Japanese soul) in 1936, and Shinya's daughter, Violeta Shinya, talked about "Reflejos del Japón Antiguo" (Reflections of ancient Japan) in 1935.
84. Inspired by the Musée Social in Paris, the Argentine Social Museum was founded in 1911 in Buenos Aires. In her book *Eugenics in the Garden: Transatlantic Architecture and the Crafting of Modernity*, Fabiola López-Durán discusses the critical role the Museum played in the history of eugenics in Argentina. See her chapter 3 called "Machines for Modern Life."
85. Graciela Karina Torales, "El Instituto Cultural Argentino Japonés del Museo Social Argentino." *La Plata Hochi*.
86. Emphasis added. Schneider, "The Two Faces of Modernity," 181.
87. Torales, "El Instituto Cultural Argentino Japonés del Museo Social Argentino."
88. Shinya also encouraged his countrymen to immigrate to Argentina through his writings. In 1903, he wrote an article for the Japanese newspaper *Kokumin Shinbun*, describing Argentina as "the most appropriate country for Japanese migration." Higa, "Desarrollo histórico de la inmigración japonesa," 478.
89. "el pueblo japonés es uno de los que mejor saben respetar las leyes y las autoridades. En la Argentina, en donde residen más de 4.000, no hay ningún preso japonés en sus cárceles." Shinya, *Imperio del sol naciente*, 140.

90. "Yo aspiro a colaborar con la juventud argentina para hacer de esta tierra una gran nación, porque estoy convencido de que aquí en las orillas del Plata ha de formarse un pueblo modelo para el mundo civilizado, pues ningún otro país tiene los elementos y las condiciones que la providencia nos legó." Yoshio Shinya, "Llamamiento a la juventud." *El Argentin Djiji*. December 22, 1934.

CHAPTER 3

1. Akemi Kikumura-Yano's *Encyclopedia of Japanese Descendants in the Americas: An Illustrated History of the Nikkei* (2002) includes a chapter on Japanese Argentines, with contributions by Isabel Laumonier, Cecilia Onaha, and Jorge Higa.
2. Besides the writers I study in Chapter 3 and Chapter 4, there are other Nikkei authors in today's Argentina, including Virginia Higa, María Claudia Otsubo, Martín Sancia Kawamichi, Susana Tamashiro, Agustina Rabaini, and Malena Higashi.
3. It must be pointed out that Sugimura and Matayoshi were not the first Nikkei writers in Argentina. For example, the newspaper *Somos Nisei* was published between 1984 and 1985 and included articles that explore the meanings of Nisei identity in the country.
4. Higa, "The Emigration of Argentines of Japanese Descent," 262.
5. Trinh T. Minh-ha, *When the Moon Waxes Red: Representation, Gender and Cultural Politics*, 159.
6. Higa, "Desarrollo histórico de la inmigración japonesa," 506.
7. Higa, "Desarrollo histórico de la inmigración japonesa," 475.
8. Laumonier, "Japanese Argentine Historical Overview," 72.
9. Masterson and Funada-Classen, *The Japanese in Latin America*, 89.
10. The remigration process emerged again after World War II as the Japanese unsatisfied with their living conditions in Paraguay, Bolivia, and the Dominican Republic emigrated clandestinely to Argentina for better economic opportunities. Federación de Asociaciones Nikkei en la Argentina, *Historia del inmigrante japonés en la Argentina: Período de Preguerra (Tomo II)*, 305.
11. Okihiro, "Turning Japanese Americans," 9.
12. Okihiro, "Turning Japanese Americans," 9.
13. Tigner, "The Ryukyuans in Argentina," 213.
14. In his novel *Los siete locos* (1929), Roberto Arlt makes a reference to a Japanese-owned bar in Buenos Aires. Japanese cafés and bars could be found in several major cities in Argentina by 1920, sometimes used as meeting places for the Bohemian society. In Córdoba, for example, Japanese immigrants owned some of the most thriving cafés. Laumonier, "Japanese Argentine Historical Overview," 75-76.
15. Laumonier, "Japanese Argentine Historical Overview," 73. Japanese immigrants formed various *kenjin-kai* based on the town of their origin. The biggest association, the Okinawa *kenjin-kai*, was established in 1951.
16. Okihiro, "Turning Japanese Americans," 10.
17. Masterson and Funada-Classen, *The Japanese in Latin America*, 321.
18. "Yo quiero que ustedes encuentren en mí no sólo una aliada, sino a una amiga." Federación de Asociaciones Nikkei en la Argentina, *Tomo II*, 111.
19. Emphasis added. "Esta colectividad japonesa que uniéndose se honra y nos honra a nosotros con su convivencia, debe tener la sensación más absoluta de que para nosotros, en esta tierra, sus miembros son tan argentinos como nosotros, tienen el mismo respeto que nuestros hombres, y no hay diferencia alguna entre un hombre japonés y un hombre

argentino." Federación de Asociaciones Nikkei en la Argentina, *Tomo II*, 110.
20. "como si fuera nuestro abnegado padre y a la inmortal Evita como a nuestra tierna madre, a quienes les prometemos ser hijos honrados y obedientes." Rein Raanan, Aya Udagawa, and Pablo Adrián Vázquez, "Los muchachos peronistas japoneses: el movimiento justicialista y los *nikkei*," 99–100.
21. Rein, Udagawa and Vázquez, "Los muchachos peronistas japoneses," 97.
22. "El peronismo es nacional, popular y japonés," *Anticipos*, March 2, 2020.
23. "El peronismo es nacional, popular y japonés," *Anticipos*, March 2, 2020.
24. Aguiló points out how Buenos Aires redefined itself as a racially diverse city after 2001: "The capital city is presented as more *mestiza* in order to be seen as more Western—that is, able to keep up with the standards of modernity identified with diversity trends in the United States and Europe. The paradox exemplifies how these international conceptions of racial and ethnic heterogeneity were appropriated and re-signified in Argentina." Aguiló, *The Darkening Nation*, 19.
25. Chisu Teresa Ko, "From Whiteness to Diversity: Crossing the Racial Threshold in Bicentennial Argentina," 2534.
26. Ko, "From Whiteness to Diversity," 2543.
27. Stuart Hall, "Cultural Identity and Diaspora," 234.
28. Hall, "Cultural Identity and Diaspora," 236.
29. Emphasis in original. Hall, "Cultural Identity and Diaspora," 244.
30. Homi K. Bhabha, *The Location of Culture*, 114.
31. Bhabha, *The Location of Culture*, 1–2.
32. Bhabha, *The Location of Culture*, 37. Gayatri Spivak criticizes the theory of hybridity from a different angle, claiming that abundant scholarly discussions on postcolonialism have allowed some migrant populations in the metropolitan area to appropriate their status as "the triumphant self-declared hybrid" (361). For her, the problem lies in the unequal cultural relations of "*neo*-colonialism," or what she calls a "hybridist postnational talk" that seeks to celebrate "globalization as Americanization." Spivak, *A Critique of Postcolonial Reason: Toward a History of the Vanishing Present*, 361.
33. Cristián Trouvé, "Héctor Dai Sugimura: sin perder la ternura." *Generacón E*. October 29, 2019.
34. In his online article for *Generacón E*, Cristián Trouvé refers to Sugimura's second novel, called "ladá," but I have been unable to locate this book anywhere.
35. Héctor Dai Sugimura, *Buscadores en mis últimas vidas*, 10.
36. "Yo te puse de nombre Dai porque ibas a ser un gato, un gran gato." Sugimura, *Buscadores en mis últimas vidas*, 34.
37. Sugimura, *Buscadores en mis últimas vidas*, 55.
38. "Por lo visto se trataba de una comunidad oriental. Me eran muy familiares esas caras y costumbres, lo que me dio la pauta de que probablemente fui un miembro de esa sociedad." Sugimura, *Buscadores en mis últimas vidas*, 19.
39. "a quienes no perdieron la magia de creer en lo increíble, ni la sensibilidad para percibir lo creíble y, especialmente, a quienes las han extraviado." Sugimura, *Buscadores en mis últimas vidas*, 5.
40. "¡Aléjate de mí, gato sucio!"; "¡No me molestes, estoy ocupado!" Sugimura, *Buscadores en mis últimas vidas*, 21.
41. "¿Qué le pasa a la gente de este nuevo mundo? Yo entiendo que no soy un animal muy atractivo, pero no he hecho nada malo para que me traten de esa manera." Sugimura, *Buscadores en mis últimas vidas*, 21.

42. "el tipo de familia que todos envidiarían." Sugimura, *Buscadores en mis últimas vidas*, 33.
43. "un hombre poco hablador, frío"; "una mujer activa [que] hacía dos o tres cosas a la vez." Sugimura, *Buscadores en mis últimas vidas*, 33.
44. "Le importaba que estudiasen más, para que pudieran el día de mañana ingresar a una respetable universidad." Sugimura, *Buscadores en mis últimas vidas*, 33.
45. Christiane Kazue Nagao, "Representación de la cultura japonesa en la literatura argentina. Marcas de procesos de transculturación," Congreso ALADAA (Asociación Latinoamericana de Estudios de Asia y África), September 8–9, 2004.
46. Rajagopalan Radhakrishnan, "Is the Ethnic 'Authentic' in the Diaspora?" 203. In his discussion of the differences between the first generation and the second generation of Indian Americans in the United States, Radhakrishnan argues that it is impossible to articulate a single definition of "home" or "Indian identity." He points out that "[t]he tensions between the old and new homes create the problem of divided allegiances that the two generations experience differently. The very organicity of the family and the community, displaced by travel and relocation, must be renegotiated and redefined."
47. Bhabha, *The Location of Culture*, 37.
48. "Me enamoré desde el primer momento en que la vi. Su manera de retarme, de mirarme, de abrazarme. Su pelo, sus ojos, su tez angelical, sus pequeños y calentitos pechos." Sugimura, *Buscadores en mis últimas vidas*, 24.
49. Sugimura, *Buscadores en mis últimas vidas*, 55.
50. "una actitud constante de búsqueda." Sugimura, *Buscadores en mis últimas vidas*, 44.
51. Minh-ha, *When the Moon Waxes Red*, 157.
52. Hall, "Cultural Identity and Diaspora," 236.
53. Mercedes Giuffré, "Gaijín: búsqueda identitaria e inmigración oriental en Argentina: A propósito de la novela de Maximiliano Matayoshi." *Signos Universitarios: Revista de la Universidad del Salvador (Migraciones y Migrantes II)*, 205.
54. Matayoshi stated that he wrote the novel based on the history of his father, Tetsuji Matayoshi, who had arrived in Argentina in 1951. Mercedes Giuffré, "En busca de la identidad argentina. Entrevista con Maximiliano Matayoshi," *Sitio al Margen*. December 2003.
55. In her dissertation, María Teresa Rinaldi compares Matayoshi's novel to Brazilian films, *Gaijin, Os Caminhos da Liberdade* (1980) and *Gaijin, Ama-me Como Sou* (2005), both of which are directed by Tizuka Yamasaki.
56. Maximiliano Matayoshi, *Gaijin*, 209, 223.
57. "con Julieta no me molestaban los silencios." Matayoshi, *Gaijin*, 139.
58. "Aún era muy fácil conversar con ella, los silencios no eran incómodos y no necesitábamos tantas palabras para entendernos." Matayoshi, *Gaijin*, 232.
59. "La historia que contaba papá era mucho mejor: las estrellas fugaces eran las almas de las personas bondadosas que, en la noche, veían a todos los que amaban y después regresaban junto a las otras estrellas." Matayoshi, *Gaijin*, 74.
60. "Nos habló de los hombres chinos que mataban a sus hijos y golpeaban a sus esposas, de los niños que les pegaban a sus padres y maestros, y de los abuelos chinos que debían trabajar todo el día sin descanso." Matayoshi, *Gaijin*, 22.
61. Matayoshi, *Gaijin*, 23.
62. Matayoshi, *Gaijin*, 151.
63. "¿Qué hacía yo en aquella casa? Había viajado miles de kilómetros durante meses para planchar ropa durante el resto de mi vida. Debí haberme quedado en Japón." Matayoshi, *Gaijin*, 169.

64. Matayoshi, *Gaijin*, 127.
65. "unos chicos que jugaban fútbol dejaron escapar la pelota, que se detuvo cerca de mí. Che, chino, pasame la pelota. La pateé pero de alguna forma no se dirigió hacia donde yo quería. Chino boludo, volvé a China, chin chu lin, gritaron y dejé de escuchar los otros insultos." Matayoshi, *Gaijin*, 204.
66. Susana Reinoso, "Premiaron a un argentino por su primera novela." *La Nación*. January 3, 2003.
67. "Trece años atrás me había embarcado para cruzar todos los océanos en busca de poder, algún día, regresar a casa. Y para lograrlo aprendí a planchar, aprendí un idioma y también aprendí que existen tierras desde donde ni siquiera se puede imaginar el mar, crucé aquellas tierras y ahora me encontraba otra vez dispuesto a cruzar océanos." Matayoshi, *Gaijin*, 245.
68. Svetlana Boym, *The Future of Nostalgia*, 251.
69. Matayoshi, *Gaijin*, 18.
70. Matayoshi, *Gaijin*, 63.
71. "De modo que ahora yo tenía un apellido que no era mío, vivía en un país al que no pertenecía, y con una familia de la que no formaba parte." Matayoshi, *Gaijin*, 241.
72. "Yo conocía a unos chicos que se habían ido y a otros que decían que era como América, pero mejor: los argentinos no matan a los japoneses." Matayoshi, *Gaijin*, 15.
73. "Intenté pensar en otra cosa, en cómo sería Argentina sin tanques, sin soldados americanos y sin muerte." Matayoshi, *Gaijin*, 21.
74. "siempre me pareció que aquella casa funcionaba como un refugio para todos los japoneses que, como yo, comenzaban una nueva vida en Argentina." Matayoshi, *Gaijin*, 139.
75. Matayoshi, *Gaijin*, 42–43.
76. Emphasis in original. "*Buenas tardes, ¿cómo estás?*, dijo en castellano. *Very good*, respondí y no pude evitar reírme." Matayoshi, *Gaijin*, 119.
77. "Cuando conseguí dar con una radio en inglés, agradecí las clases de Kiyoshi y redacté lo que faltaba del informe." Matayoshi, *Gaijin*, 227–28.

CHAPTER 4

1. For example, see Kushigian (1991), Tinajero (2003), Gasquet (2007), López-Calvo (2008), Hagimoto (2013), Camayd-Freixas (2013), Rivas and Lee-DiStefano (2016) and Torres-Rodríguez (2019).
2. Mabel Moraña, *Crítica impura: estudios de literatura y cultura latinoamericanos*, 214.
3. Laura J. Torres-Rodríguez, *Orientaciones transpacíficas: La modernidad mexicana y el espectro de Asia*, 25.
4. Masiello, *The Art of Transition*, 144.
5. Masiello, *The Art of Transition*, 145.
6. Christina Civantos, *Between Argentines and Arabs: Argentine Orientalism, Arab Immigrants, and the Writing of Identity*, 3.
7. Gasquet, *Oriente al Sur*, 295.
8. Lisa Lowe, *Critical Terrains: French and British Orientalisms*, 4.
9. Lowe, *Critical Terrains*, 20.
10. I borrow the term "gendering orientalism" from Retina Lewis who studies the contributions of women (French and British female artists) in the construction of Orientalism. She claims that "gender, as a differentiating term, was integral to the structure of [Orientalist]

discourse and individual experience of it." Retina Lewis, *Gendering Orientalism: Race, Femininity, and Representation*, 18. From a social science perspective, Maryam Khalid refers to the idea of "gendered orientalism" in order to examine the images of America's War on Terror using postcolonial and feminist lens. According to her, "gendered orientalism creates categories of people according to race and gender, defining through these categories what 'men' or 'women,' 'us' and 'them,' 'Afghan/Arab/Muslim' and 'Western' are and do." Khalid, "Gender, Orientalism and Representations of the 'Other' in the War on Terror," 27. Furthermore, my analysis is also inspired by Chisu Teresa Ko's 2019 study that discusses the topics of "self-orientalism" and "inter-imperiality" in *Flores de un solo día*.

11. See, for instance, Ahmed (1992), Badran (1995), Lewis (1996), and Abu-Lughod (2013).
12. Emphasis in original. Sara Ahmed, *Queer Phenomenology: Orientations, Objects, Others*, 115.
13. Anne Anlin Cheng, *Ornamentalism*, 2.
14. Masiello, *The Art of Transition*, 154.
15. See, for example, Geirola (2005), Martinetto (2006), Lattanzi (2013), Rinaldi (2013), Har-Kim (2017), and Ko (2019).
16. Emphasis in original. Gustavo Geirola, "Chinos y Japoneses en América Latina: Karen Tei Yamashita, Cristina García y Anna Kazumi Stahl," 119.
17. Chisu Teresa Ko, "Self-Orientalism and inter-imperiality in Anna Kazumi Stahl's *Flores de un solo día*," 4.
18. "Si Aimée es linda, la madre lo es en mayor grado, de facciones japonesas que, por su armonía, expresan una belleza universal." Anna Kazumi Stahl, *Flores de un sólo día*, 17.
19. "la dejan vivir en un universo conocido y previsible. Le permiten la felicidad; casi siempre se muestra feliz, silenciosa pero sin angustia, sin aire de enfermedad mental." Stahl, *Flores de un sólo día*, 17.
20. "un espacio cálido y fácil, que se abría entre dos personas y se llenaba no de palabras sino de las cosas que hacían juntas." Stahl, *Flores de un sólo día*, 29).
21. "ella siempre hablaba con los ojos: miraba a las personas—a las que conocía—y podía expresar un millón de cosas en un instante, directo a la mente y al corazón de la otra persona." Stahl, *Flores de un sólo día*, 275–6.
22. Stahl, *Flores de un sólo día*, 128.
23. "Le cuesta no poder comunicarse con la madre de Aimée. No sabe qué piensa, qué quiere o necesita." Stahl, *Flores de un sólo día*, 19.
24. Minobu Ohi, *History of Ikebana*, 4.
25. In the history of *ikebana*, the tradition of the "heaven-earth-man" triangle was established in the early nineteenth century. Ohi, *History of Ikebana*, 31–32.
26. "Hanako da a las flores forma, altura y aire, definición; y recibe de ellas color y calidez o frialdad, la curva o el ángulo severo, y de esa sociedad a la larga lo que emerge es una expresión, la sugerencia (casi más completa de lo que podría hacerse por medio de las palabras) de un sentimiento, una postura o actitud." Stahl, *Flores de un sólo día*, 133.
27. Ko, "Self-Orientalism and inter-imperiality," 7.
28. "La hija la guiaba, una mano femenina de huesos pequeños dento de la otra más chica pero gordita, acolchada, una mano de niña." Stahl, *Flores de un sólo día*, 56.
29. "una pequeña persona locuaz y enérgica a quien sólo le faltaba el idioma para desenvolverse." Stahl, *Flores de un sólo día*, 45.
30. Emphasis in original. "La voz de ese hombre y la densa solidez de su cuerpo le dan fuerza, porque confirman el pertenecer, la idea de que ella está donde debe estar, que éste es *su* lugar." Stahl, *Flores de un sólo día*, 81.

31. "Eran como dos gotas de agua arrojadas al petróleo; más allá de su similitud y su unión, enfrentaban juntas lo extremo foráneo, y vivían juntas la lenta transición." Stahl, *Flores de un sólo día*, 11.
32. "Son las dos de la misma estatua; caminan al mismo tiempo; se semejan en los movimientos fluidos de los brazos delicados, las piernas delgadas. Preparan la comida, y están juntas en ese silencio que comparten, que no es frío, sino cálido y continente, como un ambiente en sí." Stahl, *Flores de un sólo día*, 69.
33. "el sostén, el piso, las paredes y el techo, la firmeza del mundo." Stahl, *Flores de un sólo día*, 175.
34. Stahl, *Flores de un sólo día*, 175.
35. "Todo comenzaría más tarde que en otras ciudades, que en las más sajonas por lo menos." Stahl, *Flores de un sólo día*, 187.
36. Many of the stories in *Catástrofes naturales* narrate the life of Japanese immigrants in New Orleans after World War II. One of the salient features of these earlier works by Stahl is the insertion of Japanese conversational phrases into Spanish texts. Anna Kazumi Stahl, *Catástrofes naturales*, 31, 39, 42, 66. Moreover, Aimée appears as a character in some of the stories, most explicitly in "Rigor."
37. Debra A. Castillo, "I Call it New Orleans," 98.
38. Castillo, "I Call it New Orleans," 99.
39. Stahl, *Flores de un solo día*, 180, 198.
40. Stahl, 198.
41. Stahl, 252.
42. Stahl, 362.
43. Stahl, 360.
44. Stahl, 80.
45. Stahl, 80–81.
46. Ette, *Transarea*, 39.
47. Ette, *Transarea*, 39.
48. "Su expresión demostraba la dulce seguridad característica en ella, lo opuesto de la duda." Stahl, *Flores de un sólo día*, 166.
49. Laura Galarza, "Las hojas del viento," *Página/12*, May 8, 2016.
50. "No vas a esperar a que se cuele la luz por la ventana." Alejandra Kamiya, *Los árboles caídos también son el bosque*, 7.
51. "[u]n desayuno perfecto requiere pescado perfecto y el pescado más fresco está en los alrededores del mercado de Tsukiji." Kamiya, *Los árboles caídos también son el bosque*, 7.
52. "Vas a girar la llave y vas a apoyar la cabeza en la puerta como si fuera una almohada en la que vas a descansar." Kamiya, *Los árboles caídos también son el bosque*, 11.
53. Like Kamiya's story, the Argentine author Miguel Sardegna's "Mar de árboles" in *Hojas que caen sobre otras hojas* (2017) also deals with suicide as well as bullying in Japan. While Kamiya's setting is the ordinary family scene in the kitchen, Sardegna writes about Aokigahara on the flank of Mount Fuji, commonly known as Japan's "Suicide Forest."
54. "una grieta en la lisura de tu plan." Kamiya, *Los árboles caídos también son el bosque*, 7.
55. "ningún ángulo debe desafinar, ningún color puede chocar o apagarse." Kamiya, *Los árboles caídos también son el bosque*, 9.
56. "sonriendo más con los ojos que con los labios que no se despegan." Kamiya, *Los árboles caídos también son el bosque*, 10.
57. Ministry of Health, Labour and Welfare of Japan, "Dai 3 shou: Heisei 30 nenjyu ni okeru jisatsu no uchiwake" (Chapter 3: The Details of Suicide in 2018), March 23, 2019. The causes

for their death include "domestic problems," "health issues," and "financial difficulties," among others.

58. In February 2021, the *New York Times* published an article on the increasing rates of suicide among Japanese women, specifically addressing the impact of COVID-19. As the article mentions, "the rising psychological and physical toll of the pandemic has been accompanied by a worrisome spike in suicide among women." Motoko Rich and Hikari Hida, "As Pandemic Took Hold, Suicide Rose Among Japanese Women," *New York Times*, February 22, 2021.
59. Kamiya, *Los árboles caídos también son el bosque*, 10.
60. "silencio cómodo, liviano como el aire del que está hecho, y en el que se expresa mejor el sabor de lo que comemos." Kamiya, *Los árboles caídos también son el bosque*, 27.
61. "sé muchas cosas de él así, sin saberlas, apenas intuyéndolas." Kamiya, *Los árboles caídos también son el bosque*, 28.
62. Kamiya, *Los árboles caídos también son el bosque*, 28.
63. "A mí, que nací y me crié en Argentina, me da pereza buscar palabras en el diccionario. A él no. El español de mi padre japonés es más vasto y más concreto que el mío." Kamiya, *Los árboles caídos también son el bosque*, 29.
64. "Viendo los gestos de mi padre puedo llegar al pasado, a Japón o a la historia de mi padre, que es la mía." Kamiya, *Los árboles caídos también son el bosque*, 28.
65. "Siento lo que está al acecho, y una certidumbre parecida a la de que al día lo sucede la noche, una especie de vértigo." Kamiya, *Los árboles caídos también son el bosque*, 29.
66. "Ahora veo claramente, casi puedo tocar, los granos de arroz que se desprenden." Kamiya, *Los árboles caídos también son el bosque*, 30.
67. Kamiya, *Los árboles caídos también son el bosque*, 107.
68. "él partió no cuando salió del Japón sino cuando decidió quedarse en Argentina." Kamiya, *Los árboles caídos también son el bosque*, 107.
69. "Los otros chicos se estiraban con los índices y me decían 'china'. Yo les decía que era japonesa y ellos decían que era lo mismo. Yo no les respondía. No entendía por qué decían eso, ni muchas otras cosas. Me gritaron, me empujaron y algunos me golpearon. Todos ellos parecían muy enojados conmigo." Kamiya, *Los árboles caídos también son el bosque*, 108.
70. Kamiya, *Los árboles caídos también son el bosque*, 110. In the late nineteenth century, children of mixed race were called *ainoko* (offspring between parents of different breeds), which is now considered a derogatory term because it evokes images of racial impurity and illegitimacy. This term was replaced by *konketsu* (mixed blood) and *konketsuji* (mixed-blood child) in the twentieth century. During the late 1960s and 1970s, the Japanese word *haafu* (half) became popularized and continues to be used in today's Japanese society to refer to a person of mixed-race. See Okamura (2017) for more information.
71. "Soy japonesa en Argentina y argentina en Japón, así, con las minúsculas para mí y las mayúsculas para el país." Kamiya, *Los árboles caídos también son el bosque*, 110.
72. "los árboles que se caen no son retirados sino que se dejan para que formen parte del paisaje." Kamiya, *Los árboles caídos también son el bosque*, 113.
73. "No la conocí salvo por historias que contaba mi papá y una foto que vi una vez en la que busqué a la mujer fuerte que mantuvo sola a su familia y a la de su marido, perdiendo todo varias veces durante la guerra." Kamiya, *Los árboles caídos también son el bosque*, 111.
74. "Siento que soy una parte de algo mucho más grande. Algo que empezó del otro lado del

mundo, donde la gente acomoda los zapatos cuando se los saca, y sigue acá, donde la gente los deja como quiere." Kamiya, *Los árboles caídos también son el bosque*, 114.

CHAPTER 5

1. Lucía Rud, "Representaciones de las migraciones y diásporas de Asia del Este en el audiovisual argentino," *Nuevo mundo mundos nuevos*. June 25, 2020.
2. Joanna Page, *Crisis and Capitalism in Contemporary Argentine Cinema*, 6.
3. Page, *Crisis and Capitalism*, 7.
4. See chapter 5 of Page's book for her analyses of *Bolivia* and *Vladimir en Buenos Aires*.
5. The equivalent of "cuento chino" in English is "old wives' tale."
6. Clara Zappettini, dir., *La otra tierra: Japoneses en Argentina*, Argentina Televisora Color, 1986. The film is part of a TV series about different immigrant groups living in Argentina, including the Irish, the Spanish, and Bolivians. The episode about Japanese immigrants was uploaded by Archivo Histórico RTA on YouTube: https://www.youtube.com/watch?v=rQAIHU_5dfQ&t=9s. More recently, there is a new series called *Migrantes Latinoamérica* produced by Canal Encuentro, which focuses on a diverse range of ethnic minorities in Latin America. The stories about Argentina feature, for example, Syrians, Germans, Colombians, Cubans, Koreans, and Japanese. See *Migrantes Latinoamérica: Japoneses en Argentina* on YouTube: https://www.youtube.com/watch?v=MD2boEQOrmw.https://www.youtube.com/watch?v=MD2boEQOrmw
7. Yosefa Loshitzky, *Screening Strangers: Migration and Diaspora in Contemporary European Cinema*, 9
8. Interestingly, people still leave positive feedback in the YouTube comment section of the documentary in 2021. For example, one comment by "naty Martin" reads, "The greatest respect for the Japanese community." Another comment by "Cellser Casanova el terrible 4" says, "I am fascinated to learn these stories and to know that we have many Japanese who have been part of our Argentine history planting their attractive cultures and everything we can learn from them."
9. *Samurai*, directed by Gaspar Scheuer (Buenos Aires: AireCine, Metaluna Productions, and San Luis Cine, 2013), DVD. The film features some Nikkei actors such as Kazuomi Takagi, Miki Kawashima, Nicolás Nakayama, and Yoshio Jorge Takashima, who also appeared in *La otra tierra*. In fact, Takashima has been active in the Argentine media scene since at least the 1990s. His TV shows and movies include *El mundo de Gasalla* (1990), *Los Libonatti* (1991), *Cha cha cha* (1995–96), *Epitafios* (2004), *¿Dónde está Kim Basinger?* (2009), and *Devoto, la invasión silenciosa* (2020).
10. Gaspar Scheuer, "Gauchos y samurái," *Revista Sake*. April 1, 2014.
11. López-Calvo, *The Affinity of the Eye*, 6–7.
12. Nitobe's book is considered one of the first attempts to define Japan's national identity. Its influence later became manifest in the formation of *Nihonjinron* ("theory about the Japanese") in the postwar era.
13. Besides *Martín Fierro* and its sequel *El regreso de Martín Fierro* (1879), other classic texts of gaucho literature include Eduardo Gutiérrez's *Juan Moreira* (1880), Ricardo Güiraldes's *Don Segundo Sombra* (1926) and Benito Lynch's *El romance del gaucho* (1930). It is also worth remembering that the romanticized symbol of the gaucho was associated with the notion of whiteness in early-twentieth-century Argentina. As Aguiló points out, the

characterization of the gaucho as the paradigm of the Argentine race meant "a romanticized pure-blooded *criollo* stripped of past references to blackness and *mestizaje*." Aguiló, *The Darkening Nation*, 45.

14. For an analysis of the critique of Argentine modernity in *Samurai* (alongside two other films *Un cuento chino* and *Mujer conejo*), see Ko (2016).
15. *Un cuento chino*, directed by Sebastián Borensztein (Buenos Aires: Aliwood Mediterráneo Producciones, Castafiore Films, Gloriamundi Films and Royal Cinema Group, 2011), DVD.
16. Currently, there are over 22,000 people of Korean descent in Argentina and 200,000 Chinese Argentines.
17. Corina Courtis, *Construcciones de alteridad: Discursos cotidianos sobre la inmigración coreana en Buenos Aires*, 93–102.
18. Kim, "Asia-Latin America as Method," 115.
19. Dan Adaszko and Ana Lía Kornblit, "Xenofobia en adolescentes argentinos. Un estudio sobre la intolerancia y la discriminación en jóvenes escolarizados," 174.
20. Adaszko and Kornblit, "Xenofobia en adolescentes argentinos," 174.
21. Adaszko and Kornblit, "Xenofobia en adolescentes argentinos," 176.
22. Paul Byrnes, "A soul stripped bare." *Sydney Morning Herald*. August 25, 2012.
23. Another parallel between Poncho Negro and Roberto is that they are both veterans of war. While the former participated in the Paraguayan War, the latter joined the 1982 Malvinas War (Falklands War) against the United Kingdom.
24. Hilary Chung and Luciano Bernadette argue that "In *Chinese Takeaway* no spoken Chinese is subtitled, thus aligning the audiences' vertical relationship with the Chinese migrant Jun and the reclusive Buenos Aires shopkeeper Roberto's horizontal relationship with him." Hilary Chung and Luciano Bernadette, "The Dis/locat/ing Migrant as an Agent of Transposition: Borensztein's *Un cuento chino* and Segre's *Io sono Li*," 196.
25. Chung and Bernadette, "The Dis/locat/ing Migrant," 201.
26. Chisu Teresa Ko, "Between Foreigners and Heroes: Asian-Argentines in a Newly Multicultural Nation," 282.
27. *Silencio roto: 16 Nikkeis*, directed by Pablo Moyano (Buenos Aires: Tupasimi Producciones, 2015), DVD.
28. In an interview with the online radio program *Japón Hoy* (3/18/15), Shizuko Kaneshiro, a member of the Familiares de los Desaparecidos de la Colectividad Japonesa claims that there are more than 16 Nikkei *desaparecidos*: "I even think that today many people, many Japanese, must have relatives who are still missing, but they don't say it." "Japón Hoy, 8va temporada, Programa 02 (18/03/2015)." March 18, 2015. Accessed December 20, 2022. https://www.youtube.com/watch?v=_Brd2c91WxU).
29. Silence also plays a significant role in religious observances in the West as a form of deference to a divine force or spiritual awareness, such as in the Quaker tradition.
30. Cheryl Glenn, *Unspoken: A Rhetoric of Silence*, 9.
31. Slavoj Žižek, *Lacan: The Silent Partners*, 224.
32. Ailín Bullentini, "Nunca más queremos el silencio." *Página/12*. June 11, 2017.
33. Motoday Nagazane, "Imperial Rescript: The Great Principles of Education," 227.
34. "Japón Hoy, 8va temporada, Programa 02 (18/03/2015)." March 18, 2015.
35. The film also shows an interview with the ambassador of Japan, who admits that the officials at the time were aware of the violation of human rights but were in no position to obtain information about particular cases involving citizens of Japanese descent.

36. Diego Ardouin, "Desaparecidos de la colectividad japonesa durante la dictadura militar del 76–83," *Argentina Centro de Medios Independientes*. November 30, 2010.
37. Ardouin, "Desaparecidos de la colectividad japonesa." See also Ishida (2015).
38. Ardouin, "Desaparecidos de la colectividad japonesa."
39. Chie Ishida, "Gunseika Aruzenchin no imin community to 'nikkei shisshousha no seijisanka," 82.
40. When he was abducted, Higa was a student of literature and sociology as well as a contributor to the two newspapers for the Japanese community, *Akoku Nippo* and *La Plata Hochi*.
41. I want to acknowledge my gratitude to Chie Ishida for providing me with a copy of his unpublished poem.

CONCLUSION

1. Fernando Krapp, *Una isla artificial: Crónicas sobre japoneses en Argentina*, 28.
2. Marina Do Pico and Manuel Tacconi, "Alejandra Kamiya: 'Construyo mi lugar escribiendo,'" *Atletas*. September 14, 2019.
3. Mauro Yakimiuk, "Paula Brecciaroli: 'El personaje de Otaku es una condensación de prejuicios, anécdotas y superposiciones de muchos fanáticos que conocí en mi vida.'" July 10, 2016.
4. "Te miro y me cuesta creer que cumplís cuarenta, hijo;" "¿Cuándo vas a dejar del mundo de la fantasía para bajar un poquito a la realidad?" Paula Brecciaroli, *Otaku*, 14; 59.
5. "Ellos siempre en la vanguardia." Brecciaroli, *Otaku*, 54.
6. "La gente no se tocaba en las calles, en quince días no había visto una sola pareja caminar de la mano o besarse en público (a menos que fueran extranjeros), pero en muchos baños públicos había máquinas expendedoras que por cinco yenes entregaban pequeños tubos de plástico de colores estridentes, que escondían en su interior tangas usadas por adolescentes niponas." Lucía Puenzo, *En el hotel cápsula*, 75.
7. "Los siglos no parecían haber pasado del otro lado del portón"; "más bien parecía un albergue de peregrinos suspendido en el tiempo." Puenzo, *En el hotel cápsula*, 78, 79.
8. Other contemporary novels that deal with Japan include Miguel Sardegna's *Hojas que caen sobre otras hojas* (2017) and Mori Ponsowy's *Okasan* (2019).

Bibliography

Abu-Lughod, Lila. *Do Muslims Women Need Saving?* Cambridge, MA: Harvard University Press, 2013.

Adamovsky, Ezequiel. "Race and Class through the Visual Culture of Peronism." In *Rethinking Race in Modern Argentina*, edited by Paulina L Alberto and Eduardo Elena, 155-83. Cambridge, UK: Cambridge University Press, 2016.

Adaszko, Dan, and Ana Lía Kornblit. "Xenofobia en adolescentes argentinos. Un estudio sobre la intolerancia y la discriminación en jóvenes escolarizados." *Revista Mexicana de Sociología*. 70, 1 (2008): 147-96.

Aguiló, Ignacio. *The Darkening Nation: Race, Neoliberalism and Crisis in Argentina*. Cardiff: University of Wales Press, 2018.

Ahmed, Leila. *Women and Gender in Islam*. New Haven, CT: Yale University Press, 1992.

Ahmed, Sara. *Queer Phenomenology: Orientations, Objects, Others*. Durham, NC: Duke University Press, 2006.

Albarracín, Julia. *Making Immigrants in Modern Argentina*. Notre Dame, IN: University of Notre Dame Press, 2020.

Alberto, Paulina L., and Eduardo Elena, ed. *Rethinking Race in Modern Argentina*. Cambridge, UK: Cambridge University Press, 2016.

Allinson, Gary D. *The Columbia Guide to Modern Japanese History*. New York: Columbia University Press, 1999.

Andrews, George Reid. *The Afro-Argentines of Buenos Aires 1800-1900*. Madison: University of Wisconsin Press, 1980.

Ardouin, Diego. "Desaparecidos de la colectividad japonesa durante la dictadura militar del 76-83." *Argentina Centro de Medios Independientes*. November 30, 2010. Accessed December 15, 2022. http://argentina.indymedia.org/news/2010/11/762655.php.

El Argentin Djijo. "Conferencia de G. Yoshio Shinya: Pronunciada en el Instituto Cultural Argentino Japonés, el día jueves 26 de Junio de 1941." June 28, 1941. Accessed December 15, 2022. https://rakusai.nichibun.ac.jp/hoji/contents/ArgentinDjijo/PDF/1941/06/19410628aja10.pdf.

Asakawa, Kan'ichi. *The Russo-Japanese Conflict: Its Causes and Issues*. Shannon: Irish University Press, 1972 [1904].

Assadourian, Carlos Sempat. *El tráfico de esclavos en Córdoba, 1588-1610, según las actas de protocolos del Archivo Histórico de Córdoba*. Córdoba, Argentina: Dirección General de Publicaciones, 1965.

The Association of Nikkei and Japanese Abroad, "Who are 'Nikkei and Japanese Abroad'?" Accessed December 15, 2022. https://web.archive.org/web/20210129195448/http://www.jadesas.or.jp/en/aboutnikkei/index.html.

Azuma, Eiichiro. *In Search of Our Frontier: Japanese America and Settler Colonialism in the Construction of Japan's Borderless Empire*. Oakland: University of California Press, 2019.

Badran, Margot. *Feminists, Islam and Nation*. Princeton, NJ: Princeton University Press, 1995.

Benfey, Christopher. *The Great Wave: Gilded Age Misfits, Japanese Eccentrics, and the Opening of Old Japan*. New York: Random House, 2004.

Bhabha, Homi K. *The Location of Culture*. London and New York: Routledge, 1994.

Bird, Isabella Lucy. *Unbeaten Tracks in Japan: A Record of Travels in the Interior, Including Visits to the Aborigines of Yezo and the Shrines of Nikko and Ise*. London: George Newnes, 1900.

Borensztein, Sebastián, dir. *Un cuento chino*. Buenos Aires: Aliwood Mediterráneo Producciones, Castafiore Films, Gloriamundi Films and Royal Cinema Group, 2011. DVD.

Boym, Svetlana. *The Future of Nostalgia*. New York: Basic Books, 2001.

Briones, Claudia. "Mestizaje y blanqueamiento como coordenadas de aboriginalidad y nación en Argentina." *Runa* 23, 1 (2002): 61-88.

Brown, Jonathan C. *A Brief History of Argentina*. 2nd ed. New York: Checkmark Books, 2003.

Bujaldón de Esteves, Lila. "Eduardo Wilde and Japan: The Japanese Image of an Argentine Writer in the 19th Century." In *ICLA '91 Tokyo: The Force of Vision, II: Vision in History; Vision of the Other*, edited by Earl Miner, Toru Haga, Gerald Gillespie, Margaret Higonnet and Sumie Jones, 456–65. Tokyo: International Comparative Literature Association, 1995.

———. "Otro viajero argentino al Japón: Jorge Max Rohde (1892-1979)," *Boletín de Literatura Comparada* XXIV-XXV (1999-2000): 93–112.

———. "Anna Kazumi Stahl, 'nuestra' escritora transnacional." *Revista de Culturas y Literaturas Comparadas* 5 (2015): 1–10.

Bullentini, Ailín. "Nunca más queremos el silencio." *Página/12*. June 11, 2017. https://www.pagina12.com.ar/43466-nunca-mas-queremos-el-silencio.

Brecciaroli, Paula. *Otaku*. Buenos Aires: Paisanita Editora, 2015.

Byrnes, Paul. "A Soul Stripped Bare." *The Sydney Morning Herald*. August 25, 2012. https://www.smh.com.au/entertainment/movies/a-soul-stripped-bare-20120823-24n7n.html.

Calichman, Richard F. *What is Modernity?: Writing of Takeuchi Yoshimi*. New York: Columbia University Press, 2005.

Camayd-Freixas, Erik. *Orientalism and Identity in Latin America: Fashioning Self and Other from the (Post)Colonial Margin*. Tucson: University of Arizona Press, 2013.

Castillo, Debra A. "I Call it New Orleans." *Contemporary Women's Writing* 1, 1–2 (December 2007): 98–117.

Ching, Leo. "Yellow Skin, White Masks: Race, Class and Identification in Japanese Colonial Discourse." In *Trajectories: Inter-Asia Cultural Studies*, edited by Kuan-Hsing Chen, 65–86. London and New York: Routledge, 1998.

Cheng, Anne Anlin. *Ornamentalism*. New York: Oxford University Press, 2019.

Chung, Hilary, and Luciano Bernadette. "The Dis/locat/ing Migrant as an Agent of Transposition: Borensztein's *Un cuento chino* and Segre's *Io sono Li*." *Studies in European Cinema* 11, 3 (2015): 191-211.

Civantos, Christina. *Between Argentines and Arabs: Argentine Orientalism, Arab Immigrants, and the Writing of Identity*. Albany: State University of New York Press, 2006.

Clifford, James and George Marcus, ed. *Writing Culture: The Poetics and Politics of Ethnography*. Berkeley, Los Angeles and London: University of California Press, 1986.

Courtis, Corina. *Construcciones de alteridad: Discursos cotidianos sobre la inmigración coreana en Buenos Aires*. Buenos Aires: Eudeba, 2000.

Domecq García, Manuel. *Guerra Ruso-Japonesa 1904-1905: Estudio sobre la preparación y eficiencia de la Marina Japonesa*. Buenos Aires: Ministerio de Marina, 1917.

Do Pico, Marina and Manuel Tacconi. "Alejandra Kamiya: 'Construyo mi lugar escribiendo." *Atletas*. September 14, 2019. Accessed November 16, 2021. http://atletasrevista.com/alejandra-kamiya.

Dove, Patrick. *The Catastrophe of Modernity: Tragedy and the Nation in Latin American Literature*. Lewisburg, PA: Bucknell University Press, 2004.

Durán, Manuel. "La huella del Oriente en la poesía de Octavio Paz." *Revista iberoamericana*. 37, 74 (1971): 97-116.

Elena, Eduardo. "Argentina in Black and White: Race, Peronism, and the Color of Politics, 1940s to the Present." In *Rethinking Race in Modern Argentina*, edited by Paulina L. Alberto and Eduardo Elena, 184-210. Cambridge, UK: Cambridge University Press, 2016.

Eskildsen, Robert. "Of Civilization and Savages: The Mimetic Imperialism of Japan's 1874 Expedition to Taiwan." *The American Historical Review* 107, 2 (2002): 388-418.

Ette, Ottmar. *Transarea: A Literary History of Globalization*. Berlin: De Gruyter, 2016.

Federación de Asociaciones Nikkei en la Argentina. *Historia del inmigrante japonés en la Argentina: Período de Preguerra (Tomo I)*. Buenos Aires: Federación de Asociaciones Nikkei en la Argentina, 2004.

———. *Historia del inmigrante japonés en la Argentina: Período de Posguerra (Tomo II)*. Buenos Aires: Federación de Asociaciones Nikkei en la Argentina, 2005.

Forn, Juan. *María Domecq*. Buenos Aires: Emecé, 2007.

Galarza, Laura. "Las hojas del viento." *Página/12*, May 8, 2016. https://www.pagina12.com.ar/diario/suplementos/libros/10-5846-2016-05-08.html.

Garasino, Facundo. "Cultural Propaganda by Japanese Migrants in Buenos Aires: Experiencing Locally the Transnational Expansion of the Japanese Empire." Paper presented at the symposium *Japanese Diaspora to the Americas: Literature, History, and Identity* at Yale University, May 2019.

———. "Immigrant Propaganda: Translating Japanese Imperial Ideology into Argentine Nationalism." In *The Japanese Empire and Latin America*, edited by Pedro Iacobelli and Sidney Xu Lu. Honolulu: University of Hawai'i Press, 2023.

Gasquet, Axel. *Oriente al Sur: El orientalismo literario argentino de Esteban Echeverría a Roberto Arlt*. Buenos Aires: Eudeba, 2007.

Geirola, Gustavo. "Chinos y Japoneses en América Latina: Karen Tei Yamashita, Cristina García y Anna Kazumi Stahl." *Chasqui: revista de literatura latinoamericana* 34, 2 (November 2005): 113-30.

Giuffré, Mercedes. "En busca de la identidad argentina. Entrevista con Maximiliano Matayoshi." *Sitio al Margen*. December 2003. Accessed June 6, 2014. http://www.almargen.com.ar/sitio/seccion/entrevistas/matayoshi/.

———. "Gaijín: búsqueda identitaria e inmigración oriental en Argentina: A propósito de la novela de Maximiliano Matayoshi." *Signos Universitarios: Revista de la Universidad del Salvador (Migraciones y Migrantes II)* 23, 40 (2004): 201–6.

Glenn, Cheryl. *Unspoken: A Rhetoric of Silence*. Carbondale: Southern Illinois University Press, 2004.

Goicoa, Rodríguez J. *Japón en la Argentina*. Buenos Aires: Unión Industrial Argentina, 1938.

Gómez Carrillo, Enrique. *El Japón heroico y galante*. Guatemala: Editorial Cultural, 2009 [1912].

Gómez, Silvina and Cecilia Onaha. "Asociaciones voluntarias e identidad étnica de inmigrantes japoneses y sus descendientes en Argentina." *Migracione* 23 (2008): 207–35.

González-Stephan, Beatriz. "Economías fundacionales: Diseño del cuerpo ciudadano." In *Cultura y tercer mundo 2: Nuevas identidades y ciudadanías*, edited by Beatriz González-Stephan, 17–47. Caracas: Editorial Nueva Sociedad, 1996.

———. "The Teaching Machine for the Wild Citizen." In *The Latin American Subaltern Studies*, edited by Ileana Rodríguez, 313–40. Durham, NC: Duke University Press, 2001.

Hagimoto, Koichi. "From Hegel to Paz: Re-reading Orientalism in Latin American Writing." *Hipertexto* 17 (2013): 16–31.

———. *Between Empires: Martí, Rizal, and the Intercolonial Alliance*. New York: Palgrave Macmillan, 2013.

———. "Borges and Japan." *Chasqui: revista de literatura latinoamericana* 44, 2 (November 2015): 205–15.

Hall, Stuart. "Cultural Identity and Diaspora." In *Theorizing Diaspora: A Reader*, edited by Jana Evans Braziel and Anita Mannur, 233–46. Malden: Wiley-Blackwell, 2003.

Hanscom, Christopher P., and Dennis Washburn, eds. *The Affect of Difference: Representations of Race in East Asian Empire*. Honolulu: University of Hawai'i Press, 2016.

Har-Kim, Michelle. "American Antipodes: Anna Kazumi Stahl's *Flores de un solo día*." In *The Routledge Handbook of Asian American Studies*, edited by Cindy I-Fen Cheng, 83–100. New York: Routledge, 2017.

Hegel, G. W. F. *Lectures on the Philosophy of World History*. Translated by H. B. Nisbet. Cambridge, UK: Cambridge University Press, 1980 [1937].

Higa, Juan Carlos. "Poema del silencio." Unpublished poem. Buenos Aires, 1968.

Higa, Marcelo G. "Desarrollo histórico de la inmigración japonesa en la Argentina hasta la Segunda Guerra Mundial." *Estudios Migratorios Latinoamericanos* 10, 30 (1995): 471–512.

———. "The Emigration of Argentines of Japanese Descent to Japan." In *New Worlds, New Lives: Globalization and People of Japanese Descent in the Americas and from Latin America in Japan*, edited by Lane Ryo Hirabayashi, Akemi Kikumura-Yano, and James A. Hirabayashi, 261–78. Stanford, CA: Stanford University Press, 2002.

Higashide, Seiichi. *Adiós to Tears: The Memoirs of a Japanese-Peruvian Internee in U.S. Concentration Camps*. Seattle: University of Washington Press, 2000.

Imai, Keiko. *Aruzenchin no shuyōshi ni miru nihon ninshiki*. Tokyo: Jōchi Daigaku Iberoamerika Kenkyūjo, 2006.

Ishida, Chie. "Gunseika Aruzenchin no imin community to 'nikkei shisshousha no sei-jisanka." *Contact Zone* 7 (2015): 56–82.

Jacobowitz, Seth. "A Bitter Brew: Coffee and Labor in Japanese Brazilian Immigrant Literature." *Estudios Japoneses* 41 (2019): 13–30.

Jacobson, Matthew Frye. *Whiteness of a Different Color: European Immigrants and the Alchemy of Race.* Cambridge, MA: Harvard University Press, 1999.

"Japón Hoy, 8va temporada, Programa 02 (18/03/2015)." Japón Hoy TV, posted Jan. 19, 2016. https://www.youtube.com/watch?v=_Brd2c91WxU.

Kakuzō, Okakura. *Ideals of the East: The Spirit of Japanese Art.* New York: Cosimo Classics, 2007 [1903].

Kaminsky, Amy K. *The Other/Argentina: Jews, Gender, and Sexuality in the Making of a Modern Nation.* Albany: State University of New York Press, 2021.

Kamiya, Alejandra. *Los árboles caídos también son el bosque.* Buenos Aires: Bajo la Luna, 2016.

Keevak, Michael. *Becoming Yellow: A Short History of Racial Thinking.* Princeton, NJ: Princeton University Press, 2011.

Khalid, Maryam. "Gender, Orientalism and Representations of the 'Other' in the War on Terror." *Global Change, Peace and Security* 23, 1 (2011): 15–29.

Kikumura-Yano, Akemi, ed. *Encyclopedia of Japanese Descendants in the Americas: An Illustrated History of the Nikkei.* Walnut Creek, CA: AltaMira Press, 2002.

Kim, Junyoung Verónica. "Desarticulando el 'mito blanco': Inmigración coreana en Buenos Aires e imaginarios nacionales." *Revista de crítica literaria latinoamericana* 36, 71 (2010): 169–93.

———. "Asia-Latin America as Method: The Global South Project and the Dislocation of the West." *Verge: Studies in Global Asia* 3, 2 (2017): 97–117.

Ko, Chisu Teresa. "From Whiteness to Diversity: Crossing the Racial Threshold in Bicentennial Argentina." *Ethnic and Racial Studies* 37, 14 (2014): 2,529–46.

———. "'Argentina te incluye': Asians in Argentina's Multicultural Novels." *Symposium: A Quarterly Journal in Modern Literatures* 69, 1 (2015): 1–13.

———. "Toward Asian Argentine Studies." *Latin American Research Review* 51, 4 (2016): 271–89.

———. "Between Foreigners and Heroes: Asian-Argentines in a Newly Multicultural Nation." In *Rethinking Race in Modern Argentina*, edited by Paulina L. Alberto and Eduardo Elena, 268-288. Cambridge, UK: Cambridge University Press, 2016.

———. "Self-Orientalism and inter-imperiality in Anna Kazumi Stahl's *Flores de un solo día*." *Latin American and Caribbean Ethnic Studies* 14, 1 (2019): 70–89.

Kohl, Alejandro. *Higienismo argentino. Historia de una utopía: la salud en el imaginario colectivo de una época.* Buenos Aires: Editorial Dunken, 2006.

Krapp, Fernando *Una isla artificial: Crónicas sobre japoneses en Argentina.* Buenos Aires: Tusquets Editores, 2019.

Kushigian, Julia A. *Orientalism in the Hispanic Literary Tradition: In Dialogue with Borges, Paz, and Sarduy.* Albuquerque, N.M.: University of New Mexico, 1991.

Kushner, Barak, and Sherzod Muminov, eds. *The Dismantling of Japan's Empire in East Asia: Deimperialization, Postwar Legitimation and Imperial Afterlife.* London: Routledge, 2016.

La Nación. "China y Japón: La declaración de guerra." August 2, 1894.

———. "Guerra Rusojaponesa: Notas militares y navales." April 2, 1904.

———. "El imperio del sol levante: Progresos sorprendentes." May 9, 1904.

———. "La 'nación' en el imperio del sol naciente." June 20, 1905.

Lattanzi, Stefano. "Anna Kazumi Stahl: El mundo hispanoamericano en los relatos de una autora internacional." *Les Ateliers du SAL* 3 (2013): 158–72.

Laumonier, Isabel. "Japoneses: Esa otra inmigración." *Todo es Historia* 263 (May 1989): 62–91.

———. "Japanese Argentine Historical Overview." In *Encyclopedia of Japanese Descendants in the Americas: An Illustrated History of the Nikkei*, edited by Akemi Kikumura-Yano. Walnut Creek, CA: AltaMira Press, 2002.

Lenton, Diana. "The *Maleón de la Paz* of 1946: Indigenous *Descamisados* and the Dawn of Perón." In *The New Cultural History of Peronism: Power and Identity in Mid-Twentieth-Century Argentina*, edited by Mathew B. Karush and Oscar Chamosa, 85–112. Durham, NC: Duke University Press, 2010.

Lesser, Jeffrey. *A Discontented Diaspora: Japanese Brazilians and the Meanings of Ethnic Militancy, 1960–1980*. Durham, NC: Duke University Press, 2007.

———. "In Search of the Hyphen: Nikkei and the Struggle over Brazilian National Identity." In *New Worlds, New Lives: Globalization and People of Japanese Descent in the Americas and from Latin America in Japan*, edited by Lane Ryo Hirabayashi, Akemi Kikumura-Yano, and James A. Hirabayashi, 37–58. Stanford, CA: Stanford University Press, 2002.

Lesser, Jeffrey and Raanan Rein. "Challenging Particularity: Jews as a Lens on Latin American Ethnicity." *Latin American and Caribbean Ethnic Studies* 1, 2 (September 2006): 249–63.

Lewis, Retina. *Gendering Orientalism: Race, Femininity, and Representation*. London and New York: Routledge, 1996.

López-Calvo, Ignacio. *Imagining the Chinese in Cuban Literature and Culture*. Gainesville: University Press of Florida, 2008.

———. *The Affinity of the Eye: Writing Nikkei in Peru*. Tucson: University of Arizona Press, 2013.

———. "Worlding and Decolonizing the Literary World-System: Asian-Latin American Literature as an Alternative Type of Weltliteratur." In *Re-mapping World Literature: Writing, Book Markets and Epistemologies Between Latin America and the Global South*, edited by Gesine Muller, Jorge J. Locane, and Benjamin Loy, 15–31. Berlin and Boston: De Gruyter, 2018.

———. *Japanese Brazilian Saudades: Diasporic Identities and Cultural Production*. Denver: University Press of Colorado, 2019.

———. *The Mexican Transpacific: Nikkei Writing, Visual Arts, Performance*. Nashville, TN: Vanderbilt University Press, 2022.

López-Durán, Fabiola. *Eugenics in the Garden: Transatlantic Architecture and the Crafting of Modernity*. Austin: University of Texas Press, 2018.

Loshitzky, Yosefa. *Screening Strangers: Migration and Diaspora in Contemporary European Cinema*. Bloomington: Indiana University Press, 2010.

Lowe, Lisa. *Critical Terrains: French and British Orientalisms*. Ithaca: Cornell University Press, 1991.

Martelli Giachino, María Laura. "Violeta Shinya, la primera intelectual nikkei." *Alternativa Nikkei*, accessed December 15, 2022. https://alternativanikkei.com/violeta-shinya-la-primera-intelectual-nikkei.

Martinetto, Vittoria. "Extranjera para sí misma: Diálogo entre identidad y creación en Flores de un solo día de Anna Kazumi Stahl." *Artifara: Revista de lenguas y literaturas ibéricas y latinoamericanas*, no. 6 (2006). https://www.ojs.unito.it/index.php/artifara/article/view/2976/2865.

Masiello, Francine. *The Art of Transition: Latin American Culture and Neoliberal Crisis*. Durham, NC: Duke University Press, 2001.

Masterson, Daniel M., and Sayaka Funada-Classen. *The Japanese in Latin America*. Urbana and Chicago: University of Illinois Press, 2004.

Matayoshi, Maximiliano. *Gaijin*. México: Universidad Nacional Autónomade México, 2003.

Mendes, Ana Cristina, and Lisa Lau. "India through re-Orientalist Lenses: Vicarious Indulgence and Vicarious Redemption." *Interventions: International Journal of Postcolonial Studies*. 17, 5 (2015): 706–27.

Mignolo, Walter D. *The Darker Side of Western Modernity: Global Futures, Decolonial Options*. Durham, NC: Duke University Press, 2011.

———. "Foreword. On Pluriversality and Multipolarity." In *Constructing the Pluriverse: The Geopolitics of Knowledge*, edited by Bernd Reiter, ix–xvi. Durham, NC: Duke University Press, 2018.

Milanesio, Natalia. "Peronists and Cabecitas, Stereotypes and Anxieties at the Peak of Social Change." In *The New Cultural History of Peronism: Power and Identity in Mid-Twentieth-Century Argentina*, edited by Mathew B. Karush and Oscar Chamosa, 53–84. Durham, NC: Duke University Press, 2010.

Minh-ha, Trinh T. *When the Moon Waxes Red: Representation, Gender and Cultural Politics*. New York: Routledge, 1991.

Ministry of Health, Labour and Welfare of Japan. "Dai 3 shou: Heisei 30 nenjyu ni okeru jisatsu no uchiwake" (Chapter 3: The Details of Suicide in 2018). Ministry of Health, Labour and Welfare, March 23, 2019. https://www.mhlw.go.jp/content/H30kakutei-03.pdf.

Ministry of Foreign Affairs of Japan. "Amigos Across the Ocean: Episodes in Japan-Latin America Relations." Accessed December 15, 2022. https://www.mofa.go.jp/region/latin/latin_e/episode.html#Argentina's.

———. "Japan-Argentina Relations (Basic Data)." Accessed December 15, 2022. https://www.mofa.go.jp/region/latin/argentine/data.html.

Mishra, Pankaj. *From the Ruins of Empire: The Revolt Against the West and the Remaking of Asia*. Picador, Farrar, Straus and Giroux: New York, 2012.

Morais, Fernando. *Dirty Hearts: The History of Shindō Renmei*. Translated by Seth Jacobowitz. London: Palgrave Macmillan, 2021.

Moraña, Mabel. *Crítica impura: estudios de literatura y cultura latinoamericanos*. Madrid: Iberoamericana/Vervuert, 2004.

Moyano, Pablo, dir. *Silencio roto: 16 Nikkeis*. Buenos Aires: Tupasimi Producciones, 2015. DVD.

Nagazane, Motoday. "Imperial Rescript: The Great Principles of Education." In *Society and Education in Japan*. Translated by Herbert Passin. New York: Teachers College, Columbia University Press, 1965.

Nagao, Christiane Kazue. "Representación de la cultura japonesa en la literatura argentina. Marcas de procesos de transculturación." Congreso ALADAA (Asociación Latinoamericana de Estudios de Asia y África). September 8–9, 2004. http://www.transoxiana.org/ALADAA_2004/dct/NAGAO%20Christiane.doc.

Nitobe, Inazō. *Bushidō: The Soul of Japan*. Rutland: Tuttle Publishing, 1969 [1899].

Nouzeilles, Gabriela. *Ficciones somáticas: Naturalismo, nacionalismo y políticas médicas del cuerpo (Argentina 1880-1910)*. Rosario, Argentina: Beatriz Viterbo, 2000.

Ohi, Minobu. *History of Ikebana*. Translated by Seiko Aoyama. Tokyo: Shufunotomo, 1962.

Okamura, Hyoue. "The Language of 'Racial Mixture' in Japan: How *Ainoko* became *Haafu*, and the *Haafu-gao* Makeup Fad." *Asia Pacific Perspectives* 14, 2 (2017): 40-79.

Okihiro, Gary Y. "Turning Japanese Americans." In *Encyclopedia of Japanese Descendants in the Americas: An Illustrated History of the Nikkei*, edited by Akemi Kikumura-Yano, 9-28. Walnut Creek, CA: AltaMira Press, 2002.

Olsen, Dale A. *The Chrysanthemum and the Song: Music, Memory, and Identity in the South American Japanese Diaspora*. Gainesville: University Press of Florida, 2004.

Page, Joanna. *Crisis and Capitalism in Contemporary Argentine Cinema*. Durham, NC: Duke University Press, 2009.

Pardue, David. "Leopoldo Lugones y el haikú." *Chasqui: revista de literatura latinoamericana*. 23, 2 (1994): 86-94.

Pappier, Andrea. "Inmigración china en Argentina: el barrio chino de Bs. As. como caso de estudio cultural." In *Memoria electrónica del XIII congreso internacional de ALADAA*. Bogotá: Secretaría General de ALADAA, 2011.

Perón, Juan Domingo. *Apuntes de historia militar: Guerra Ruso-Japonesa de 1904-1905*. Buenos Aires: Talleres Gráficos de la Escuela Superior de Guerra, 1933.

"El peronismo es nacional, popular y japonés." *Anticipos*. March 2, 2020. https://diarioanticipos.com/2020/03/02/el-peronismo-es-nacional-popular-y-japones.

Pratt, Mary Louise. *Imperial Eyes: Travel Writing and Transculturation*. 2nd ed. London and New York: Routledge, 2008 [1992].

Puenzo, Lucía. *En el hotel cápsula*. Buenos Aires: Editorial Mansalva, 2017.

Raanan, Rein, Aya Udagawa, and Pablo Adrián Vázquez. "Los muchachos peronistas japoneses: el movimiento justicialista y los *nikkei*." *Revista de la Carrera de Sociología* 9, 9 (2019): 96-123.

Radhakrishnan, Rajagopalan. "Is the Ethnic 'Authentic' in the Diaspora?" In *Defining Travel: Diverse Visions*, edited by Susan L. Robertson, 200-210. Jackson: University Press of Mississippi, 2001.

Rafael, Vicente L., and Mary Louise Pratt. "Introduction." *American Quarterly* 73, 3 (September 2021): 419-37.

Reinoso, Susana. "Premiaron a un argentino por su primera novela." *La Nación*, January 3, 2003.

Rich, Motoko, and Hikari Hida. "As Pandemic Took Hold, Suicide Rose among Japanese Women." *New York Times*, February 22, 2021. https://www.nytimes.com/2021/02/22/world/asia/japan-women-suicide-coronavirus.html.

Rinaldi, María Teresa. "Soles de oriente en Latinoamérica: Producción cultural *nikkei* en Brasil y Argentina," PhD diss. University of California, Merced, 2013.

Rivas, Zelideth María, and Debbie Lee-DiStefano, editors. *Imagining Asia in the Americas*. New Brunswick, NJ: Rutgers University Press, 2016.

Robertson, Roland. *Globalization. Social Theory and Global Culture*. London: Sage, 1992.

Roediger, David R. *Working Toward Whiteness: How America's Immigrants Became White: The Strange Journey from Ellis Island to the Suburbs*. New York: Basic Books, 2006.

Rohde, Jorge Max. *Viaje al Japón*. Buenos Aires: M. Gleizer, 1932.

Roskelly, Hephzibah. "Cultural Translator: Lafcadio Hearn." In *Literary New Orleans: Essays and Meditations*, edited by Richard S. Kennedy, 16–28. Baton Rouge: Lousiana State University Press, 1992.

Rud, Lucía, "Representaciones de las migraciones y diásporas de Asia del Este en el audiovisual argentino." *Nuevo mundo mundos nuevos*, June 25, 2020. https://journals.openedition.org/nuevomundo/80888.

Ruggiero, Kristin. *Modernity in the Flesh: Medicine, Law, and Society in Turn-of-the-Century Argentina*. Stanford, CA: Stanford University Press, 2004.

Sakai, Naoki. "Civilizational Difference and Criticism: On the Complicity of Globalization and Cultural Nationalism." *Modern Chinese Literature and Culture* 17, 1 (Spring 2005): 188–205.

Sakata, Yoshio and John Whitney Hall. "The Motivation of Political Leadership in the Meiji Restoration." *Journal of Asian Studies* 16, 1 (1956): 31–50.

Sardegna, Miguel. *Hojas que caen sobre otras hojas*. Buenos Aires: Conejos, 2017.

Sarlo, Beatriz. *Una modernidad periférica: Buenos Aires 1920–1930*. Buenos Aires: Nueva Visión, 2007 [1988].

Scheuer, Gaspar, dir. *Samurai*. Buenos Aires: AireCine, Metaluna Productions, and San Luis Cine, 2013. DVD.

———. "Gauchos y samurai." *Revista Sake*, April 1, 2014. https://sakerevista.wordpress.com/2014/04/01/gauchos-y-samurai.

Schneider, Arnd. "The Two Faces of Modernity: Concepts of the Melting Pot in Argentina." *Critique of Anthropology* 16, 2 (1996): 173–98.

Shimazu, Naoko. *Japanese Society at War: Death, Memory and the Russo-Japanese War*. Cambridge, UK: Cambridge University Press, 2009.

Shinya, Yoshio. *Imperio del sol naciente: Su maravillosa evolución moderna*. Buenos Aires: Librería Cervantes, 1934.

———. "Llamamiento a la juventud." *El Argentin Djiji*, December 22, 1934. https://rakusai.nichibun.ac.jp/hoji/contents/ArgentinDjijo/PDF/1934/12/19341222aja10.pdf.

Sirimarco, Ángel. "Dedicada a la colectividad japonesa." *La Plata Hochi*. September 11, 1954.

Sone, Hiromi. "Prostitution and Public Authority in Early Modern Japan." Translated by Akiko Terashima and Anne Walthall. In *Women and Class in Japanese History*, edited by Hitomi Tonomura, Anne Walthall and Wakita Haruko, 169–85. Anne Arbor: Center for Japanese Studies, The University of Michigan, 1999.

Spivak, Gayatri Chakravorty. *A Critique of Postcolonial Reason: Toward a History of the Vanishing Present*. Cambridge, MA: Harvard University Press, 1999.

Stahl, Anna Kazumi. *Flores de un sólo día*. Buenos Aires: Booket, 2007 [2002].

———. *Catástrofes naturales*. Buenos Aires: Sudamericana, 1997.

Sugimura, Héctor Dai. *Buscadores en mis últimas vidas*. Buenos Aires: Editorial Almagesto, 1995.

Tablada, José Juan. *En el país del sol (obra VIII)*. México: Universidad Nacional Autónoma de México, 2006 [1919].

Takenaka, Ayumi. "The Japanese in Peru: History of Immigration, Settlement, and Racialization." *Latin American Perspectives* 31, 3 (2004): 77–98.

Takeuchi, Yoshimi. "Overcoming Modernity." In *What is Modernity?: Writing of Takeuchi Yoshimi*. Translated by Richard F. Calichman, 103–48. New York: Columbia University Press, 2005.

Tanaka, Stefan. *Japan's Orient: Rendering Pasts into History*. Berkeley: University of California Press, 1995.

Taussig, Michael. *Mimesis and Alterity: A Particular History of the Senses*. New York and London: Routledge, 1993.

Taylor, David. "Shaking the Buddhas: Lafcadio Hearn in Japan, 1890–1904." In *Asian Crossings: Travel Writing on China, Japan and Southeast Asia*, edited by Steve Clark and Paul Smethurst, 163–78. Hong Kong: Hong Kong University Press, 2008.

Tejedor, Francesca Arena de. *Argentina y Japón: Se conocieron en el violento amanecer del mundo moderno*. Buenos Aires: Centro Naval, Instituto de Publicaciones Navales, 1992.

Tigner, James Lawrence. "The Ryukyuans in Argentina." *The Hispanic American Historical Review* 47, 2 (May 1967): 203–24.

Tinajero, Araceli. *Orientalismo en el modernismo hispanoamericano*. West Lafayette, IN: Purdue University Press, 2003.

Tobin, Joseph J. "Introduction: Domesticating the West." In *Re-made in Japan: Everyday Life and Consumer Taste in a Changing Society*, edited by Joseph J Tobin, 1–41. New Haven: Yale University Press, 1992.

Torales, Graciela Karina. "El Instituto Cultural Argentino Japonés del Museo Social Argentino." *La Plata Hochi*, February 3, 2021. http://www.laplatahochi.com.ar/index.php?option=com_content&view=article&id=261.

Torres-Rodríguez, Laura J. *Orientaciones transpacíficas: La modernidad mexicana y el espectro de Asia*. Chapel Hill: North Carolina Studies in the Romance Languages and Literatures, 2019.

Trouvé, Cristián. "Héctor Dai Sugimura: sin perder la ternura." *Generacón E*, October 29, 2019. https://generacione.com.ar/hector-dai-sugimura-sin-perder-la-ternura.

Tsurumi, Rebecca Riger. *The Closed Hand: Images of the Japanese in Modern Peruvian Literature*. West Lafayette, IN: Purdue University Press, 2012.

Van der Oye, David Schimmelpenninck. "Rewriting the Russo-Japanese War: A Centenary Retrospective." *Russian Review* 67, 1 (2008): 78–87.

Wijeyeratne, Subodhana. "A Race to War: Japanese Public Intellectuals and Racial Explanations of the Russo-Japanese War." *Asia-Pacific Journal* 18, 19, no. 4 (October 2020): 1–17.

Wilde, Eduardo. *Curso de higiene pública: Lecciones en el colegio nacional de Buenos Aires*, 2nd ed. Buenos Aires: Imprenta y Librería de Mayo, 1885 [1878].

———. *Por mares y por tierras*. Buenos Aires: Jacobo Peuser, 1899.

———. *Viajes y observaciones*. Buenos Aires: Belmonte, 1939.

Yakimiuk, Mauro. "Paula Brecciaroli: 'El personaje de Otaku es una condensación de prejuicios, anécdotas y superposiciones de muchos fanáticos que conocí en mi vida.'" *Entre vidas* (blog), July 10, 2016. http://entrevidasmm.blogspot.com/2016/07/paula-brecciaroli-el-personaje-de-otaku.html.

Zaia Okinawa Kenjin Rengokai. *Aruzenchin no Uchinanchu Hachiju-nenshi*. Buenos Aires: Zaia Okinawa Kenjin Rengokai, 1994.

Zappettini, Clara, dir. *La otra tierra: Japoneses en Argentina, 1986 (parte I)*. Argentina Televisora Color, 1986. Posted by Archivo Prisma, Oct. 28, 2015. https://www.youtube.com/watch?v=rQAIHU_5dfQ&t=0s.

Žižek, Slavoj. *Lacan: The Silent Partners*. London and New York: Verso, 2006.

Index

árboles caídos también son el bosque, Los (Kamiya), 94–100
Argentina
  cinema, 101–2
  Conquest of the Desert, 8, 44, 49
  Dirty War, 114
  economic crisis of 2001, 71–72, 101, 127n40, 143n24
  Japanese immigrants, 4–7, 33, 69–72, 126n12, 126n17, 127n23
  newspapers, 15, 50, 137nn29–30
  See also modernity; Perón, Juan Domingo; Sarmiento, Domingo Faustino; whiteness

Benjamin, Walter, 28
Bhabha, Homi, 73, 76, 81
Borges, Jorge Luis, 16, 60, 138n43
Brazil
  anti-Japanese propaganda, 3–4, 33
  Estado Novo, 4
  Japanese immigrants, 3–5, 33, 126n12, 130n71
  See also Shindō Renmei
Brecciaroli, Paula, 122–23
Buscadores en mis últimas vidas (Sugimura), 73–77
bushidō, 108, 138n43, 149n12

Catholicism, 6, 127n26
China
  Chinese immigrants in Argentina, 33, 110–11, 150n16

Confucianism, 11, 108, 115–16
Manchuria, 29, 42, 55, 57–58
Sino-Japanese War, 11, 46, 49, 56
Conquest of the Desert, 8, 44, 47, 49
cuento chino, Un (Borensztein), 17, 111–14

desaparecidos, 114. *See also Silencio roto: 16 Nikkeis* (Moyano)
Domecq García, Manuel, 15–16, 45, 51
  Guerra Ruso-Japonesa 1904–1905, 51–55

Ette, Otmar, 94, 130n76

Flores de un solo día (Stahl), 87–94
Fukuzawa, Yukichi, 11, 128n56

Gaijin (Matayoshi), 77–83
Gasquet, Axel, 27, 43, 85, 126n5, 131n10
Gómez Carrillo, Enrique, 30, 134n61, 138n43
Guerra Ruso-Japonesa 1904–1905 (Domecq García), 51–55

Hall, Stuart, 72–73, 77
Hearn, Lafcadio, 23–24, 38–40, 42–43, 135nn78–79
Hegel, G. W. F., 27, 87, 131n14
Hernández, José, 108
hybridity, 72–73, 81, 143n32
hygiene, 15, 23–24, 30–32, 61, 131n15, 132n27. *See also* "hygiene utopia"
"hygiene utopia," 31, 132n27

Imperio del sol naciente (Shinya), 56–63
Inazō, Nitobe, 108, 149n12. *See also* *bushidō*

Japan
    aesthetics, 34–35, 37–38
    haiku, 73, 130n73
    hygiene, 15, 23–24, 30–32, 61, 131n15, 132n27
    ikebana, 61, 88–91
    Meiji Restoration, 11–12, 29, 44, 60, 106–7, 115
    spirituality, 37–40, 53, 123
    and westernization, 10–12, 60, 128n53–55
    women, 33–36, 40–41, 86–91, 96–100, 135n91, 148n58
    See also *bushidō*; Japanese diaspora; Japanese imperialism; Nikkei; Okinawa (Ryukyu); whiteness
Japanese Argentine Cultural Institute, 55, 61–62, 139n54
Japanese diaspora, in Latin America, 2–3, 68–69, 126n17, 128n51
Japanese Empire. *See* Japanese imperialism
Japanese imperialism, 11–12, 29, 41–43, 45–48, 53, 134n75. *See also* Russo-Japanese War; Shinya, Yoshio

Kamiya, Alejandra, 17–18, 84
    Los árboles caídos también son el bosque, 94–100
Kim, Junyoung Verónica, 3, 111, 127n35
Ko, Chisu Teresa, 3, 72, 87, 126n7
Korea, 11–13, 38, 47, 58–59, 129n61
Korean immigrants in Argentina, 7, 10, 110–11, 150n16

Lowe, Lisa, 85–86

Matayoshi, Maximiliano, 17, 68
    Gaijin, 77–83
Mexico, 33, 128n51, 130n70

Mignolo, Walter, 17, 118, 129n62, 130n75
Min-ha, Trinh T., 68, 77
"model minority," 18, 33, 63, 104
modernismo, 24–25, 30, 85
modernity
    Argentine, 13–14, 32, 129n66
    European, 13
    Latin American, 31
    transpacific, 2, 12–16, 18, 42, 45, 106–9, 130n70
multiculturalism, 10, 16, 72
    in *Flores de un solo día* (Stahl), 90–94
    in *Gaijin* (Matayoshi), 81–83
Museo Social Argentino, 61

Nación, La (newspaper), 49–51, 137n29
Nikkei, 5, 125n2
    desaparecidos, 114
    global Nikkei literature, 123–24
    Issei, 6, 76, 81, 99, 104–5
    literature, 16–19, 122, 142n2
    Nisei, 6, 76, 97, 99, 105, 142n3
    Sansei, 99, 105
    See also *Silencio roto: 16 Nikkeis* (Moyano)

Okinawa (Ryukyu), 11, 42
    immigrants, 69, 78, 126–27n22, 142n15
    Okinawa imin joseishi, 103
Orientalism
    Argentine, 27, 126n5
    gendering, 85–86, 145–46n10
    Latin American, 26
    See also Said, Edward
ornamentalism, 35, 86, 133n54
otra tierra: Japoneses en Argentina, La (Zappettini), 18, 102–5

Paraguay, 10, 142n10
    Paraguayan War, 44, 48, 108, 150n23
Paz, Octavio, 38, 60
Perón, Juan Domingo, 8–9, 50–51, 70–72, 128n44

Peru
　anti-Japanese propaganda, 4
　Japanese immigrants, 4–6
Plata Hochi, La (newspaper), 1, 151n40
Por mares y por tierras (Wilde), 23–24, 29–36
"positive prejudice," 4–5
Pratt, Mary Louise, 3, 35–26
Prensa, La (newspaper), 28, 137n29
Puenzo, Lucía, 123

race, 7, 39, 57, 59, 127n35. *See also* racism; Russo-Japanese War; whiteness; Yellow Peril
racism, 3–4, 10, 111
　in *Flores de un solo día* (Stahl), 92
　in *Gaijin* (Matayoshi), 80
　in *Los árboles caídos también son el bosque* (Kamiya), 98
Radhakrishnan, Rajagopalan, 76, 144n46
Rohde, Jorge Max, 15, 23–25
　and Lafcadio Hearn, 38–40
　Viaje al Japón, 36–43
Russian Empire, 15, 47, 52. *See also* Russo-Japanese War
Russo-Japanese War, 15, 42, 45–51, 71, 130n72, 137nn21. *See also* *Guerra Ruso-Japonesa 1904–1905* (Domecq García)

Said, Edward, 27, 85. *See also* Orientalism
Saigō, Takamori, 106–08
Samurai (Scheuer), 17, 106–9
Sarlo, Beatriz, 14–15
Sarmiento, Domingo Faustino, 8, 13–14, 25, 108
settler colonialism, 11–12, 56, 140n59
Shindō Renmei, 45, 69, 136n3
Shinya, Yoshio, 15–16, 45, 55–56
　Imperio del sol naciente, 56–63
silence, 5, 114–15, 118, 150n29
　as mode of communication, 78–79, 88–91, 96–97

　See also *Silencio roto: 16 Nikkeis* (Moyano)
Silencio roto: 16 Nikkeis (Moyano), 17, 114–19
Spivak, Gayatri, 86, 143n32
Stahl, Anna Kazumi, 17–18, 86–87
　Catástrofes naturales, 91, 147n36
　Flores de un solo día, 87–94
Sugimura, Héctor Dai, 17, 73
　Buscadores en mis últimas vidas, 73–77

Tablada, José Juan, 30, 34, 134n61
Taiwan, 11, 47
Takeuchi, Yoshimi, 12, 129n60
Taussig, Michael, 60
Tinajero, Araceli, 26–27, 85
Torres-Rodríguez, Laura, 85, 130n70

United States
　Asian American Studies, 3
　in *Flores de un solo día* (Stahl), 91–94
　in *Gaijin* (Matayoshi), 81–82
　internment camps, 4, 10, 69

Viaje al Japón (Rohde), 36–43

whiteness
　in Argentina, 7–10, 14, 17, 83, 127n35, 149–50n13
　in Japan, 13, 45–48, 129n61, 137n21
　in United States, 128n46
Wilde, Eduardo, 15, 23–25, 28
　Por mares y por tierras, 23–24, 29–36
World War II, 12, 57
　and anti-Japanese movement, 4, 69, 128n51
　Japan-Argentina relations during, 5–6

Yellow Peril, 46, 136n8
Yoshiwara, 35–36, 133n55, 134n61

www.ingramcontent.com/pod-product-compliance
Lightning Source LLC
Chambersburg PA
CBHW030655230426
43665CB00011B/1104